BLER
DSON
RAMBLER

THE COMPLETE BOOK OF

AMC CARS

AMERICAN MOTORS CORPORATION 1954–1988

PATRICK R. FOSTER & TOM GLATCH

FOREWORD BY VINCE GERACI

motorbooks

Quarto.com

First Published in 2024 by Motorbooks, an imprint of The Quarto Group,
100 Cummings Center, Suite 265-D, Beverly, MA 01915, USA.

T (978) 282-9590 F (978) 283-2742

EEA Representation, WTS Tax d.o.o.,
Žanova ulica 3, 4000 Kranj, Slovenia.
www.wts-tax.si

28 27 26 3 4 5

ISBN: 978-0-7603-8701-6

Digital edition published in 2024

eISBN: 978-0-7603-8702-3

Library of Congress Cataloging-in-Publication Data available

Design and Page Layout: Silverglass Design
Cover Images: Randy Leffingwell (front); Tom & Kelly Glatch (back/top); Pat Foster Historical Collection (back/bottom, flaps, case, endpapers)

Photography: Courtesy of Pat Foster Historical Collection and Tom Glatch, except where noted

All production numbers courtesy of Tom Glatch

Printed in Huizhou City, Guangdong, China TT012026

To the countless men and women who worked the assembly lines and ran the machines to build the automobiles; and to the designers, engineers, and planners that created them . . . this is *your story*!

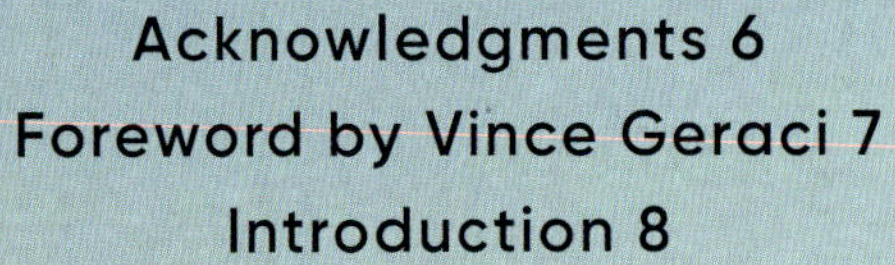

Acknowledgments 6

Foreword by Vince Geraci 7

Introduction 8

CHAPTER 1

1954–1957: In the Beginning 13

CHAPTER 2

1958–1963: The Great Rambler Years 39

CHAPTER 3

1964–1969: Rambler's Decline and AMC's Rise 71

CHAPTER 4

1970–1974: The New Generation Cars 115

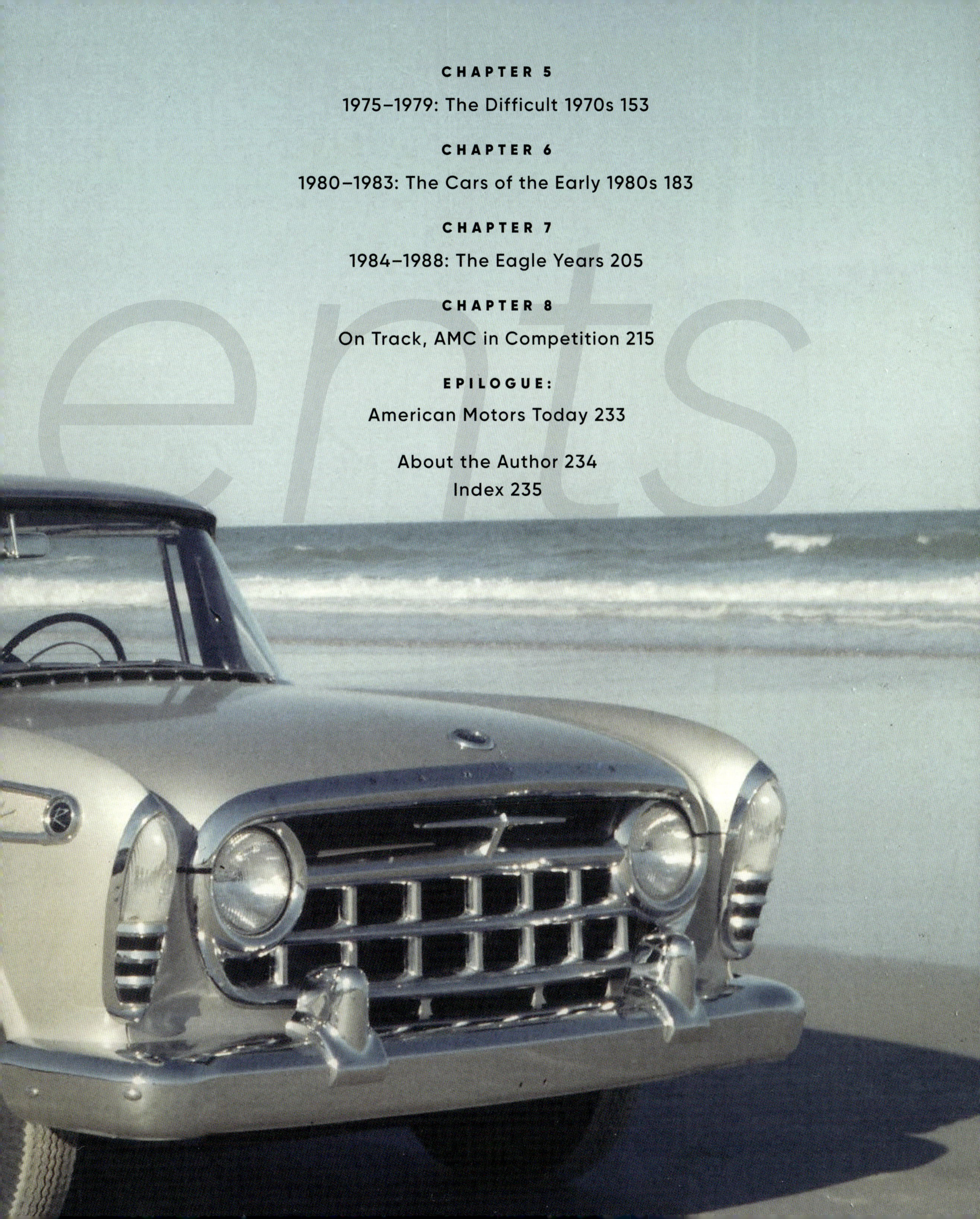

CHAPTER 5

1975–1979: The Difficult 1970s 153

CHAPTER 6

1980–1983: The Cars of the Early 1980s 183

CHAPTER 7

1984–1988: The Eagle Years 205

CHAPTER 8

On Track, AMC in Competition 215

EPILOGUE:

American Motors Today 233

About the Author 234

Index 235

Acknowledgments

American Motors created some of the finest automobiles this nation has produced, though you might not know that based on recent magazine articles and internet misinformation. This book was created to right those wrongs, to tell the true stories, and I could not have done that without Pat Foster's knowledge, research, guidance, and historical documents. The Kenosha History Center is a trove of information, and Jonathan Martens, their exhibitions and collections specialist, helped me visualize what the city was like during AMC's heyday. Joe Skibinski of the Indianapolis Motor Speedway archives supplied photos of the AMC-powered Indy 500 racers while Chas Howe supplied photos and information on his dad's "Brand X" Javelin oval track stock car. Alan Strang, who bought the last AMC made; Thomas Benvie, who supplied AMX SS and other production data; members of the American Motors Owners Association (AMO); the grandchildren of Plant Manager Julius Riedl; and many others contributed American Motors lore.

Then there are the owners of the automobiles my wife Kelly and I photographed for this book: knowledgeable, passionate—and fun! Two of the owners are in their twenties, dedicated caretakers of their grandparents' cars. Another just purchased the 100th AMC product he's owned over the years. Mike Spangler and Cheryl Samuel, two of the finest people you will find in the automobile hobby, again opened their collection of AMC prototypes for us. This is a living history that must be preserved, and these people are doing just that. A sincere thank-you to you all!

Finally, Kelly helped scout locations, gathered information from owners, listened to ideas, and tolerated my obsessive desire to create something truly special. This year we celebrated our thirtieth wedding anniversary photographing one of the Ramblers for this book. What a journey it's been!

—Tom Glatch

I'd like to thank AMC Designer Vince Geraci for all his help over the years, and for his friendship—one of the most treasured I've known. I would also like to thank co-author Tom Glatch, who actually wrote the majority of this book's text, due to time constraints and health issues I was going through during the year and a half we worked on it. Thanks, Tom!

—Patrick Foster

Foreword

By Vincent Geraci, Retired Head of AMC Styling

Within the pages of this book, you'll learn about one of the most unique and significant automobile companies ever: American Motors Corporation. AMC was a place I worked at and loved for many years. It was unique both in the products we built and the relationships we enjoyed. Our cars and Jeep vehicles were often revolutionary in nature and set trends that still exist today. American Motors introduced many "firsts," some of which forced larger automakers to play catch up. The amazing success of the Rambler in the 1950s and 1960s, for example, forced the "Big Three" to introduce compact and mid-size cars or lose a substantial part of the market. The AMC Javelin is one of the most beloved pony cars of all time. Eagle pioneered and introduced four-wheel-drive passenger cars, a trend accelerating to this day. The AMC Gremlin, a project I worked on, was America's first subcompact car. The list of innovations goes on and on, as you'll see in this book.

America lost its "Last Independent Automaker" when Chrysler acquired American Motors in 1987, though Jeep lives on as one of its crowning achievements. There will probably never be another American Motors car built, and certainly there will never be another company like it. Thus, it is up to you, dear reader, the men and women who today collect, restore, and preserve thousands of AMC cars and Jeeps, to keep alive the legend of the little automaker that could. American Motors was a one-timer—an utterly unique company never to be duplicated again. It's up to you to not only preserve the products, but also to preserve the memory and the legacy of one of America's best automakers. It's a trust I turn over to you, and I hope you will always keep the story alive.

Introduction

Before AMC

This is a story of the American dream, of the triumph of the underdog succeeding against the odds, and of a company that survived and even thrived using guts, creativity, determination, innovation, and hard work. They manufactured cars with names like Gremlin, Spirit, Eagle, American, and Rebel. This is the story of American Motors.

American Motors was born, not out of a desire to expand and conquer, but in a desperate effort to survive in troubled times.

Nash-Kelvinator Corporation and Hudson Motor Car Company had both been successful businesses. Unlike many other small automakers, they had survived the Great Depression, then made major capital investments during World War II to supply war materiel for President Roosevelt's "Arsenal of Democracy." They continued growing after the end of hostilities, feeding America's frenzy for new automobiles following years of economic depression and war rationing.

By the late 1940s, both companies had invested in completely new automobiles: Hudson released its radical Step-Down series, with its low-slung design in 1948, while Nash debuted the Ambassador and 600 series a year later. Both featured aerodynamic Airflyte styling refined by the first wind-tunnel testing ever performed on an automobile.

In 1951, two years before the Chevrolet Corvette arrived, Nash had introduced the Nash-Healey, America's first sports car by a major automaker. This Italian-built beauty featured a Nash drivetrain and a striking two-seat convertible body. Hudson offered its own Italian crossover in 1953: the limited-production Italia, a European-style grand touring coupe.

The early 1950s also saw the companies roll out "compact" and "subcompact" models—the first-ever instance of those styles. Nash's popular Rambler appeared in 1950, and by 1954 the company had added the imported subcompact Metropolitan. In the same years Hudson launched its smaller Jet compact model, positioned to compete with the Rambler. As late as the first half of 1953, automobiles from both companies were selling well, with Nash factories working overtime to meet demand.

The big Hudson models, Wasp and Hornet, were now built on the Nash body shell with a new, distinctive appearance. The fender wells were open, a bright new grille graced the front, and overall styling was clean and uncluttered, at least by the standards of the day. Shown is a Hudson Hornet four-door sedan.

Only the Strongest

Success was fleeting, however: by mid-1953, the postwar economic boom was on the wane, and the end of the Korean War contributed to an economic recession. The government's Bureau of the Budget described the recession as "relatively mild and brief," yet the sharp drop in annual consumer spending hit America's smaller businesses hard. The nation's gross domestic product dropped 2.2 percent, while unemployment peaked at 6 percent. Then, as now, consumers deferred purchases of expensive items while they rode out the economic uncertainty. The giant automakers had deep reserves to draw on in this period, but small, independent automakers like Hudson, Nash, Packard, Studebaker, and Kaiser-Willys were forced to reinvent themselves or lose everything.

As the economic downturn took hold, the independents were caught in the middle of a historic battle: the 1953–1954 sales war between Ford and Chevrolet. The end of the Korean War meant the lifting of restrictions on auto production that had been enacted to save raw materials for military production.

ORIGINS: NASH-KELVINATOR

Nash Motors was founded in 1916 by Charles W. Nash. The former president of General Motors, Nash had left that company to purchase the Thomas B. Jeffery Company of Kenosha, Wisconsin, known for their Rambler. The man himself was described by one of his associates in 1926, on Nash Motors' tenth anniversary: "The candor and friendliness of this strong, quiet man, who is efficient, progressive, and yet unassuming in manner, accounts in large measure for the success he has attained since that day more than thirty years ago when he took his first factory job."

Nash implemented just-in-time supply chains and continuous improvement decades before business consultants were throwing such terms around to describe methods for improving corporate efficiency and growing profit margins. But in 1937, the seventy-three-year-old Nash saw that it was time to turn the business over to a younger man. He chose George W. Mason, the forty-six-year-old president of appliance maker Kelvinator. Mason would only agree to the move if Nash purchased Kelvinator; like General Motors' alliance with Frigidaire and Ford's with Philco, the merger would mean diversifying and expanding Nash's business. The company born from this agreement was the Nash-Kelvinator Corporation.

Sensing an opportunity, Henry Ford II sought to reclaim Ford's long-held top sales position, which it had lost to General Motors in 1938 and only taken back twice since. Ford stoked his plants to a record increase in manufacturing. New cars arrived, often without orders, at overstocked and nearly overwhelmed dealers, forcing them to sell at any price to move the inventory. The company had built 671,733 cars in 1952, doubling that number to 1,247,542 in 1953 and reaching 1,165,942 in 1954. Chevrolet responded in kind, assembling 1,346,475 cars in 1953 and 1,143,561 the following year.

The effect on the economy was so profound, economist Timothy F. Bresnahan wrote, that "conduct in 1955 comes from a competitive model, in nearby years, from a collusive one." Simply put, Ford and Chevrolet artificially flooded the market in 1953–1954 to gain a sales advantage, while market demand drove production in 1955. The effects were like the Japanese dumping of automobiles in the United States in the 1980s: only the strongest could survive.

The independent automakers accounted for around 6 percent of the total market in this period and, sadly, many wound up as collateral damage in Ford and Chevy's two-year sales battle. The independents were in deep trouble.

A New Dawn

Gossip has always traveled at lightning speed in Detroit. And in the autumn of 1953 the rumor mill was working overtime. The Monday, October 12, 1953, issue of *Time* magazine reported: "Nash and Hudson are secretly dickering to merge. The deal, involving assets of $320 million, would be the biggest auto merger since Chrysler bought Dodge in 1928. Reason for the move: the two independents think that it would help them cut costs and strengthen their sales organizations to meet intense competition expected from autos' Big Three in 1954–55." The rumors were well founded: George Mason, the president and chairman of Nash-Kelvinator, had been courting Hudson's chairman, Abraham E. Barit, about a merger. And on March 25, 1954, the *New York Times* reported that "Stockholders of Nash-Kelvinator Corporation and Hudson Motor Car Company today approved plans to merge the two concerns into a new company to be known as American Motors Corporation (AMC)."

As usual, some shareholders protested. One asked, "What does Hudson bring Nash that Nash hasn't got? They haven't been successful." A Nash-Kelvinator vice president, H. G. Perkins, replied, "The possibility of cutting manufacturing costs is very prominent here." Yet the financials for the companies the *Times* reported begged the same question: "Hudson reported last week that its 1953 operations had brought a loss of more than $10,000,000. Nash-Kelvinator had net earnings of $14,123,000 in its fiscal year ended Sept. 30, 1953."

George Mason had more in mind than combining his company with Hudson. As early as 1946, he had wanted to merge Nash, Hudson, and the Packard Motor Car Company. The resulting company would still have been a distant fourth to the Big Three—Nash and Hudson combined held 3.2 percent of market share in 1954, while Packard held a little over half a percent—but imagine the company's lineup: Packard would offer large luxury cars, equal or superior to Cadillac, Lincoln, and Imperial, while Nash and Hudson would compete in the middle market against Buick, Oldsmobile, Mercury, Dodge, and DeSoto. The Nash Rambler would fill a unique niche in the compact car market, taking sales from Ford, Chevy, and Plymouth.

Unfortunately, Packard CEO James J. Nance demanded the chairmanship of the proposed new company, something Mason couldn't accept. Having headed General Electric's Hotpoint brand from 1945 to 1951, when he took the reins of Packard, Nance had only nominal experience in the automotive business at the time Mason approached him. The chairmanship was off the table, so Packard declined to merge, leaving their relationship in the form of a vaguely worded reciprocity agreement in which Packard would sell engines and transmissions to American Motors, while AMC would supply stampings to Packard's production line. Packard ended up buying Studebaker later in 1954. Instead of one large company positioned to take on the Big Three, there would be two medium-size ones.

The merger that formed AMC, minus Packard, was finally announced by the *New York Times* on April 22, 1954: "Directors of Hudson Motor Car Company and Nash-Kelvinator Corporation today approved the merger of the two companies into American Motors Corporation. The $355,000,000 concern will be the auto industry's fourth largest, behind General Motors, Ford, and Chrysler. The consolidation will be completed formally next Friday with the filing of the merger agreement with state authorities in Michigan and Maryland. At recent meetings, Nash and Hudson stockholders voted overwhelmingly for the consolidation." George Mason told the *Times* the merger would "give American Motors the increased financial strength, the enlarged facilities and the volume sales and service outlets" to make it more competitive.

On May 1, 1954, it became official, and American Motors Corporation came into being.

1954-1957

CHAPTER

1

IN THE BEGINNING

To reduce development and manufacturing costs, George Mason's plan was to build the big Hudson Hornet and shorter Wasp models on Nash Ambassador and Statesman platforms at his company's Kenosha plants. Both makes had been fabricated using unit-body construction, but Nash decided on the more modern Budd-type construction for its new lines, adopting a process still used on automobiles today. Hudson cars would have distinctive styling and use their own legacy drivetrains.

The concept was hardly new. General Motors had made an art of building brands with unique personas based on common architectures—Chevrolet, Pontiac, Buick, Oldsmobile, and even some Cadillacs shared most components—yet each

OPPOSITE TOP: Top executives of the new American Motors pose together in late April 1954. *Left to right:* H. C. Doss, vice president of Nash Sales; N. K. VanDerzee, vice president of Hudson Sales; Charles T. Lawson, vice president of Appliance Distribution; and George Walter Mason, AMC chairman and CEO. Before the year was out, Doss would resign because of disagreements with AMC executive George W Romney, Charles Lawson would become executive vice president of the Appliance Division, and George Mason would be dead following a brief illness.

OPPOSITE BOTTOM: New to the Hudson line for 1954 was this sharp Hudson Hornet Club Sedan, a lower-priced version of the top-selling Hornet. Introduced in March to try to spur sales demand, the Hornet Special line also included Club Coupe and four-door sedan models.

LEFT: The four-door Rambler Cross Country station wagon proved surprisingly popular despite being the highest-priced model in the Rambler line. In fact, the Cross Country was the top-selling Rambler this year, and the Custom four-door sedan was the number two Rambler in terms of sales volume, with the Deluxe two-door Rambler coming in third.

ABOVE: The limited-production Hudson Italia was something new on the market: a prestige grand touring coupe from an American brand. With beautiful styling and a body hand built by Carrozzeria Touring in Italy, the $4,800 Hudson Italia was not a hot seller. Only twenty-six cars were built, and selling even that number proved difficult. Sales exec Roy D. Chapin Jr. was forced to strong-arm some of his dealers to unload them.

RIGHT: Actor William Holden drove this handsome Nash-Healey roadster in the movie *Sabrina*, which also starred Audrey Hepburn and Humphrey Bogart. This marked the final year for Nash-Healey production.

LEFT: Another slow-selling Hudson failure was the 1954 Jet, despite the addition of lower-priced models for the year. Sturdy and well built, the Jet's styling didn't appeal to enough buyers to ensure its success. Part of the pre-merger wrangling between Hudson and Nash executives involved replacing the Jet with a Rambler-based car and writing off the investment in the Jet.

BELOW: The new, imported Nash Metropolitan made a moderate impact during the difficult 1954 selling year. Tagged at a mere $1,445 for the two-door hardtop version and $1,469 for this attractive convertible, Mets were comfortable, inexpensive, and economical. Hudson dealers were soon able to offer a 1954 Hudson version, their first benefit resulting from the Hudson-Nash merger.

brand had distinctive designs and engines. Ford did the same with its midmarket Mercury line, as did Chrysler with Dodge, Plymouth, and DeSoto.

Now it was American Motors' turn to save costs by building with common elements styled in unique ways. The task was daunting, with new Hudson designs based on the Nash platforms, renderings approved, clay models built, and Hudson drivetrains adapted to the Nash vehicles. Then engineering drawings would be drafted, giant stamping dies machined, assembly lines modified, prototype vehicles tested, promotional materials created . . . the task list goes on and on. Most manufacturing lead times in Detroit are measured in years, and a project of this magnitude could easily take two years or more. But it was May, and the new model years were traditionally expected to begin in September.

ABOVE: The Hudson line for 1954 also included this sharp Super Wasp Hollywood hardtop two-door, seen here with optional wire wheel covers and two-tone paint. Note the trademark roof-mounted radio antenna. The Super Wasp series featured a larger, more powerful six-cylinder engine than the regular Wasp cars.

RIGHT: Two premium cars in the 1954 Nash lineup were the Nash Ambassador Country Club two-door hardtop and the Nash Rambler Custom four-door sedan. The four-door Rambler model was new this year and performed well in sales, an indication that Americans were interested in smaller cars so long as they were attractive and roomy enough for a family.

American Motors' small staff performed a miracle, the first of many to come: they completed the project in just ten months, and the 1955 Nash and Hudson models would appear in show rooms by February 1955.

Then this shocking item appeared in the October 11, 1954, edition of the *Detroit News*: "Services for George W. Mason, president and chairman of the board of the American Motors Corp., were held today at Christ Church Cranbrook. Burial was in White Chapel Memorial Cemetery. Mr. Mason died Friday at the age of 63." Mason had succumbed to a brief bout of pancreatitis. His sudden illness and death meant that he had no time to formally name a successor.

Thankfully, he had been grooming George Wilcken Romney for the top leadership role since 1948. Romney had been at Mason's side through all the merger negotiations. Now, the forty-seven-year-old was the leader of the fledgling American Motors Corporation. As he often said, "Pursuit of the difficult makes you strong." People would soon see just how strong.

1955

Another new Rambler model for 1954 was the baseline Rambler Deluxe two-door sedan, priced at $1,550. Nash was forced to hold this volume-selling model off the market until raw materials were available. This year Rambler offered its broadest array of models to date, with prices ranging from $1,550 to $2,050.

Hudson

For beautiful performance, twice the safety, three times softer ride, surging V-8 power . . . drive the 1955 Hudson Hornet.

For Hudson, 1955 opened a whole new chapter in company history, and their advertising attempted to portray all its advantages. The big Hudson Hornet now rode on the Nash Ambassador's 121.25-inch (308-centimeter) wheelbase. AMC designer Allan Kornmiller, under Director of Automotive Styling Edmund "Ed" Anderson, ably differentiated the Hudson's style from the bulbous, ungainly "bathtub" look of the Nash; only two body panels were shared, the roof and the rear deck. A large Hudson-like grille led the way, and from most angles the Nash heritage was less obvious. Strangely, in this era of increasingly longer, lower, wider automobiles, the formerly low-slung Hornet was now three inches (eight centimeters) taller due to the Nash architecture.

The Hornet was available in both two-door hardtop and four-door sedan versions; there was no two-door sedan this year. Power continued to be Hudson's famous "National Champion" 308-cu.-in. L-head straight six, producing 210 horsepower. The Twin-H option was still available—this was the same engine that propelled the earlier Hornet to seventy-nine victories on the NASCAR stock car circuit, with an additional 10 horses. Optional was Packard's modern 320-cu.-in. OHV V-8 generating 208 horsepower. The lower-priced

MAKE	NASH		RAMBLER	HUDSON		METROPOLITAN
Model	Statesman	Ambassador		Wasp	Hornet	Series II
Passengers	6	6	5	6	6	3
Doors	2 or 4	2 or 4	2 or 4	2 or 4	2 or 4	2
Wheelbase (inches)	114.25	121.25	100 (2dr) or 108 (4dr)	114.25	121.25	85
Engine (Standard)	195.6 cu.in., F-Head I-6, 110 hp	252.6 cu.in., OHV I-6, 120 hp	195.6 cu.in., F-Head I-6, 90 hp	202 cu.in., L-Head I-6, 110 hp or 120 hp	308 cu.in., L-Head I-6, 160 hp or 170 hp	73.1 cu.in., OHV I-4, 42 hp
Engine (Optional)		320 cu.in., OHV V-8, 208 hp				
Production	15,272	10,580	81,237	7,191	13,130	6,096
	25,852			20,321		

Total American Motors Production: 108,292 Market Share: 3.2%

ABOVE: Nash stylists came up with a clever, low-cost facelift for the 1954 Nash senior cars. The heavy-looking chrome headlamp rings of prior years were now painted in the body color with about an inch of chrome appearing at the outer edge; this made the cars look longer. The thick chrome grille of 1952–1953 was replaced by a lighter floating grille, which afforded a more modern appearance.

BELOW LEFT: For 1955, the senior Hudson cars used the same basic body shell as the big Nash cars and were built on the same assembly line. Here we see the new 1955 Hudson Hornet Hollywood Hardtop. Note the open wheelwells and modified C-pillar.

BELOW RIGHT: With the start of 1955 production, all American Motors cars except the imported Metropolitan were built either in the Kenosha, Wisconsin, main plant or, for a time, in El Segundo, California. Here we see the first 1955 Hudson built in Kenosha as it comes off the final assembly line.

LEFT: There were no major changes to the Metropolitan for 1955. Both the Nash and Hudson sales organizations were selling the little Met, which was often purchased by customers who might otherwise have bought some other European-built import. It was a nice addition to what dealers could offer and was successful in luring new customers into Nash and Hudson showrooms.

BELOW: The senior Nash models, Statesman and Ambassador, were treated to a facelift for 1955. New front fenders arched forward aggressively and featured raised wheelwells. Headlamps were moved from the fenders to inside a new oval grille. It was controversial, but within a few years nearly all cars would place headlamps within the grille or flanking it, rather than mounted to the fender.

Hudson Wasp now shared the Nash Statesman's 116.25-inch (295-centimeter) wheelbase, literally a shortened Ambassador. The Wasp continued to use Hudson's 202-cu.-in. L-head six, generating 110 horsepower, or 120 horsepower in "Twin H" form. Two-door hardtop and four-door sedan styles were offered.

One major benefit of the common Nash heritage of the Hornet and Wasp was the innovative "Weather Eye" climate control system. Weather Eye was the first modern heater for automobiles, developed by Nash engineer Nils Erik Wahlberg in the mid-1930s, offering thermostatic control of both hot and cool air.

Then, in 1954, Nash's Kelvinator division helped develop the first modern "All-Season Air Conditioning" system. Prior to this innovation, air conditioning required large, expensive systems with trunk-mounted condensers, found on only the most luxurious of autos. *Popular Mechanics* in its May 1954 issue praised the new All-Season breakthrough: "Nash, the company that pioneered the heater that brings in air from outside the car, now offers the industry's first combination heater and air conditioner. The entire system mounts forward of the dashboard. There are no parts in the trunk.

RIGHT: The 1955 Hudson Wasp Custom four-door sedan with monotone paint displays the fresh appearance and good styling that debuted that year. No longer based on Hudson's famed Step-Down chassis, the big Hudsons didn't handle or corner as well as earlier models, to the disappointment of performance buffs.

BELOW: The Rambler was now sold under both the Hudson and Nash brands, with differences limited to badges. Styling changes on both included open front fenders and a sharp new grille. This year the Rambler boasted the highest resale value among all low-priced cars.

Pricewise, it is the lowest in the industry, selling for $395 factory installed, or $300 below competitive combinations."

Hudson also gained Nash's Twin Travel seating, with reclining front seat backs that could fold into beds. If the new Hudson's instrument cluster and steering wheel looked familiar, that was because they were leftover 1954 components.

It was a fine new automobile, but the highly competitive 1954 market limited sales to just 20,321 Hornet and Wasp units.

Hudson dealers had their hands full adapting to other changes. Gone was the boxy, unloved Hudson Jet compact, though it was fairly new, having been introduced in 1953. The Jet's development had cost around $16 million, but its sales were disappointing—only 35,367 had been sold in two years—compounding the company's losses on this model.

The Hudson Italia sports car was also a casualty in this period. Based on the Jet, only twenty-six Italias were built. A sports car might offer a brand credibility and prestige, but these were desperate times for American Motors and the company couldn't afford the resources to field such halo products.

Help was on the way for those embattled Hudson dealers who stuck with the company. A new compact was on the horizon, one that would quickly turn heads and turn profits: the Rambler.

Nash

Icy-Cool Nash Starts Travel Boom!

"Thanks to Nash, thousands of families look forward to a new kind of vacation," declared a 1955 advertisement. The family could enjoy peering through the new wraparound Scena-Ramic windshield, staying warm or cool in All-Season comfort, and relaxing on Twin Travel Bed seating—Nash made travel by automobile a pleasure.

Riding on a 121.25-inch (308-centimeter) wheelbase, the premium Ambassador was available in two versions: the Ambassador Six, powered by the familiar Nash 252.6-cu.-in. 120-horsepower OHV inline six; and the Ambassador Eight, powered by Packard's fine 320-cu.-in. 208-horsepower V-8. The Statesman was four inches shorter and featured the Nash 195.6-cu.-in. L-head six, producing 110 horsepower.

Both cars were completely restyled in 1952, though they continued the envelope design of enclosed front and rear wheels and rounded forms loved by George Mason. At least designer Ed Anderson was able to open the front wheel arches a few inches on both models for 1955, adding a distortion-free wraparound windshield, the largest in the business. Up front, the Ambassador and Statesman received a new oval grille that enclosed Safety View headlights. Based on Pininfarina's Nash-Healey sports car, the design as worn by the big, broad Nash gave the car a rather bloated look.

According to the National Automobile Dealers Association (NADA), resale value for the Nash line was one of the best in the business, but only 25,852 buyers chose to travel in such style—at such value—that year. Instead, they were drawn by the deals the Chevy-Ford sales war made available.

This year American Motors purchased Packard-built V-8 engines and Twin-Ultramatic transmissions to offer in its finest car lines: Ambassador and Hornet. The engines were powerful, but the improved Twin-Ultramatics proved troublesome. Studebaker-Packard charged high prices for the powertrains, which forced AMC to raise the V-8 models' prices to uncompetitive levels.

Nash or Hudson Rambler

A Whole New Ideal in Automobiles.

American Motors gave Hudson dealers their best sales opportunity in the form of the popular Rambler line, confusingly branded as either the Hudson or Nash Rambler. The difference? A Hudson emblem in the updated grille and Hudson hubcaps.

Tom McCahill had loved Ramblers for years. The legendary road tester for *Mechanix Illustrated* loved the 1955 Rambler even more:

> Right from the opening gun the Rambler held its resale value dollar with Ford and Chevy. Here was a truly different item, just right for thousands of people who want an easy handling car that could get an extra eight or ten miles out of each gallon of fuel and still have all the comfort of its nearest competitors—Ford, Chevy and Plymouth. For the price of an awfully plain Ford or Chevy you can buy a Rambler with the best air-conditioner in the business, the best heater and a lot of other small refinements not usually found in the low-priced field.

This was the sixth year for the Rambler, a vehicle that defied the "bigger is better" logic of the 1950s. George Mason had believed America needed a smaller car, but one that "also had to be big enough to appeal to families as their primary car." At 175.8 inches (447 centimeters) long, with a diminutive 100-inch (254-centimeter) wheelbase for two-door sedan, wagon, and convertible models—and a comfortable 108-inch (274-centimeter) on four-doors—the Rambler was truly compact, but with the room and comfort families wanted. Ramblers were also well equipped and appointed. Powered by the same 90-horsepower, 195.6-cu.-in. L-head six-cylinder engine as the larger Nash Statesman, the Rambler was also a surprisingly spritely performer.

Wisconsin Governor Walter J. Kohler Jr. usually ordered a big Nash for his own use. Here we see his choice for 1955: a handsome Ambassador Custom four-door sedan. Notice the "1" license plate. Nash cars had been produced in Kenosha, Wisconsin, since 1916.

WIS 55
1
OFFICIAL

ROAD TEST: 1955 NASH AMBASSADOR CUSTOM V-8

Publication: *Motor Life*, July 1955
Author: *Motor Life* Staff

The Nash has always been noted for comfort, reliability, and some "different" touches unobtainable on most cars. The 1955 Ambassador V-8 retains all these features and adds one that will be new to most loyal Nash followers—performance that is far better than that of any Nash in the past.

From the outside the two major changes from 1954 are the grille-mounted headlights and the wraparound windshield, which Nash claims is the largest in the industry. The headlight treatment is derived from the Nash-Healey and looks good.

To go with its fine performance, the Nash also offers good handing qualities. . . . Steering is light and easy yet retains a remarkable degree of road feel, more so than in many of its competitors. The Nash rode uncommonly well over very rough gravel roads—which were in very poor shape due to spring thaw and heaving, incidentally. This will be important to a lot of potential Nash owners because it has traditionally appealed to many sportsmen who use it for hunting and fishing expeditions.

The Nash not only goes well but is pretty good in the brakes department . . . "panic" stops from 30, 45, and 60 mph resulted in extremely good stopping distances for a car its size.

This new Nash is all that its forerunners were with new and better performance. The added "go" makes it an even better all-round family car than it's been in the past. The men in the family will like the added zip. The ladies will go for the comfort, power features, and attractive interiors. Almost everyone will like the roominess and reliability.

Knowing the highly maneuverable Rambler would appeal to women, the company brought in a German-born designer, Helene Rother, to create the interiors. Having escaped war-torn Europe, fleeing first to Paris and then to the US, Rother championed the needs of women in automotive design as an independent consultant for the company. In 1948 she became the first woman to deliver a paper to the Society of Automotive Engineers, telling her male audience, "Women very often asked me, when do we get the new fabrics—the ones we can wash and clean, the more colorful ones?" She continued, "Perhaps our new stylists fear to use colors that are too extreme. This results in our being presented again and again with gray

Attempting to keep pace with the rapidly improving power and performance of its competitors, Nash again equipped the Statesman L-head six-cylinder engine with two single-barrel carburetors in 1955. With 110 horsepower, it was still underpowered, but neither Nash or Hudson produced a V-8 engine in this period.

and tan interiors." Mason promised Rother she could use the Rambler as her artistic palette.

Not only was the Rambler unique in the marketplace at the time, it also convinced George Romney to join Nash instead of taking an executive position at Packard. "I was shown prototypes of the Rambler," he said, "and was convinced that here was something different, unique. I felt it was the car of the future."

New designs appeared that helped bring the Rambler current with the times. One feature that held the company back, the enclosed wheels of Nash's Airflyte design, had been a nonnegotiable for the late George Mason. Designer Anderson removed them for the 1955 Rambler, opening up the front wheel arches and widening the front wheels' track.

Tom McCahill was delighted: "My only serious beef about these cars has always been that due to their former all-round envelope bodies you needed more room to make a U-turn than you would to land a B-36. In '55 they've beaten this by cutting a hole out of the fenders for the wheels so that what was the lousiest turning car in the world can now claim to have the shortest turning radius in America." He concluded, "In summing up: the 1955 Ramblers, regardless of grille ornament, are still good cars and excellent buys in the low-price field if they happen to fill what you need in transportation." In American Motors' first, shortened model year, 81,237 buyers agreed, including 25,214 sold through Hudson dealers.

Nash or Hudson Metropolitan

40 Million Miles of Raves.

As small as the Rambler was, American Motors had something even smaller in its back pocket: the Metropolitan. Another Mason project, this was a subcompact that Nash and independent designer William J. Flajole had begun developing in the late 1940s. The goal was to create a smaller auto, one that would appeal to buyers as a second car or to city dwellers challenged by congested streets and limited parking. Like other Nashes, it featured unibody construction and Airflyte design, only in miniature.

To save money, Mason had contracted with British manufacturers Fisher & Ludlow Ltd. to produce the bodies and Austin Motor Company Ltd. to supply the suspension components, Austin's 1,200 cc (73-cu.-in.) 42-horsepower OHV four-cylinder engine with three-speed manual transmission, and final assembly. With Great Britain still struggling to rebuild after World War II, producing the Metropolitan cost Nash just $1,018,475.94 in tooling, along with significant savings in assembly labor.

Introduced in 1954, the Metropolitan continued into 1955 priced at $1,527 for the coupe and $1,551 for the convertible. Americans responded, snapping up 6,096 cars that year.

The Results

American Motors reported a net loss of $6,900,000 for fiscal-year 1954, but much of that could be attributed to the costs of merging Nash and Hudson. They produced 108,292 automobiles and captured 3.4 percent of the US market in calendar year 1955.

1956

Hudson

1956 Hornet has new Safety-Torque V-8 power . . . smart, new V-Line styling . . . 3 times smoother ride.

After a shortened 1955 model year, Hudson returned with a new look and new power. The November 1955 issue of *Popular Science* reported, "New Hudson, new Nash veer apart. These brother autos now offer more individuality in styling, new luxury, higher horsepower. A little more of everything, from torque to tones, is the word from American Motors on its big cars for 1956. The planned dissociation of Hudson and Nash in appearance, despite the use of many of the same body parts, is perhaps the biggest change this year."

With Hudson, V-Line styling was big news. American Motors brought in independent industrial designer Richard Arbib to give their big cars a new look. A graduate of the Pratt Institute in Brooklyn, Arbib joined General Motors' Styling Section in 1939 while running the Detroit Institute of Automobile Styling. After the war he designed commercial vehicles for Henney Motor Company before going off on his own. Arbib was well known for his renderings of futuristic automobiles and spacecraft. He even designed the first electric

Created by independent designer Richard Arbib, the Hudson Wasp and Hornet models were given a facelift for 1956. New frontal styling emphasized the Hudson V motif. At first glance it conveyed a more modern appearance, but overall, it may have looked a little too busy.

LEFT: A closer look at the senior Hudson's new frontal styling shows rich detail and a lot of bright chrome, a hallmark of auto design for the decade. Note the peaked headlamp rings, and the body-color intake vents placed atop the fenders, complete with crosshatch grille-work done in miniature.

BELOW: In order to offer a Hornet at a much lower price than the V-8 models, it was decided to continue offering the big Hornet Six, complete with optional Twin-H-Power (i.e., two carburetors). The Hornets equipped with this engine offered surprisingly good performance, though big, medium-priced cars equipped with a six were rapidly losing their appeal.

wristwatch, the Hamilton Ventura, along with other watches for the company. (He was also known for his romantic involvement with pinup legend Bettie Page.)

Arbib emphasized the Hudson's V-8 power, including a large gold anodized "V" in the grille and large "V" shapes in the side trim. He also added small finlike caps on the rear fenders following the trend of the 1950s.

Power on the smaller Wasp continued to be Hudson's 202-cu.-in. L-head six, in both standard 120- and 130-horsepower Twin H versions. The big Hornet continued with the Hudson 308-cu.-in. L-head straight six, producing 210 or 220 horsepower with Twin H and Packard's updated 352-cu.-in. V-8.

But the Detroit rumor mill was working overtime again. Leo Donovan's "Detroit Listening Post" column in the January 1956 *Popular Mechanics* reported:

> Just about the time you are reading this, American Motors will start building its own V-8 engines at Kenosha, Wis. Both the Hudson and Nash cars have been using Packard V-8 engines and transmissions. Beginning in January, they will be available with their own V-8s, in addition. The new engine will be smaller than the Packard, of course. (After all, Packard's is the biggest in the business.) And the new AM engine will come in a variety of sizes, including one small enough for the Rambler. With the new V-8 engine, the Rambler should be a bomb—it's plenty peppy right now with its six.

Packard's James Nance was doing more than gouging American Motors on the price of its engine: he also reneged on their agreement to buy stampings from AMC. Thankfully, engineers Ralph Isbrandt and David Potter had been developing a thoroughly modern V-8 engine for their former employer, Kaiser. The last thing George Romney needed was another large development expense, but the V-8 gave American Motors a powerplant on a par with what the Big Three offered. And thanks to the previous design work at Kaiser, the new engine took just eighteen months from drawing board to production.

ABOVE: The beautiful Nash Ambassador Country Club hardtop for 1956 offered beautiful styling, V-8 power, the lowest-cost air conditioning on the market, and reclining front seats that could convert into twin beds. Note the front edge of the front fender in this photo and compare with changes made on later production Ambassadors..

RIGHT: An Ambassador produced a little later in the model year. Note the front fenders now have a band of chrome around the front arches and the area surrounding the grille is painted a contrasting color. These changes were first introduced only on Ambassador Customs, then on all Ambassadors, and finally on all Nash senior models in an attempt to address complaints about the front-end styling.

There's New Magic Every Mile
In NASH—the World's Finest Travel Car

PHOTOGRAPHED IN DISNEYLAND

Faced with falling sales of its largest cars, the Nash Motors Division of American Motors fielded a new Ambassador Special line of cars in mid-1956. Based on the shorter-wheelbase Statesman chassis, it was powered by AMC's new 250-cu.-in. V-8. The new V-8 engine family was designed in-house and was more budget friendly than the overpriced Packard engines. This Country Club hardtop listed for $2,462, some $610 less than the regular Ambassador hardtop.

Hudson's new model, the Hudson Hornet Special, sported the new 250-cu.-in. V-8 as of April 1956, built on the Wasp's 116.25-inch (295-centimeter) wheelbase. Priced at $2,405 for the four-door sedan and $2,512 for the two-door hardtop, the Hornet Special was just $191 more than the six-cylinder Wasp. It was also significantly less than the Packard-powered Hudson V-8, starting at $3,026.

It didn't matter: Hudson production was just 8,152 units, less than half the previous year's dismal numbers. To put this into perspective, in 1956 Cadillac built one-and-a-half times more cars—in a single month.

Nash

Announcing Blazing V-8 Power with Traditional Nash Economy!

Motor Trend summed up the new Nash Ambassador and Statesman models in December 1955 like so: "This year, there's a newness that can still be credited to a grille which remains unchanged, yet one which is unique enough to draw glances and comment from all quarters; add to this restyled parking lights, vastly different taillights, higher rear fenders and tricky body panel chrome work, and you have an outline of the Nashes."

Nash called it "Speedline Styling," adding a one-piece wraparound rear window to match the windshield pioneered the year before.

Like Hudson, Nash switched to the new AMC 250-cu.-in. Torque-Flo V-8 in April 1956, paired with a three-speed manual transmission, optional overdrive, or an optional Flashaway three-speed automatic from GM's Hydra-Matic division. As with Hudson, the availability of this new engine gave Nash the power to bring out a new Ambassador Special model. Based on the shorter Statesman body, the Ambassador Special could move from a standstill to 60 miles per hour (97 kilometers per hour) in a quick 14.6 seconds according to *Motor Trend*, which also saw a surprising 19 miles per gallon (8 kilometers

In a gutsy and fateful move, AMC president George W. Romney decided to move up introduction of the all-new Rambler planned for 1957 to the 1956 model year. It cost a great deal of time and money, but the resulting car attracted a great deal of attention from the motoring press and public. To reduce costs, it was decided to offer the new Rambler in four-door models only; sedan, hardtop, station wagon, and hardtop station wagon. Seen here is the four-door Custom hardtop.

per liter) at a constant 45 miles per hour (71 kilometers per hour), a common cruising speed in the days before interstate highways.

Advertising touted the Special's fuel economy and American Motors' advanced Double Safe unibody construction with over eight thousand spot welds. The famous Twin Travel Bed, unique All-Season Air Conditioning, and large trunk were also on display in a five-minute promotional film narrated by Ed Zern, an outdoor sportsman who wrote for the *New York Times, Field & Stream*, and others. Senior Nash prices started at $2,139 for the Statesman, $2,939 for the Custom Ambassador Eight with Packard V-8 power, and $2,355 for the Ambassador Special four-door sedan—every version a great value for the money.

The company poured all their effort into these cars, but production was unimpressive. For all models, the total produced was a mere 22,263 units, nearly half the previous year's output.

MAKE	NASH			RAMBLER	HUDSON			METROPOLITAN
Model	Statesman	Ambassador	Ambassador Special		Wasp	Hornet	Hornet Special	Series III
Passengers	6	6	6	5	6	6	6	3
Doors	2 or 4	2 or 4	2 or 4	4	2 or 4	2 or 4	2 or 4	2
Wheelbase (inches)	114.25	121.25	114.25	108	114.25	121.25	114.25	85
Engine (Standard)	195.6 cu.in., F-Head I-6, 110 hp	252.6 cu.in., OHV I-6, 120 hp	250 cu.in., OHV V-8, 190 hp	195.6 cu.in., OHV I-6, 120 hp	202 cu.in., L-Head I-6, 120 hp or 130 hp	308 cu.in., L-Head I-6, 165 hp or 175 hp	250 cu.in., OHV V-8, 190 hp	90.9 cu.in., OHV I-4, 52 hp
Engine (Optional)		352 cu.in., OHV V-8, 220 hp				352 cu.in., OHV V-8, 220 hp		
Production	7,438	10,680	4,145	66,573	2,519	4,638	1,757	9,068
	22,263				8,914			

Total American Motors Production: 106,818 Market Share: 2.1%

Nash and Hudson Rambler

Lots more fun! Much less cost! Make the Smart Switch to Rambler!

The hype was real, the 1956 Rambler was all new, and it was outstanding. After the expenses associated with merging Hudson into the company and the resulting losses of 1955, American Motors was bleeding red ink and running out of money—and time. George Romney threw everything he had left into bringing out a new Rambler, the one shining star in the American Motors lineup.

Bill Reddig, a young designer who reported to Anderson, was working on a major update to the look of the 1957 Rambler. Since Rambler was the only American Motors product selling in any volume, Romney committed $5.4 million to bringing those changes to show rooms a year earlier than planned.

"There were darn few of us (in Styling) and we were working like hell," said Reddig. "We were working long hours and we got tired, but Romney, in his shirtsleeves, was coming in several times a day to see how things were going. He didn't have a whip; he was so full of enthusiasm it was contagious, and Ed was right out there on the boards, with a stylus in his hand, working with the clay modelers to get the look exactly as he wanted it."

Built on the 108-inch (274-centimeter) wheelbase of the previous four-door and station wagon Ramblers, no 100-inch (254-centimeter) two-door or convertible version would be offered. Gone was any hint of the previous "bathtub" style, replaced now with a contemporary design (dubbed the Solid Gold Look) with an open "greenhouse" for visibility and a dramatic reverse-slope C-pillar called the Fashion Safety Arch. The large chrome grille was die-cast for strength (not stamped) and the forward-leaning front fender edges continued the design language used on the large Nash without dating the look. Add two- and three-tone paint schemes, and the new Rambler was quite handsome. *Popular Mechanics* summed it up: "Distinct and different, the all-new Rambler can be recognized at any angle from its wide-open competition-type grille to the pronounced arch over the rear window."

BELOW LEFT: The new Ramblers were popular overseas. Shown is a 1956 Hudson Rambler Custom four-door hardtop at a European auto show. Hudsons drew a lot of attention (and sales) in the United Kingdom at the time.

BELOW RIGHT: A scene from the Milwaukee Body Plant final assembly line: three workers carefully install the windshield in a 1956 Rambler Custom. After body assembly was completed, the vehicle would be shipped by truck to the Kenosha main plant. By the way, this three-man installation job today is done by a single, self-guided robot.

AMC faced pushback in 1956 on the Rambler Custom's two-toning for its basket-handle roof pillar. Moving quickly to address this, the company introduced a revised Custom trim midyear by eliminating two-toning on the C-pillar. Similar to what would be used on the 1957 Rambler Custom, differences appear on close examination.

Powering the new Rambler was the familiar 195.6-cu.-in. straight six but modernized with an overhead valvetrain. This increased output by 33 percent, to 120 horsepower, and improved fuel efficiency, returning a class-leading 24.35 mpg (10.35 kilometers per liter) in the 1956 Mobilgas Economy Run.

As before, Hudson and Nash dealers sold versions that were identical, apart from the emblems. The basic Deluxe four-door sedan cost as little as $1,829, while the Custom Cross Country station wagon started at $2,494. The new Rambler lived up to its hype: while sales were less than the previous year, automobile sales in general were down from the record numbers of 1955. With 66,573 built (including 20,496 sold through Hudson dealers), the new Rambler was very much a hit.

Nash and Hudson Metropolitan

Amazing New, Blazing New.

In December 1955, the tiny Metropolitan received a much-needed power boost in the form of a larger 1,493 cc (90.9-cu.-in.) engine that produced 52 horsepower. The new Series III Metropolitan 1500 also got stylish two-tone paint treatments, with Caribbean Green, Sunburst Yellow, or Coral Red over Snowberry White.

According to the July 1956 issue of *Sports Car Illustrated*, "The current Metropolitan has few defects in the light-car frame of reference. The most serious gripes registered by owners, aside from seating capacity, concern the excessively large turning circle and the somewhat inaccessible luggage space. Otherwise, the Metropolitan goes, stops, steers, handles, and rides well. Its fuel economy is excellent and its top speed and acceleration are adequate."

Nash and Hudson sold another 9,068 of these small wonders, a small victory for those beleaguered dealers.

The Results

American Motors reported a net loss of $19,700,000 in 1955, some of that due to the development of the new Rambler, for the fiscal year. They produced 106,818 automobiles and captured 2.1 percent of the US market.

1957

Hudson

Way up in power, way down in price!

The 1957 Hudson was a true value. Richard Arbib continued the V-Line styling of the previous model, toned down a bit with a silver "V" on the grille. The faux fins on the rear fenders were now body color, too. A major update was a new, flatter roof stamping, which mitigated the bathtub look and, along with 14-inch (36-centimeter) wheels, lowered the overall height by 2 inches (5 centimeters). Hudson and Nash also joined the $13,074 Cadillac Eldorado Brougham as the only models to pioneer quad headlamps—a bold move, since many states had not yet legalized this innovative headlight feature.

American Motors also discontinued the shorter, slow-selling Wasp in this year. Hudsons now started at $2,000 and included the big Hornet body, in four-door sedan and two-door hardtop versions, powered by the newest engine in the AMC family, the 220-horsepower, 327-cu.-in. V-8, a bored-out version of the 250-cu.-in. Torque-Flo introduced the previous year. Despite the Hornet's great value, however, buyers rejected the big Hudson, and just 4,180 were produced.

Nash

World's newest, finest travel car!

You could see the U.S.A. in your Chevrolet, but it would be so much more enjoyable in a Nash. The famous '57 Chevy lacked the large Scena-Ramic windshield, Weather Eye and optional All-Season Air Conditioning for climate control, Twin Travel Bed reclining front seats, and the 220-horsepower, 327-cu.-in. V-8. In one automotive package, Nash made a compelling case for people who liked to travel the highways and byways of America.

Like the Hudson, the updated Nash lost much of its former soap-bar shape of old by applying a flatter roof, smaller wheels, and quad headlights. Still, the basic design dated to 1952, and the market now demanded lower, longer, wider—and fins. Or smaller cars, like the Rambler.

Only 10,330 Nash Ambassadors left the Kenosha plant.

ABOVE: Because it had been treated to restyling in 1956, the Hudson Hornet was given only minor appearance updates for the following year. It received the new American Motors 327-cu.-in. V-8, though, so its performance could be maintained while its price stayed low. This was the final year for the Hudson in America, and only the Hornet V-8 was offered, though some six-cylinder models were produced for export markets.

BELOW: Painted tail fins on a 1957 Hornet sedan: the Hornet's tail fins were grafted on in pieces because AMC lacked the money to fully retool the fenders, a detail added in an effort to keep up with the styling trends of the latter half of the decade. Sales were low, however, mainly due to worries that the Hudson brand was on its way out.

Rambler

You don't know what a thrill driving can be.

Imagine American Motors' hot new 327-cu.-in. V-8, derived from the big Ambassador and Hornet—featuring higher compression, four-barrel carb, and mechanical lifters—loaded into the compact Rambler. The 1957 Rambler Rebel was a true factory hot rod, available at any Nash or Hudson dealer.

The exterior dimensions of the AMC V-8 were the same regardless of displacement, so if the 250-cu.-in. engine fit the Rambler's engine compartment, so did the bored-out 327. Transmission options were the Flashaway Hydra-Matic or three-speed manual with overdrive.

Motor Trend's Joseph H. Wherry compared "Detroit's Stock Rods" in the April 1957 issue and discovered that the Rebel was the second quickest of the group in 0-to-60-mile-per-hour (0-to-97-kilometer-per-hour) acceleration. The car's 7.5-second blast was faster than the 375-horsepower Chrysler 300C, only beaten by the 7.0-second 283-horsepower Corvette with its new Rochester Ram-Jet mechanical fuel injection. Just as shocking as the Rebel's speed was its thrift, as it won in its class in the 1957 Mobilgas Economy Run, recording 21.62 miles per gallon (9.2 kilometers per liter).

The Rebel could have been even quicker. The plan was to offer Bendix Electrojector electronic fuel injection as a $395 option. The revolutionary multipoint injection system increased the Rebel's power from 255 to a striking 288 horsepower, five more than the

ABOVE: The 1957 Nash Ambassador, last of the breed, received a stylish facelift this year. A new oval grille, new front fenders bearing quad headlamps, and open front wheelwells gave the Ambassador a great new look. A redesigned roof panel and smaller wheels helped lower the roofline, while the new standard 327-cu.-in. American Motors V-8 provided exciting performance.

RIGHT: Do big cars get any better-looking than this? The 1957 Ambassador has more than just style: it has presence, something that helps it take over the scene wherever it goes. The styling is aggressive, bold, and utterly unique. And it has performance to put others to shame.

ROAD TEST: 1957 RAMBLER REBEL

Publication: ***Hot Rod*****, August 1957**
Author: Ray Brock

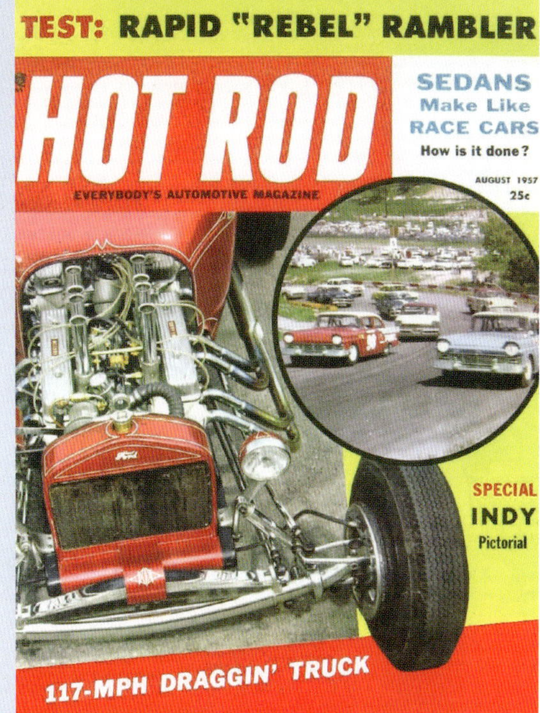

In keeping with HRM's policy of trying to give our readers a true report on Detroit's "super-stocks" or "performance models" as they are sometimes called, we selected the American Motors Corporation's new Rambler Rebel for our guinea pig this month. There is only one model available in the Rebel series and it is easily distinguished from other Rambler cars. . . . The thing that really makes it differ from the other Ramblers, though it doesn't show from the outside but is readily apparent either by lifting the hood or by tickling the throttle. The big difference is in the power department.

The engine is a 327-cubic-inch V-8 with 255 horsepower that was developed by American Motors and used with a smaller 250-inch displacement in the 1956 Hudson Hornet and Nash Statesman cars.

In the transmission department two types are available, the standard shift with overdrive or the "Flashaway" Hydra-Matic. For the stick shift transmission, a Borg & Beck 10-inch pressure plate and disc are used. The "Flashaway" Hydra-Matic, with which our test car was equipped, is made by the Detroit Gear Division of General Motors and is basically the same as the Olds Jetaway or Pontiac Strato-Flight.

While we had the Rebel placed at our disposal by the Southern California American Motors zone office, we made the rounds of several speed shops in the Los Angeles area seeking interesting bits of information and met repeated requests for a trial ride from performance-minded people. We obliged whenever possible and were quite impressed by comments we received on the Rebel. All thought that the acceleration was very good, 9.4 seconds to a true 60 mph with our Hydra-Matic (3.15 rear end) equipped test car. The same car with standard transmission and a 4.10 rear end is reliably reported to better 8 seconds flat. Our guest critics were also impressed by the workmanship on the car. The Rebel is not a cheap car in price or quality. Body work, interior material and trim, paint, door fit, etc. were all excellent.

Standing ¼-mile acceleration was accomplished in 17 seconds flat with speed of 84 mph at the end of the. . . . It is quite a car and a trial run in one might surprise you.

fuelie Corvette. Those extra 33 horses could have easily propelled the Rebel past the 'Vette in acceleration. Unfortunately, the cutting-edge system was not ready for prime time, and only a handful of Rebels were produced with it. Chrysler also tried the Bendix system on their high-end 1958 Chrysler 300D, DeSoto Adventurer, Dodge D-500, and Plymouth Fury performance cars, with the same unreliable results. It would be another ten years before the Electrojector appeared on a production vehicle, though at that time it was offered by the German Bosch company as their D-Jetronic system.

Differentiating the Rebel four-door hardtop sedan from lesser Ramblers was a unique Silver-Gray paint and a full-length gold-anodized aluminum trim piece along

RIGHT: he 1957 Rambler Custom four-door sedan, showing off its newly designed side trim. Note the V-8 badge on the C-pillar, indicating that this car is equipped with the AMC 250-cu.-in. V-8. This was the first year for a V-8 Rambler; though it didn't make a real impact on sales for the year, the car attracted many new buyers who otherwise might not have bought a Rambler.

BELOW RIGHT: This 1957 Rambler Custom four-door station wagon boasts new side trim plus three-tone paint: gold body, black side spear, and white roof. Buyers loved the Custom series because it provided more luxury than a comparable Chevy or Ford, at lower prices and with far better fuel economy. The station wagons in particular were hot sellers.

the side of the car, like the trim on Chrysler's upscale Plymouth Fury and DeSoto Adventurer that year.

For value, though, the Rebel had the others beat. Where a Chrysler 300C started at $4,929, and a fuel-injected Corvette went for about $4,053, you could pick up a Rebel for a mere $2,786. Every one of the 1,500 limited-edition models sold.

The Rebel may have grabbed all the headlines and drawn crowds to the show rooms, but the rest of the Rambler line continued much like the year before, albeit with more compelling options. No longer a Nash or a Hudson, the Rambler was now a brand of its own, sold by both dealer networks.

Two distinct models were offered: the Rambler Six with the 120-horsepower, 195.6-cu.-in. OHV six, and the Rambler V-8 powered by the 190-horsepower, 250-cu.-in. engine from the previous year's Ambassador and Hornet Special—both featured Hydra-Matic or three-speed manual transmissions, with overdrive optional on the manual. Six-cylinder sedans appeared in Deluxe, Super, and Custom trim, wagons in Super and Custom, and

MAKE	NASH	RAMBLER			HUDSON	METROPOLITAN
Model	Ambassador	Six	V-8	Rebel	Hornet	Series III
Passengers	6	6	6	6	6	3
Doors	4	4	4	4	4	2
Wheelbase (inches)	121.25	108	108	108	121.25	85
Engine (Standard)	327 cu.in., OHV V-8, 225 hp	195.6 cu.in., OHV I-6, 125 hp	250 cu.in., OHV V-8, 190 hp	327 cu.in., OHV V-8, 255 hp	327 cu.in., OHV V-8, 225 hp	90.9 cu.in., OHV I-4, 52 hp
Production	3,561	68,757	14,442	1,500	4,108	15,317
		84,699				

Total American Motors Production: 107,685 Market Share: 1.8%

the non-Rebel hardtop in Super trim. For V-8 models there were sedans and wagons in Super and Custom trim, plus a hardtop station wagon and sedan in Custom only.

By the end of the 1957 model year, a stunning 91,469 Ramblers had been produced. George Romney's $5.6 million investment in the Rambler seemed to be paying off.

Metropolitan

Join the personal car set!

The year didn't see a sea change when it came to sales, though, like the Rambler, the Metropolitan (making a name for itself as the Met) was now a separate make. The grille emblem changed from either Hudson or Nash to an "M" for Metropolitan—and more people than ever were joining the personal car set by owning one.

In 1950, US homes averaged one automobile per family, but by 1957 that number had increased by more than a quarter, to 1.3 autos per family. More American households were becoming two-car families, and the Metropolitan, with its features and interior design catering to women, was clearly a unique option. More than fifteen-thousand buyers thought so, up 40.7 percent from 1956.

The Metropolitan got new two-toning for 1956, a style that was carried over unchanged to this 1957 model. A mid-1955 change in the Metropolitan included this trim/two-toning as standard equipment, along with a larger, 1500 cc four-cylinder engine that provided much better acceleration *and* better fuel economy. A new grille graced the front end.

The Results

American Motors reported a net loss of $11,833,200 for fiscal year 1957. Those loses came mostly in the first half of the year, while the rest of the year trended positive. The company produced 107,685 automobiles and captured 1.8 percent of the US market. "I knew we were on the right track," George Romney told *Time* magazine. "The question was: Would the car-buying public discover that in time?"

1958-1963

CHAPTER

2

THE GREAT RAMBLER YEARS

For George Romney, model year 1958 would either be the most successful one in American Motors' short existence—or the company would fail completely. Romney was hardly a gambling man. Born in 1907 in a Mormon colony in Mexico, as a young adult he'd devoted two years to Mormon missionary work. *Time* magazine commented, "In an industry noted for hard drinking and tough talk, Romney does not drink (not even tea or coffee), or smoke, or swear." He would not gamble in the traditional sense, either. Yet with the 1958 models nearing their introduction date, Romney had just pushed in all his chips and rolled the dice.

He'd spent the previous three years building on the work of his predecessor, George Mason. Unproductive or unneeded plants were rationalized, existing models

OPPOSITE TOP: American Motors' top volume-selling car was the six-cylinder Rambler series. The line offered four-door sedans and station wagons in Deluxe, Super, and Custom trim, plusa hardtop sedan in Super trim. *Tom & Kelly Glatch*

OPPOSITE BOTTOM: The 1958 model year saw AMC's first full-year profit, though the company had been running in the black at the close of 1957. All corporate and administrative functions were carried out in the American Motors headquarters building at 14250 Plymouth Road in Detroit. Originally the headquarters for Kelvinator Corporation, the building was subsequently used as Nash-Kelvinator headquarters before becoming AMC's home.

LEFT: Like the Nashes before them, Ramblers were famed for offering optional reclining front seats that could be folded down to form twin beds. By adding pillows, bedding. and cushions to level out the surface area. two people could sleep in comfort all night. Optional screens could be purchased to keep out bugs when the windows were left open.

Another new series for 1958 was the Ambassador by Rambler, which replaced the Nash Ambassador and Hudson Hornet as AMC's big car. Produced by mating the senior Rambler's main body with a longer 117-inch (297-centimeter) wheelbase and updated frontal styling and trim, the Ambassador offered a total of six models in two series: Super and Custom. This Rambler display includes an Ambassador hardtop sedan *center*, flanked by an Ambassador Custom four-door sedan, and a Rambler Rebel station wagon in the background.

were reduced to include only the most popular, and then, for 1958, Romney let the withering Nash and Hudson brands die. Assembly lines were repurposed, tooling for Nash and Hudson products scrapped.

Only one year, 1957, saw American Motors carrying all its four brands: Nash, Hudson, Rambler, and Metropolitan. For 1958 there would be just two: Rambler and Metropolitan. Roy D. Chapin Jr., AMC's sales manager at the time, commented, "The decision really was one that said 'we've got to spend our money and our effort and our concentration on the Rambler.'"

Yet again the United States was plunged into an economic recession, this time worse than the recession of 1953; the economy dropped 3.7 percent in the fourth quarter of 1957 alone. With over five million Americans unemployed and inflation running at 2.7 percent, owners were holding on to their cars longer, causing new car sales to plummet to almost half of 1955's figures.

The 1953 recession and price war between Chevrolet and Ford had been devastating to independent automakers. What would 1958's challenges do to American Motors? There was no money left, and if Romney's plan failed, new products could not be rushed into production.

There was simply no turning back.

1958

Rambler

Get American big car room and comfort. Get European small car economy, handling ease.

The quad headlamps pioneered by Nash and Hudson the year before became part of the facelift given the 1958 Rambler, combining in what was called Jet Stream Styling. *Motor Life* magazine commented that the "front end revamping is very good; the new treatment is crisper and cleaner than before. In addition, a visual impression of greater width is created without any actual increase in dimension." The side trim was revamped, as well. In typical AMC fashion, these were minor changes that provided maximum impact, with the updated Rambler looking fresh and new.

Four-door sedan, hardtop, and station wagon bodies continued, in Custom and Super trim, plus sedan and wagon models in Deluxe trim. Two series were offered: the Rambler 6, powered by the same 195.6-cu.-in. OHV six, and the Rambler V-8, now called the Rebel, using the 250-cu.-in. two-barrel V-8 from 1957, now producing 215 horsepower. The Borg-Warner T96 three-speed manual was standard, overdrive optional, and also optional was the Flash-O-Matic automatic transmission, now with pushbutton Telovac Shifting controls.

Although the 327-V-8 Rebel of the previous year had been unceremoniously discontinued, the new mainstream Rebel "is now able to reach a true 60-mph from a standstill in an estimated 12.0 seconds," reported *Motor Trend*. Not Corvette quick like the 1957 version, but plenty entertaining just the same.

What had been the Rambler V-8 became the Rambler Rebel series for 1958. These cars were different from the 1957 limited-build Rebels: for one thing, the new Rebel line was powered by the smaller AMC 250-cu.-in. V-8. The 1958 Rebel offered more models and body styles and much lower prices. What had begun as a winning statement came to nothing: AMC discontinued its high-performance Rebel just as Detroit's horsepower wars were starting to heat up.

Ambassador by Rambler

And now . . . All New Ambassador V-8.

The termination of Nash and Hudson left a void in the large car marketplace, though both brands had been barely making an impact during their production runs. To fill the gaps, American Motors reintroduced the Ambassador name on a new car for 1958.

In another brilliant move, the Ambassador was created by lengthening the Rambler by 9 inches (23 centimeters). The Rambler's unibody was relatively easy to lengthen or shorten in the manufacturing process, while still retaining an interior as large as those found in full-size Ford and GM sedans (though it seemed deceptively smaller). On the Ambassador, length was added forward of the passenger compartment, which gave the illusion of greater luxury and mass. It was a new concept, one copied a decade later by John Z. Delorean to create the 1969 Pontiac Grand Prix from the midsize Tempest.

The new Ambassador may have shared many of its components with the Rambler—even much of the exterior sheet metal—but the visual effect was remarkable. Ambassadors were given different trim than the Rambler, including anodized side trim that swept up the rear fins, and a V-shaped front bumper that recalled the 1956–1957 Hudson. Front and rear bold letters spelling A×M×B×A×S×S×A×D×O×R told all who saw it this was a "new 270 HP Ambassador by Rambler, now featuring one of the highest power-weight ratios. It's the world's finest travel car."

That's right: all Ambassadors were powered by the same 270-horsepower, 327-cu.-in. V-8 of the 1957 Rebel, backed by the same transmissions. Both Custom and Super trim levels were offered on four-door sedan, hardtop, and station wagon bodies.

Sales of the imported Metropolitan were ramping up nicely in 1958, as this picture taken at a shipping yard attests. Americans were becoming increasingly interested in smaller, more fuel-efficient cars and were open to the idea of purchasing foreign cars. This was likely an effect of so many Americans having served overseas during World War II.

RAMBLER CLASSIC: BUYERS' PROFILE

In its March 1963 issue, *Popular Mechanics* polled owners of that year's Classics to find out who they were and why they'd selected the car.

"Rambler owners, it seems, are no ordinary breed. They are a practical and thrifty group who look on their motor cars as proof of their good sense, rather than as impressive symbols of their personal affluence. Although they appreciate the styling of Rambler's brand-new body, some 67.8 per cent stated that their purchase of a 1963 Rambler was most influenced by a desire for economy. Perhaps the many ministers, farmers, government workers, schoolteachers, and retired people among them help to explain the emphasis on thrift.

"The second-ranking influence to buy, mentioned by 18.7 per cent of all owners, was size, indicating an appreciation of Rambler's exemplary combination of compact exterior dimensions with roomy interiors for the passengers."

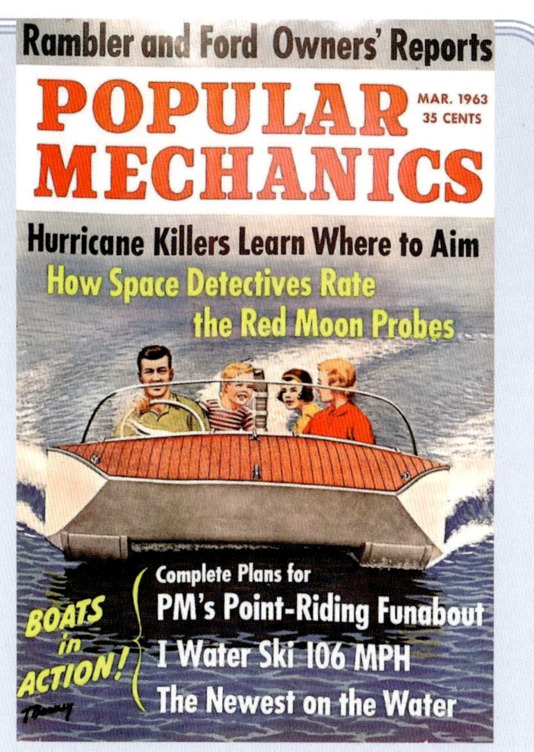

Sales were brisk, with 14,570 Ambassadors sold in this year. The numbers were about the same as Nash and Hudson in the previous year, but since they shared the Rambler's DNA, were now profitable to produce.

Rambler American

Here by Popular Demand.

AMC's product planners saw a gap in the company's offerings, between the 108-inch (274-centimeter) wheelbase of the four-door Rambler and the subcompact, 85-inch (216-centimeter) wheelbase found on the Metropolitan. There was talk of stretching the Metropolitan into a four-seater, but due to the losses incurred in the previous years—and the capital spent on updating the Rambler and creating the Ambassadors for 1958—resources were tight for fielding another new product.

Sales manager Roy Chapin Jr. recalled a discussion with management. "Grins lighted up our faces . . . 'Why, we already have such a car,' one of us exclaimed. 'Our tools are still intact for the 100-inch Rambler.'" The original Rambler two-door, introduced in 1951, had been canceled after 1955 to make way for the all-new four-door Rambler. Everything required to manufacture the two-door was still in storage.

All styling chief Ed Anderson and his team had to do was take the 1955 Rambler and give it an inexpensive makeover. Existing stamping dies would be modified to open the wheel arches to eliminate the dreaded Airflyte bathtub look, the hood's scoop and bulky

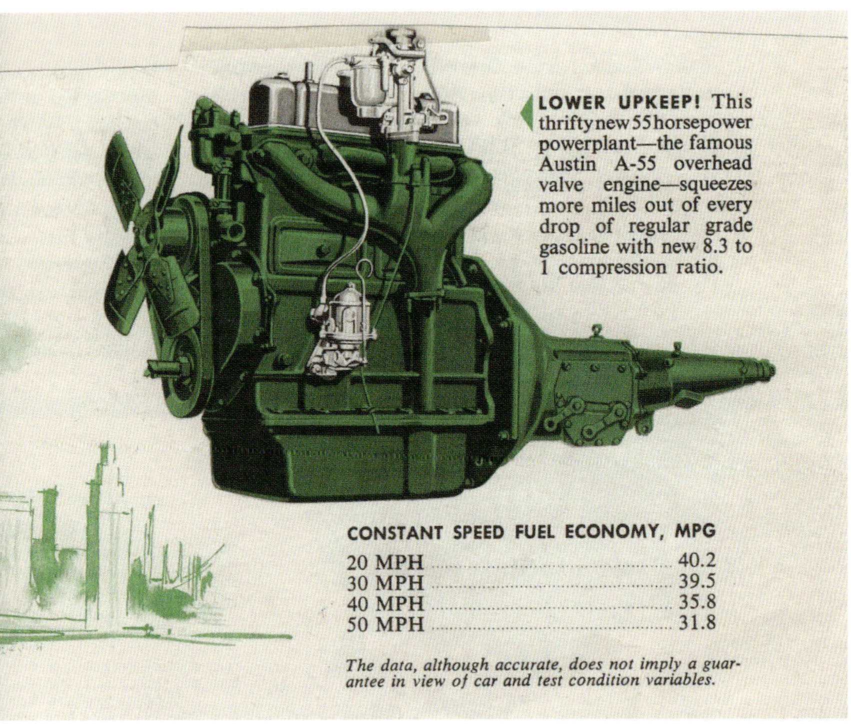

The Metropolitan was built in the United Kingdom by Austin, a large British automaker with excess production capacity. Although designed entirely in the US, the Met was built with English components, including its 1500 cc four-cylinder Austin engine. As the chart shows, at a steady 40 miles per hour (64.3 kilometers per hour), the Met could achieve 35.8 miles per gallon (15 kilometers per liter)—excellent gas mileage for the time.

ornament would be taken off, and the raised ridge on the trunk lid removed. Anderson added a new grille stamping and a lower, flatter roof panel, along with a large wraparound rear window echoing the larger Rambler.

One more styling trick: Chapin suggested turning the existing taillamps upside down so the reflectors would now be on the bottom. The updates cost little to execute, and the look was fresh while also retaining a few hints of the car's Nash past.

The 195.6-cu.-in. L-head six that powered the original Nash Rambler was used again, mated to the same transmissions as the larger cars. The basic Deluxe model cost just $1,789, making it the nation's lowest-priced American car. For just $85 more, you could receive the Super, which included foam-cushion seats, armrests, twin sun visors, and other amenities.

The revived two-door was dubbed the Rambler American to separate it from the larger Rambler and foreign competitors, including the British-built Metropolitan. Though the American didn't arrive until January 1958, it made an impact: 30,640 were sold.

Rambler Metropolitan

Luxury in Miniature.

Little changed on the Metropolitan for 1958, save a switch midyear to a one-piece rear window. The car had its niche in the marketplace and was selling just fine.

A seven-page brochure compared the Met with its competition: Ford Anglia, Hillman Minx, Renault Dauphine, and the segment-leading Volkswagen Beetle. The booklet made a compelling case for the American-designed Metropolitan, illustrating how it suited American roads and driving expectations with a column-shifted manual transmission, exterior design "in the American tradition," and a wide bench seat (versus the buckets of the foreigners) with coil springs. The modern engine delivered a fairly quick 0-to-60 miles per hour (0-to-97 kilometers per hour) in 17.4 seconds, getting 33.5 miles per gallon (14 kilometers per liter) at 50 miles per hour (80 kilometers per hour). The brochure bragged of the company's 1,334 dealers nationwide (where VW only had 352). The promotion must have worked: 13,128 Metropolitans were sold (down from 15,317 the year before), despite facing direct competition from the new American.

MAKE	RAMBLER				
Model	American	Rambler 6	Rambler Rebel	Ambassador	Metropolitan
Passengers	5	6	6	6	2
Doors	2	4	4	4	2
Wheelbase (inches/ centimeters)	100/254	108/274	108/274	117/297	85/216
Engine (Standard)	195.6 cu. in., L-head I-6, 110 hp	195.6 cu. in., OHV I-6, 125 hp	250 cu. in., OHV V-8, 215 hp	327 cu. in., OHV V-8, 270 hp	90.9 cu. in., OHV I-4, 52 hp
Engine (Optional)		195.6 cu. in., OHV I-6, 138 hp			
Production	30,640	106,916	10,056	14,570	13,128

Total American Motors Production: 175,310 Market Share: 4.2%

The Results

The *New York Times* on November 25, 1958, offered this final judgement: "The American Motors Corporation, maker of Rambler cars, enjoying its most successful year, reported a net profit today of $26,085,134 for the fiscal year ended Sept. 30, 1958. 'The financial results in the 1958 fiscal year are a forceful indication that Rambler has achieved a major breakthrough in the automobile market,' Mr. Romney said."

American Motors built 162,182 cars (and imported 13,128 Metropolitans) with a 4.2 percent market share—a dramatic increase from 1.8 percent in 1957. Rambler was selling better than the midpriced Dodge, Mercury, Edsel, DeSoto, and Studebaker. In the same year, the once-glorious Packard brand folded forever (maybe they should have joined American Motors after all). *Time* magazine reported, "Ford and Chrysler together, on the other hand, sold 1,429,000 cars in the first nine months of 1958—and lost $61 million between them." In this challenging recession year, AMC was the only automaker to turn a profit.

In a surprise move, CEO George Romney ordered the 1955 100-inch (254-centimeter) wheelbase Rambler two-door sedan back into production as the 1958 Rambler American. The car received minor styling updates for a more contemporary look and was priced well below other American-made automobiles. This Deluxe two-door sedan's base price was $1,789, versus the lowest-cost Chevrolet's $2,101 price tag. A Rambler American Super was the only other model in the American line, priced at $1,874.

ABOVE: American Motors' lowest-priced family-sized car for 1959 was this Deluxe four-door sedan. The Deluxe series this year wore only two headlamps, not the four seen on the higher-priced series. These were basic cars with stark interior trim, but they were roomy, comfortable, and very economical.

RIGHT: For buyers who wanted a V-8 engine, the Rebel series offered an array of models, including this handsome Custom Cross Country station wagon. The roof rack and full wheel discs were standard equipment, and this car boasts an optional radio and wide whitewall tires. A smart, stylish family wagon.

1959

Rambler

Why pay up to $300 a foot for excess length?

The *New York Times* on September 11, 1958, described the 1959 Ramblers: "Rear fins have been blended into the door panels to provide a longer graceful line that is not extreme in style. Chrome has been curtailed and design treatments sharpened. Contrary to the trend of the Big Three—General Motors, Ford and Chrysler—to longer, lower and wider cars, the Ramblers will continue unchanged in size to conform to the American Motors theory

LEFT: Since the restyled 1958 models were so well received by the public, the 1959 Ramblers were given only minor styling updates. New full-width grilles debuted on the senior Ramblers, along with reshaped rear doors and revised side trim. The American series was indistinguishable from the prior year's offerings, but a new two-door station wagon model was added to the lineup.

BELOW: To burnish its reputation for exceptional fuel economy, American Motors entered its cars in several sanctioned fuel economy challenges. In addition, the company arranged its own economy trials, like the 1959 Rambler Coast-to-Coast Economy Run. Two 1959 Rambler Six models were driven from Los Angeles to New York: one was equipped with the standard transmission plus overdrive, the other with the optional three-speed automatic transmission. The stick-shift car achieved 36.88 miles per gallon (15.68 kilometers per liter), the automatic 32.07 miles per gallon (13.63 kilometers per liter).

of avoiding radical change and built-in obsolescence." George Romney was avoiding the enormously costly, comprehensive styling updates implemented annually by the Big Three, instead saving money by making subtle changes to kept his cars current.

The April 6, 1959, issue of *Time* magazine featured Romney on the cover. The story, titled "The Dinosaur Hunter," told readers, "The American dinosaur, to Romney, is the long, low, chrome-laden U.S. auto, i.e., any car of his Big Three competitors." His message was resonating with consumers: they were buying Ramblers like never before, over fifty thousand more than the previous year.

Ambassador by Rambler

The Modern Concept of a Luxury Car.

In an ad for the 1959 Ambassador, American Motors said, "'Too big to park.' That's what most owners say about their overgrown '59 cars. The Ambassador is the one medium-priced car that parks easily . . . is so much more agile in traffic." The Ambassador couldn't face off against competitors like Oldsmobile or Mercury directly, but it did appeal to the customer looking for an upscale automobile in a more practical package.

ABOVE: The 1959 Rambler Classic was perfect for growing "Baby Boom" families: small on the outside, room for six inside, with the economy and durability few other automobiles could deliver. *Tom & Kelly Glatch*

RIGHT: Business was red-hot in 1959. American Motors was forced to spend more on equipment to boost production of the year's cars, along with hiring many more employees. This American two-door Super sedan is receiving its final inspection before being driven off the assembly line.

Side trim now had an anodized aluminum insert between the chrome strips, with a Z-shaped lightning bolt before sweeping up in the fins. Body styles continued with four-door sedans in base Super or upscale Custom trim; four-door hardtops and a unique hardtop wagon were only available in Custom trim.

Sales data showed that buyers were spending the $215 premium for an Ambassador over the Rebel V-8. That resulted in 23,769 being built, almost double the 1958 output.

ABOVE: Although the Metropolitan didn't look different for 1959, it actually boasted several important features and upgrades. Vent windows were now standard equipment on all Mets, along with an outside-opening trunk lid. A wraparound rear window, which had debuted in mid-1958 on the hardtop models, was continued for 1959. Although the Mets weren't much less expensive than the Rambler American, they were better trimmed and included electric windshield wipers, bumper guards, cigarette lighter, two-tone paint, and more as standard equipment. These items either cost extra or were not available on the American.

Rambler American

America demanded it! Rambler built it!"

As expected, the compact American returned with few changes. Added was the option of a limited-slip Twin Grip differential, a welcome addition in Snowbelt states or rural areas where extra traction was useful. Dealers could also now install an air conditioning package, equally welcome in the South and Southwest. The Deluxe and Super trim level remained, though Deluxe sedans now included rolldown rear windows. The 90-horsepower Super Flying Scot L-head six was the only engine available.

One important addition to the lineup was a station wagon. American Motors dusted off the tooling for the old Rambler wagon and began offering it starting at a mere $2,060 in Deluxe trim, or $2,145 got you the Super, which included a cargo mat and chrome roof rack. Fold the rear seat flat and families and small businesses had 52 cubic feet (1.5 cubic meters) of cargo room.

Demand for the American was spectacular: 91,491 were built, including 32,639 wagons. By contrast, only 30,640 Americans of all models were produced the prior year.

LEFT: The 1960 Metropolitan looked the same as before, and with the start of a new decade, it was beginning to get a little stale. The enclosed wheels told everyone that it had begun life as a Nash model, while the two-tone paint and continental spare tire mount were 1950s clichés that were growing increasingly unpopular. At this point the company should have redesigned the car, but apparently George Romney had lost interest in the Met series.

MAKE	RAMBLER				
Model	American	Rambler 6	Rambler Rebel	Ambassador	Metropolitan
Passengers	5	6	6	6	2
Doors	2	4	4	4	2
Wheelbase (inches/ centimeters)	100/254	108/274	108/274	117/297	85/216
Engine (Standard)	195.6 cu. in., L-head I-6, 110 hp	195.6 cu. in., OHV I-6, 127 hp	250 cu. in., OHV V-8, 215 hp	327 cu. in., OHV V-8, 270 hp	90.9 cu. in., OHV I-4, 55 hp
Engine (Optional)		195.6 cu. in., OHV I-6, 138 hp			
Production	91,491	242,581	16,399	23,769	22,209

Total American Motors Production: 396,449 Market Share: 7.1%

As the 1959 model year progressed, enthusiasm in the Rambler line grew like a mighty force. CEO George Romney became the most famous industrialist in the world, and buyers flocked to Rambler showrooms. Amazingly, in June that year Rambler placed third in U.S. sales, edging out the giant Plymouth sales organization. As a measure of the company's success the *Kenosha Evening News* (9/18/59), reported on the annual "Rambler Jamboree" employee celebration and new model introduction at Milwaukee County Stadium, home at that time of baseball's Milwaukee Braves: "With more than 21,000 employees now working at American Motors plants in Kenosha and Milwaukee—nearly twice the 12,000 on the rolls a year ago—it is easily possible for 35,000 to 40,000 to show up at the Milwaukee Stadium."

Rambler Metropolitan

World's smartest smaller car.

The appearance of diminutive boxes for Metropolitan advertising in the lower right-hand corner of regular Rambler ads made it clear that American Motors was putting little effort into marketing the subcompact. This promotional sidelining had no effect: the car was still selling at the same rate.

One welcome update in 1959 was the inclusion of an actual trunk lid—no longer did Metropolitan owners have to pull down the vestigial rear seat back and reach into the storage compartment. Other new features included larger 5.60-13 tubeless tires and vent windows that offered added ventilation. And there was a bump in power up to 55 horsepower. The marketplace approved: the subcompact sold in record numbers, 22,209.

Here's Proof America Buys Basic Excellence...

RAMBLER

3RD IN SALES IN U.S.A. IN JUNE!

THE WALL STREET JOURNAL

WEDNESDAY, JULY 8, 1959

Here are model-by-model break-downs of retail sales:

	June	6 mos.
(1) Chevrolet	175,263	810,541
(2) Ford-(x)	153,300	676,000
(3) Rambler	43,556	190,091
(4) Plymouth-(x)	41,700	208,700
(5) Pontiac	37,387	212,147
(6) Oldsmobile	33,980	199,650
(7) Buick	22,359	133,543
(8) Dodge-(x)	15,900	78,000
(9) Mercury	13,763	78,675
(10) Studebaker	12,960	74,000
(11) Cadillac	11,721	77,134
(12) Chrysler-(x)	6,800	34,450
(13) DeSoto-(x)	4,900	25,000
(14) Edsel	3,547	24,172
(15) Lincoln	1,928	15,015
(16) Imperial-(x)	1,450	9,450

(x) Estimated

America's leading daily business paper, "The Wall Street Journal," reports that Rambler was No. 3 in sales of all cars sold in the United States in June.

Why is the Compact* Rambler the fastest growing car in sales in more than 30 years?

Because Rambler gives you basic excellence in quality, performance, room, comfort, economy and handling.

Rambler has 20 years experience in building a car with rattleproof, squeakfree, Single Unit Construction.*

Rambler is proved America's top economy car, holding the transcontinental NASCAR economy records—with both overdrive and automatic transmission.

Rambler's basic excellence gives you the highest resale value of any low-priced car.

Discover Rambler's basic excellence. Drive America's No. 1 success car at your Rambler dealer's now.

*Trademark American Motors

The Results

Time magazine said of George Romney, "Never has Detroit seen an auto executive like Romney. . . . He reserves his Sundays exclusively for church activities, often travels to other Mormon churches to set up conferences or deliver sermons." With his uncommon life of hard work and deep faith, Romney and his small, talented team delivered $48,243,361 in net profit for 1959. They produced 374,240 automobiles (and sold 22,209 Metropolitans), capturing 7.1 percent of the US market, the sixth largest share for the year.

LEFT: With Rambler sales booming, the Kenosha factory became the highest-producing automobile factory in North America, running three shifts a day plus Saturday overtime, all in an attempt to keep up with sales. The four-millionth Rambler, a 1960 four-door, was produced on December 30, 1959, on the second shift.

BELOW: The 1960 Rambler Rebel V-8 Custom Cross Country station wagon was the last word in compact performance, comfort, and usefulness—and it's a great-looking car! The white-painted roof was a popular option on all Rambler lines this year: more than just attractive, it reduced heat buildup inside the car on sunny days.

1960

Rambler

1960's Biggest Car Values.

The "Dinosaur Hunter" article in *Time* magazine had described George Romney's vision: "In 1955 he had predicted: 'By 1960, the compact car will be a top contender with present-type cars for the bulk of the market.'" Well, 1960 was here. As Romney foresaw, Rambler now had competition. The year before, Studebaker had launched their Lark compact. Now this year it was the Ford Falcon, Chevy Corvair, and Chrysler's Valiant joining the compact party, and more were on the way. Would Rambler's glory days be over?

Romney didn't believe in change for its own sake, but it was time to refresh the Rambler. Anderson and his design team must have perceived that America's tastes were changing: we were heading into a fresh, new decade, and it was time to remove the excesses of the 1950s.

Gone were the sweeping fins and soaring taillamps of the past, replaced by short, canted fins and smaller lights. The rear window was made larger, the roof panel thinner, and a new Scena-Ramic windshield with a lower cowl replaced the 1950s-looking wraparound glass, opening more of the greenhouse. (The lower cowl required a lower hood and fender line.)

It was an update that gave Rambler a look of contemporary style. The Big Three carried many of their styling excesses on into the new decade, at least for a year or two; sales for some brands, like Dodge, Plymouth, and DeSoto, were disastrous. Instead, 55,460 more Rambler Six and Rebel units were sold than the prior year.

Ambassador by Rambler

America's Only Compact Luxury Car.

Since it shared the same platform as the Rambler, the Ambassador received the same styling updates. Power continued to be the 327-cu.-in. V-8 in 250- and 270-horsepower versions, backed by the usual manual and automatic transmission choices. Deluxe models continued to be reserved for fleets, Super and top-of-the-line Custom for consumers. Four-door sedans and wagons were again offered, and Custom buyers could select the unique pillarless four-door hardtop.

Only a handful more were sold from the previous year. "It was a hedge—a kind of failsafe," remembered sales manager Roy Chapin. "If the small car gambit went bad, we had the Ambassador shell and could expand on it. As it happened, the small cars didn't go bad, so the Ambassador kind of hung around as a sidelight." With value, style, and power, the Ambassador was a good sidelight to have.

The powerful 1960 Ambassador four-door hardtop was also a pleasure to behold. This would be the final year for the Ambassador four-door hardtops, as George Romney tried to bring the series' prices closer to what mainstream buyers expected in order to build sales volume. Note the delicately canted fins and rear-mounted radio antenna. The Ambassador was packed with luxury and style.

Rambler American

The Most Imitated Car in America.

With the slew of compacts by the Big Three targeting American Motors' market, it felt like AMC copycats were everywhere. But none were as small as the American, still riding on a

Back in the early 1950s, Nash engineers said they couldn't build a four-door Rambler on the 100-inch (254-centimeter) wheelbase, but for 1960 they finally figured out a way—and it looked good. The new four-door Rambler American was a surprise addition to the line that was noticed and appreciated by car buyers.

100-inch (254-centimeter) wheelbase. The Rambler American received minor changes from the previous year, and buyers were fine with that.

One major change was in the engine: the 195.6-cu.-in. OHV six from the Rambler was now standard on the top-line Custom. *Motor Life* called the Custom "a vastly improved example of the 100-inch wheelbase vehicle. The test car, a two-door station wagon, offers the same economical operation, comfort, and relative handling ease of the former unit but—with its new muscle—also delivers the charging style of a far larger, far more powerful vehicle." A version of the American sedan with four doors was also new. Sales increased another 25 percent, to 120,603 units.

MAKE	RAMBLER				
Model	American	Rambler 6	Rambler Rebel	Ambassador	Metropolitan
Passengers	5	6	6	6	2
Doors	2	4	4	4	2
Wheelbase (inches/ centimeters)	100/254	108/274	108/274	117/297	85/216
Engine (Standard)	195.6 cu. in., L-head I-6, 90 hp	195.6 cu. in., OHV I-6, 127 hp	250 cu. in., OHV V-8, 200 hp	327 cu. in., OHV V-8, 250 hp	90.9 cu. in., OHV I-4, 55 hp
Engine (Optional)	195.6 cu. in., OHV I-6, 125 hp	195.6 cu. in., OHV I-6, 138 hp	250 cu. in., OHV V-8, 215 hp	327 cu. in., OHV V-8, 270 hp	
Production	120,603	297,378	17,062	23,798	13,103

Total American Motors Production: 471,944 Market Share: 8.1%

RIGHT: American Motors also added a new Custom trim level for the Rambler American 1960 line. Standard equipment included the 195.6-cu.-in. OHV six-cylinder engine, which provided more power and better fuel economy than the base flathead six. This 1960 Rambler American Custom two-door was a winner at the Pure Oil Economy Trials; the Custom model was put forward in the competition because it offered better gas mileage using the OHV engine.

RIGHT BOTTOM: Other standard features included on the Custom American series included finer interior trim, full wheel discs, and more brightwork. This particular car, photographed in Kenosha, is something of a mystery because its wood-look greenhouse trim wasn't available for 1960. It may have been specially built for a company executive or VIP.

Where was the Metropolitan? It had little advertising, though the cars were still present in show rooms. With a large inventory of unsold cars to manage—and with the compact American eating into the Metropolitan's market—orders for new units were halted. Still surprisingly popular (13,103 were sold in 1960), the Met was aging and even a little redundant when placed alongside the American. It would take two more years for the Metropolitan inventory to be completely sold.

ROAD TEST: 1960 RAMBLER AMERICAN CUSTOM

Publication: *Motor Life*, June 1960
Author: *Motor Life* Staff

The Rambler American, as reported on in the February 1960, issue of *Motor Life*, was a satisfactory compact automobile representing a modest compromise between efficiency, economy and practically. But, its L-head, 90-hp engine afforded it only adequate performance. For this reason, the Custom version of the Rambler American series has recently made its bow.

The Custom, fitted with the standard Rambler 195.6-cu.-in. OHV engine is a vastly improved example of the 100-inch wheelbase vehicle. The test car, a two-door station wagon with the new powerplant, offers the same economical operation, comfort and relative handling ease of the former unit but—with its new muscle—also delivers the charging style of a far larger, far more powerful vehicle.

Borrowing the theory that a more modern ohv engine in an already successful small car equals greater gasoline dollar (even though the engine is larger)—American Motors decided to place the more powerful 125-hp Rambler engine between the mounting stubs of the smaller, lighter car. The results are proof that such reasoning was worthwhile.

The station wagon test car delivered an average of 22 mpg for over 300 miles of winter driving. And when we brought out the stopwatch and put the galoshes down hard on the throttle—it turned a 0–60 mph time of 12.9 seconds—a most respectable figure for any small domestic.

The new muscle in the American is a welcome addition also to the handling qualities of the car. While both versions of the car (L-head and OHV) share the same suspension system, the added bite of the more powerful unit makes for quicker cornering without losing rear end traction and the result is a vehicle that can be thrown around bends far faster.

In conclusion, if the Rambler American was a worthy compact before—it can only be added that it's now a highly superior unit—full of pep and just as light on the fuel bill.

The Results

Ford's Edsel brand was finally dead, having cost the company around $350 million in total losses; meanwhile, American Motors reported a net profit of $48,243,361 for the fiscal year. They produced 458,841 automobiles and, along with Metropolitan sales, captured 7.5 percent of the US market. Rambler had just surpassed Pontiac and Oldsmobile for fourth in production volume.

1961

Rambler

Can big-car owners feel "at home" in a compact?

They could in a Rambler. Though compact by the standards of the day, the interior of a Rambler was deceptively large, even a little larger than a full-size Ford or Plymouth. In a Rambler, you could have economy and maneuverability and still have comfort for six.

You also had great value. Engineering Vice President Ralph Isbrandt noted, "Another feature that has resulted in vast savings to our buyers has been the guaranteed for life, ceramic-armored exhaust system. Offered as standard equipment on all Rambler models—a first in the industry."

The upscale Custom was also equipped with a revolutionary engine: AMC's popular 195.6-cu.-in. OHV six now had a die-cast aluminum cylinder block, the world's first. The casting, developed by the Doehler-Jarvis company, removed 80 pounds (36 kilograms) of weight over the front wheels, improving handling and fuel economy.

ABOVE: The Rambler senior cars bore the Classic series name for 1961 and were available in both Classic Six and Classic V-8, which was more in keeping with industry naming trends. This year the front end was extensively restyled, with a lower grille flanked by quad headlamps. The eyebrow forms over the headlamps were a unique styling touch that was also used on the American. Shown is a Classic Six Custom wagon.

RIGHT: A new interior feature on the big Ramblers for 1961 was an acoustical headliner that was said to decrease interior noise levels while also providing better insulation from heat. In addition, the new headliners never sagged (so it was claimed), and although some eventually did, they were durable over many years.

LEFT: American Motors tried something different for 1961, giving the Ambassador line new styling that was distinctive from the Classic series, as can be seen in this Custom four-door sedan. However, the bold European look of the Ambassador failed to ignite buyers to a significant degree, so the decision was made to revert to more traditional styling in the following year.

BELOW: It's easier to spot the carryover body shell in the two-door American sedans and wagons because they use the same B-pillar as before. But the slip-away wheel arches and slab sides give this car a more contemporary look. It was also more compact than ever, and quite like some of the large imported cars from Europe. Its low price and outstanding quality were major selling points.

Car Life magazine tested a Classic Six in Super trim, concluding, "In summation, the Super 6 is an economical car but not one cheaply made. Everything fits well and honestly, with no hanky-panky like putting lead in the doors. The quality of the workmanship is evident in the attention to detail (like, f'instance, the durable aluminum trim around the side windows) and the car should last as long as you like it. And, probably, then some."

The car's sales backed up this opinion: 223,057 buyers were betting on it.

Ambassador by Rambler:

America's finest compact luxury car.

Ambassador was given unique new front-end sheet metal to differentiate it from the Classic. The intent made perfect sense, separating the upscale Ambassador from the Classic with which it shared most of its components. Adding a differentiating feature like this is common in the automotive world: note how today's Lincoln Aviator looks subtly different from its inspiration, the Ford Explorer.

The result in the Ambassador's case was not as successful. With its pointed front fender edges, a lower grille, and quad headlamp placement under a brooding hood and fenders, the car's new look didn't turn buyers' heads. Instead of increasing demand, the new Ambassador lost 4,956 in sales from the previous year.

MAKE	RAMBLER				
Model	American	Classic Six	Classic V-8	Ambassador	Metropolitan
Passengers	5	6	6	6	2
Doors	2 or 4	2 or 4	2 or 4	2 or 4	2
Wheelbase (inches/ centimeters)	100/254	108/274	108/274	117/294	85/216
Engine (Standard)	195.6 cu. in., L-head I-6, 90 hp	195.6 cu. in., OHV I-6, 127 hp	250 cu. in., OHV V-8, 200 hp	327 cu. in., OHV V-8, 250 hp	90.9 cu. in., OHV I-4, 55 hp
Engine (Optional)	195.6 cu. in., OHV I-6, 125 hp	195.6 cu. in., OHV I-6, 138 hp	250 cu. in., OHV V-8, 215 hp	327 cu. in., OHV V-8, 270 hp	
Production	136,003	214,177	8,880	18,842	969

Total American Motors Production: 378,871 Market Share: 7.2%

Rambler American

America's leading economy compact car.

The Rambler American for 1961 was all new—or at least it looked that way. Anderson's assistant, Bill Reddig, had sketched out a new American a few years before, adapting his design to the original 100-inch (254-centimeter) wheelbase of the Nash Rambler unibody. To match the thoroughly modern exterior, the instrument panel received a complete redo.

The Rambler American came in for a complete restyling for 1961. Because it still used the 1950–1960 Rambler underbody, the new design had a higher beltline than desired, but overall it was a successful redo that was relatively inexpensive and uncomplicated. Some wags, however, complained that the grille design looked like it belonged on an aluminum screen door. Sales of these models were quite good despite increasing competition from the Big Three and foreign imports.

The new American's grille design came in for some complaints, as wags pointed out that it looked like it belonged on an aluminum screen door. That wasn't a big problem, since the grille was destined to be changed every year the car was in production. Even with its low price, the bumper guards and hood ornament were standard equipment.

Available bodies continued to be the familiar two-door sedan and wagon, plus the four-door sedan. New was a four-door wagon and a classy convertible with power top. The update was executed so skillfully that few would have recognized that the unibody dated from 1950: it completely shed the American of its Nash past, at least visually.

Powering the new American was the same reliable 90-horsepower 195.6-cu.-in. L-head six, a Nash design that dated from before World War II. The previous Deluxe, Super, and Custom trim levels remained, and Customs got the modern 125-horsepower overhead valve version of the straight six engine. Factory air conditioning was finally available, too, as a $359 option.

Thanks to the new American's taut design, it was slightly shorter than the previous version while claiming 50 percent more luggage space on sedans and 23 percent more cargo room on wagons. The refreshed American clearly resonated with buyers: 136,003 were produced, 16,600 more than in 1960.

The Results

American Motors reported a net profit of $23,578,894 for the fiscal year. The company produced 378,871 automobiles and, along with 969 Metropolitans sold, captured 7.2 percent of the US market, down from 8.1 percent the previous year. Yet Rambler passed Plymouth for third place in domestic market share. Over at Chrysler, the DeSoto brand, which just a few years before was one of the hotter cars in the nation, was terminated due to meager sales.

1962

Rambler

Why wait for the law to make these new brakes a "must"?

Rambler magazine advertisements asked this serious question. A burst brake line would leave a car with no stopping ability, which inspired the addition of a dual master cylinder system on all new Ramblers for 1962. Engineering Vice President Ralph Isbrandt told *Motor Trend*, "We believe the extra cost is well worth the safety it provides Rambler buyers. The system has separate hydraulic units for front and rear brakes. Should either fail through accident or neglect, the other unit will continue to operate." According to the magazine ad, "The law may require brakes like Rambler's on all cars someday. Today, they're standard equipment on

A proud couple picking up their new 1962 Rambler Classic Custom, with the woman inspecting the deep shine of the standard enamel paint finish. American Motors used enamel paint on all its cars because it was more durable and chip resistant, retaining its shine much longer than the cheap lacquer paint other companies used. New this year was a standard twin-circuit brake system, which was one of the most important safety improvements in automotive history. Only a handful of luxury cars included this feature as standard equipment, so Rambler had taken a big step ahead of its competitors. The V-8 Classic series wasn't offered this year, an odd move that could only hurt Rambler's overall sales.

Rambler (and Cadillac, no other U.S. cars)." Federal law did require a dual master cylinder system five years later, in 1967.

Rambler Ambassador

Makes downhills out of uphills.

The Ambassador name had been around since 1929, but it no longer referred to a larger luxury model. What had been the Classic V-8 was now called Ambassador, with the big 327-cu.-in. engine in 250- or 270-horsepower versions replacing the Classic's 250 V-8. In the shorter, lighter Classic body, the new Ambassador was a quick machine. Important to note, this was a Rambler Ambassador now, not an Ambassador by Rambler as it had been called in the past. Side trim was different from the Classic, its taillights were square, not round, and "V-8" badges graced the rear doors.

The new Ambassador was another way George Romney rationalized manufacturing and components to save on cost. It might have seemed counterintuitive to make a smaller luxury car, but 36,171 were produced, more than the Classic V-8 and Ambassador of the previous year combined.

Car Life magazine commented, "Make no mistake, this Rambler V-8 model is a very competitive automobile in every respect. The problem comes when one tries to classify it. Its base price, model for model, puts it $80–$100 lower than a Ford Galaxie or Chevrolet Bel Air (with V-8 engines and heaters). But in size the Rambler V-8 is something unique and this is where we feel the general public may be overlooking a good thing." Some of the public must have noticed.

Rambler American

Why buy Rambler size without Rambler quality?

Compact cars by all Big Three manufacturers were now on the market. To distinguish their own products, Rambler emphasized to potential buyers that the American wasn't new or unproven: they'd been making a roomy, solid, reliable small car since 1950. That legacy supported the company's place in the automotive landscape, although design changes were minimal: after its major update the previous year, the 1962 American looked much the same, with the exception of its new brake system.

After *Motor Trend* tested an American 400 two-door sedan, the magazine declared, "Planned obsolescence is a very costly thing for both buyer and manufacturer. This is a

LEFT: The 1962 Rambler Classic line featured new rear styling that eliminated the tail fins, whose vogue had now passed, offering a more contemporary look. Revised side trim helped neaten the exterior. Surprisingly, American Motors introduced a two-door sedan version of the Classic this year. While two-door sedans were still popular at the time, the company was already committed to bringing out an all-new Classic for 1963. Thus, this two-door sedan was a one-year only model.

BELOW: The pert and perky 1962 Rambler American convertible was even more stylish with the attractive new grille introduced on all Americans this year. Ads for the American convertible usually showed its owners having fun in pleasant settings. And in truth, it was a fun car to drive and an easy car to own. Its standard Custom Flying Scot OHV six-cylinder engine, offered 125 horsepower while returning terrific gas mileage and great reliability. These models are still extremely popular today.

Finished bodies for the 1962 Rambler American are seen here getting a complete inspection before being sent to the final assembly line to receive their drivetrains and mechanical components. In addition to the huge main assembly line in Kenosha, American Motors owned a large body plant in nearby Milwaukee, Wisconsin. Bodies were trucked from there to Kenosha for final assembly.

fact readily recognized by Detroit, but at the present, American Motors is the only domestic manufacturer that has attempted to do anything about it. That a large segment of the car buying public agrees with them is evident in the company's sales reports for the past several years. They keep selling more and more Ramblers." The proof was obvious: 125,679 had placed their faith in the American.

The Results

The November 16, 1962, edition of the *New York Times* reported that, "Roy Abernethy, president and general manager of American Motors, would also become chief executive officer of the company." George Romney, the company's dynamic leader for the last eight years, had resigned on February 12, 1962, promoting Abernethy as president and GM to allow Romney to run for the Michigan governor's seat. The move was surprisingly successful for Romney: running as a Republican in a Democratic state, he would be elected to the office for three terms.

The company saw other management changes in this period. Director of Automotive Styling Ed Anderson, a mainstay at Nash ever since George Mason hired him in 1950, left the company at the end of 1961. His replacement, thirty-nine-year-old Richard Arthur "Dick" Teague, had worked with Anderson at General Motors in the late 1940s. He went on to work as chief stylist at Packard before joining AMC in 1959.

American Motors reported a net profit of $34,240,621 for the fiscal year. They produced 442,766 automobiles and, along with the last 420 Metropolitans sold, captured 9.6 percent of the US market, up from 7.2 percent the previous year. Rambler slipped behind a resurgent Pontiac for fourth in the US market, yet its 1962 market share was the greatest the company would ever see.

MAKE	RAMBLER			
Model	American	Classic	Ambassador	Metropolitan
Passengers	5	6	6	2
Doors	2 or 4	2 or 4	2 or 4	2
Wheelbase (inches/ centimeters)	100/254	108/274	118/300	85/216
Engine (Standard)	195.6 cu. in., L-head I-6, 90 hp	195.6 cu. in., OHV I-6, 127 hp	327 cu. in., OHV V-8, 250 hp	90.9 cu. in., OHV I-4, 55 hp
Engine (Optional)	195.6 cu. in., OHV I-6, 125 hp	195.6 cu. in., OHV I-6, 138 hp	327 cu. in., OHV V-8, 270 hp	
Production	125,679	280,497	36,171	420

Total American Motors Production: 442,766 Market Share: 9.6%

Although AMC didn't offer a four-door American wagon in 1958–1960 (despite having a four-door sedan in the last year), it did offer that format, as well as a two-door version, in the second-generation Americans of 1961–1963. Three trim levels were available for 1962: base Deluxe, midrange Super, and top-line 400. Prices ranged from $2,130 to $2,320. An extensive list of optional equipment allowed buyers to tailor the car to their needs.

ABOVE: This Rambler Classic 770 two-door sedan used the same wheelbase and chassis seen on the four-door and station wagon models. All-new senior cars featuring advanced unibody design complete with Uni-Side Construction for superior door fit, reduced weight, and easier assembly was the big news at American Motors for this year. Invented by AMC, this assembly method was eventually copied by most other automakers because it greatly improved body quality. All Classics and Ambassadors were more compact than before, despite featuring longer wheelbases and increased interior space. This may have been a misstep for AMC, since size-wise it made them more comparable to the Ford Fairlane and Chevrolet Chevelle midsize cars.

RIGHT: The attractive Rambler Classic 770 station wagon for 1963, a model that families couldn't get enough of. With plenty of interior space, the new Rambler was easy to maneuver in traffic and simple to park. The Rambler's many virtues were appreciated by new car shoppers, and the 1963 fiscal year saw Rambler production top 500,000 cars for the first time ever.

1963

Rambler Classic

Motor Trend Car of the Year.

Motor Trend magazine's Car of the Year award has been one of the most prestigious in the industry since the first prize car was awarded in 1949. And for 1963, the Car of the Year was not the headline-making Corvette Sting Ray. No, it was the entire Rambler lineup: American, Classic, and Ambassador.

The 1963 Classic and Ambassador were both new from the ground up, based on a longer, 112-inch (284-centimeter) wheelbase. The unibody was revolutionary, with door frames made from two giant spot-welded stampings to replace the previous structure made from fifty-two welded pieces. Engineering's Ralph Isbrandt told *Motor Trend*, "There's no chance for door openings to vary due to human error or variations in fixtures and jigs. The result is a more rigid structure with greater quality."

LEFT: Like the Rambler Classic, the Ambassador series was available in two- and four-door sedans, plus a four-door Cross Country station wagon in two- and three-seat versions. Shown here is the handsome 990 two-door sedan, an elegant car despite its smaller size. George Romney later said the overall size and styling was "Mercedes-like." With its standard 327-cu.-in. American Motors V-8 engine, it offered terrific acceleration as well as smooth, quiet highway cruising.

BELOW: During the Cold War with the Soviet Union, Civil Defense bomb shelters were common in communities and school children practiced Civil Defense drills to prepare for a possible Russian attack. This '63 Classic 770 served Civil Defense in the St. Louis area and was equipped with a police radio and whip antenna, and flashing lights, along with J.C. Whitney seat protection. It is still in original condition. *Tom & Kelly Glatch*

RIGHT: The 1963 Rambler American series was given an attractive new grille this year, plus new series numbers: 220 for the base models, 330 for midlevel, and 440 for the top series. A new spear side accent paint scheme was available on top-line 440 models, as shown here. The hood ornament was now optional on the 220 models, standard on all the others.

BELOW: American Motors introduced a new Twin-Stick transmission option with two console-mounted levers: one for the three-speed manual transmission, the other for operating the overdrive unit. This new option was available on Rambler 440, 770, and 990 models equipped with bucket seats. It could be matched with either the six-cylinder engine or available V-8 engines.

Stronger, less costly, and 150 pounds (68 kilograms) lighter, the Classic pioneered the way all unibody cars are made today. The Classic also presented innovation in the curved glass used in its side windows, the first on a lower-priced auto.

Classic's available engines remained the same, though an all-new 287-cu.-in. V-8 with 198 horsepower was added midyear. The model featured a new transmission as a $141 option: the unique Twin-Stick three-speed manual, plus overdrive on second and third gears, with dual floorshifts (one for the transmission, one for the overdrive).

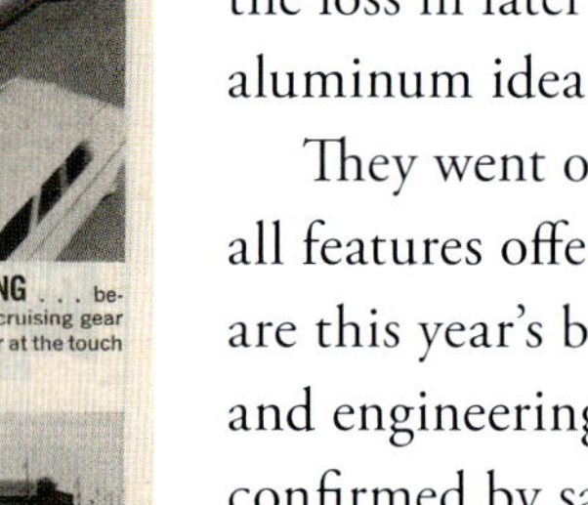

This year's Classic also dropped the aluminum six-cylinder engine. As *Motor Trend* had reported, "It is said that the cost of purchasing aluminum blocks from Doehler-Jarvis, plus the loss in later scrappage and servicing costs, have made the aluminum idea less attractive."

They went on: "In our opinion, based on close scrutiny of all features offered for 1963, the American Motors' Ramblers are this year's best examples of outstanding design achievement and engineering leadership." The success of this design was confirmed by sales of 321,019 units.

Rambler Ambassador

Treat yourself to the luxury of Rambler.

As in 1962, Ambassador was the name for AMC's luxury, 327-cu.-in. V-8–powered Ramblers, with specific trim levels designated 800 for Fleet models, along with the upgraded 880 and the luxury 990.

Car Life magazine wrote in March 1963:

> Our usually blasé test crew waxed so eloquent over the new Classic that it was eager to get its hands on the new Ambassador to see if that car, too, had taken on a new personality. Our consensus: It has—it's a luxury compact with a big kick!

MAKE	RAMBLER		
Model	American	Classic	Ambassador
Passengers	5	6	6
Doors	2 or 4	2 or 4	2 or 4
Wheelbase (inches/ centimeters)	100/254	112/284	112/284
Engine (Standard)	195.6 cu. in., L-head I-6, 90 hp	195.6 cu. in., OHV I-6, 127 hp	327 cu. in., OHV V-8, 250 hp
Engine (Optional)	195.6 cu. in., OHV I-6, 125 hp	195.6 cu. in., OHV I-6, 138 hp	327 cu. in., OHV V-8, 270 hp
Engine (Optional)	195.6 cu. in., OHV I-6, 138 hp	287 cu. in., OHV V-8, 198 hp	
Production	105,296	321,019	37,811

Total American Motors Production: 464,126 Market Share: 6.3%

> Generally, the Rambler Ambassador has fair cornering and handling characteristics. . . . Like the Rambler Classic we tested earlier this year, we found the Ambassador to be an attractive car for its price. With either Twin-Stick or automatic transmission behind its big V-8, it becomes a good performing, good looking luxury, compact.

The new Ambassador made a positive impression: 37,811 were produced, 1,640 more than the previous year.

Rambler American

Go for fun . . . save a bundle.

For its February 1963 issue, *Motor Trend* tested the Rambler American, declaring, "They've aimed their American at a much broader segment of the population—motorists who want

American Motors realized 1963 would be a tough year for the little American, as it faced increased competition, so it added a handsome two-door hardtop model to the 440 series. The roofline was styled to resemble a convertible top and came complete with bows on the interior headliner. The top-line model was offered in 440 and 440H models. The latter, seen here, included a more powerful 138-horsepower six-cylinder engine, bucket seats, and two-tone paint as standard equipment.

reliable economical transportation in a package that's conveniently small without being crowded. That American owners approve is indicated by the fact that an increasing number of them are repeat customers—and unhappy car owners seldom repeat their mistakes."

The American returned with only an updated grille design from the previous year's model. Apparently the company didn't feel the need to meddle with success. One nice addition was the optional Twin-Stick manual overdrive transmission found on the new larger Ramblers. A sporty two-door hardtop returned, a style that had been missing since 1955 on the 100-inch (254-centimeter) wheelbase cars. Trim levels were now designated 220 for base, 330 for midlevel, and 440 for the top-line, with the two-door hardtop called the 440H, which included the option of a 138-horsepower six.

ABOVE: An aerial view of the enormous American Motors main plant in Kenosha, Wisconsin, in 1963, showing areas where construction of additional production and storage space was ongoing. The AMC main plant was the most productive automobile manufacturing plant in North America, and its three-shift production ensured profitability for the company despite its having to compete with much larger firms.

RIGHT: American Motors also had a Canada-based subsidiary company that had its own manufacturing plant to serve the Canadian market and other sterling markets overseas. They produced many of the Ramblers that were sold in the UK and Europe. Two years earlier, George Romney had placed VP Roy D. Chapin Jr. in charge of export sales, leading Chapin to supercharge AMC's overseas sales as well as setting up assembly plants in export markets.

ROAD TEST: 1963 RAMBLER CLASSIC

Publication: *Car Life*, January 1963
Author: *Car Life* Staff

When an automobile manufacturer changes his basic body design only once in seven successful years, that change is usually pretty dramatic. And when the designer has that length of time in which to develop, built and test his ideas, the resulting car should be a mechanical masterpiece. Or, you might say, a Classic.

Although AM management long has deplored the "change for the sake of change" theory, when a change is made it is an outstanding one. The '63 Ramblers are infinitely more appealing esthetically and more satisfactory mechanically. While perpetuating the compact concept by an actual reduction in overall dimensions, the new Classic and Ambassador also have that luxury-of-space feeling of large, expensive cars.

This "bigger-on-the-inside, smaller-on-the-inside" paradox is the result of some clever design work by chief stylist Richard Teague's staff and a lot of "what-does-the-customer-want?" head-scratching in the sales department. The result is that the bigger Ramblers, which had begun to look a bit dowdy and bulgy around the middle by comparison with current styles, now have a youthful fleetness accented by sharply concave front and rear styling. Although there's a bit too much lavishness with the chrome (in most cases, stainless steel) trim on some models, on the whole the cars are immensely eye-pleasing.

Car Life's first meeting with the '63 Ramblers was at the AM Proving Grounds near Kenosha, Wis. . . . Further examination after their public introduction reaffirmed this impression and when we picked up the Classic 660 for testing, we decided that the car looks better each time you see it.

Motor Trend concluded, "We liked the little American. Except for the unit body, pioneered by Rambler and now in common use, it lacks fancy engineering innovations. That may be part of its charm—a straightforward, proven design with no nonsense—something for everyday folks." Everyday folks agreed: an American could be had for as little as $2,130, and 105,296 were produced.

The Results

According to the *New York Times*, "The American Motors Corporation showed a 10.4 per cent rise in profits and a new sales record in the fiscal year ended Sept. 30. Net profit reported yesterday for the fiscal year amounted to $37,807,205." Faced with greatly increased competition, AMC fell to sixth place with a 6.3 percent market share. "When they challenge me, brother," Roy Abernethy told *Time* magazine, "I take them on."

What a long way the company had come since its place on the margins back in 1958.

1964–1969

CHAPTER

3

RAMBLER'S DECLINE AND AMC'S RISE

In the United States, approximately seventy-nine million babies were born during the Baby Boom of 1946 to 1964, with three to more than four million births per year during that period. By 1964 the first wave of children born in this period was turning eighteen. As much as George Romney's Ramblers appealed to the parents of those Baby Boomers, their lives tempered by the Great Depression and World War II, this new flood of young adults would be brought up with expanding wealth and far different personal preferences.

ABOVE: The automobile transport company used most often by American Motors was Kenosha Auto Transport Corporation (KAT). They transported automobiles by truck throughout much of the country. Early in the 1964 model year, KAT was especially busy, as dealer orders for the all-new Rambler American were many times greater than for the prior model. In addition, the Classic and Ambassador series offered new styling and new models this year, further spurring early demand.

OPPOSITE TOP: American Motors unveiled a completely new Rambler American for the 1964 model year. The company was a bit late bringing it to market, since Chevrolet had debuted its new Chevy II compact for 1962, and Ford's Falcon had been on the market since the 1960 model year. The new American, however, was roomier and much more attractive than before, and competitive with the other American compacts. The American line included this stylish convertible. *Tom & Kelly Glatch*

OPPOSITE BOTTOM: Riding a much longer 106-inch (269-centimeter) wheelbase, the 1964 American sedans were much roomier inside and could hold six passengers in comfort. The frontal styling resembles the Chrysler Turbine concept cars of that era for good reason: AMC stylist Bob Nixon had formerly worked with Chrysler and had designed both cars.

On May 15, 1964, *Time* magazine declared:

> While the U.S. auto industry speeds toward its first 8,000,000-car-sales year, the only U.S. automaker failing to share in the boom is the one that needs it the most: American Motors Corp. Sales of its Big Three competitors have risen 1% above last year's level, but American Motors has so far sold 8,800 fewer cars this year than last. Last week AMC announced a 17% drop in earnings for its first fiscal half at a time when the other car makers are setting new profit records. So many Ramblers remain unsold that President Roy Abernethy, 57, next week will lay off 7,800 workers, probably will not recall them until new-model production begins in August.

Abernethy was about as opposite a personality to George Romney as two men could be. "Blunt, cigar-smoking (ten Coronas a day) Roy Abernethy started out as an apprentice Packard mechanic at 18¢ an hour in 1926," *Time* had written two years before. "By the time he joined Romney seven years ago, Abernethy had won a formidable reputation as a Packard dealer ($1,000,000 worth of cars in a single year in Hartford, Conn.) and as sales vice president of Willys Motors. At American Motors he put new life into a listless sales organization by flying 50,000 miles a year to spread Romney's gospel of the compact car."

Bob Dylan, then a young folksinger, released an album in February 1964: "The Times They Are a-Changin'." Could Roy Abernethy's American Motors follow suit and change with the times?

Under the direction of President Roy Abernethy, who replaced George Romney in 1962 when Romney left to become governor of Michigan, American Motors began to focus more attention on its pricier models, lavishing them with extra-sharp interiors and a host of new luxury options, including AM/FM radio, adjustable headrests, bucket seats in both wide and slim versions, tilt steering wheel, power windows, and, finally, electric windshield wipers—though those cost extra.

1964

American

The Luxury Six for the Man Who Wants Something Better.

"A clever bit of manufacturing design turns into a surprisingly handsome product" was *Car Life* magazine's headline for the all-new 1964 American. It really was a striking shape, illustrating the artistic prowess of Vice President of Design Dick Teague and his team. The American's chief designer, Bob Nixon, had recently moved from Chrysler, and the front-end treatment echoed experimental Chrysler Turbine cars, though Nixon said he hadn't copied the design.

Just as beautiful was the engineering prowess beneath the smooth skin. The American was built around that same doorframe structure pioneered on the 1963 Classic and Ambassador, yet if you park an American and a Classic next to each other you can't tell. The door frame was mated to a new floorpan, cowl, and roof, with shorter substructures front and back to create a 106-inch (269-centimeter) wheelbase. *Car Life* noted that "the American also

Shown on a section of the American Motors proving grounds test track, the 1964 Rambler Classic sedan (*rear*), American convertible (*middle*), and Ambassador sedan (*front*) show off their good looks for the camera. The Ambassador was unique in the market, a luxurious, top-quality automobile of compact, almost European dimensions, yet offering the power and roominess of conventional big cars. Its standard 327-cu.-in. V-8 gave it terrific performance.

utilizes the bigger cars' curved glass side windows and generally roomy interior—all the while maintaining the shortest wheelbase and overall length of any sedan built in the U.S." Engines and transmissions remained the same as in the previous year and were adequate for a car weighing 2,200 pounds (998 kilograms), while the leaf-spring rear suspension and traditional driveshaft carried over from the previous American.

Popular Mechanics asked owners of 1964 Americans their opinion of the cars. The magazine wrote, "In our previous reports, the group of Rambler owners has been heavily loaded with such un-frivolous occupations as clergymen and accountants. There still are many teachers and engineers, but this year's group seems less conservative. As an example, there's the Texas industrial supervisor who says, 'I am the proud owner of a sassy red-and-white Rambler American hardtop. Besides being economical and sturdy, it's also beautiful. Previous Ramblers looked too much like boxes on wheels.'" A South Carolina sailor opined, "It handles so well, driving through rush-hour traffic is no longer worse than the day's work." An Ohio factory worker commented, "The car is small, easy to handle, yet large enough for comfort on trips," and a pilot from the same state wrote, "It has a comfortable interior for my 6-foot 3-inch frame." It's easy to see why 160,321 were built.

RIGHT: American Motors engineers had been working on an all-new six-cylinder engine design—by 1964 it was ready for introduction. This brand-new, multi-million-dollar engine manufacturing plant was constructed for assembly of the new six, as well as for assembling rear axles, which were needed to support an expected increase in automobile sales and production. With restyled Classics and Ambassadors, plus the all-new American, it was reasonable to expect sales would go up in 1964.

BELOW: The 1964 Classic series was treated to a new grille that neatly filled in the previous convex grille area, making the car look longer than it had before. A new hood and revised side trim also helped give a fresh new appearance to the Classic models. AMC also added sharp new two-door hardtop models to the lineup, along with beautiful new interiors.

Ambassador

Insist on More in '64.

Ambassador continued to share the Classic's body, but with additional upscale equipment. There was just one trim level now, the 990, featuring a blacked-out grille that spelled out A×M×B×A×S×S×A×D×O×R in the same two- and four-door sedan, four-door wagon, and new two-door hardtop bodies as the Classic. Power came from the 327 V-8 available in both two-barrel, 250-horsepower or four-barrel, 270-horsepower versions.

It's possible buyers *were* insisting on more, as only 18,647 were assembled. Maybe the Ambassador was just too much Classic to justify the additional expense?

LEFT: The top-line Rambler Classic 770 models looked especially handsome in four-door versions, with just the right amount of chrome details to brighten their appearance without being gaudy. The Classic and Ambassador models were only mildly updated from the 1963 versions and offered good interior room and comfort in a more sensible size than the "Low-Priced Three" automobiles from Chevy, Ford, and Plymouth.

BELOW: American Motors decided to introduce its all-new six-cylinder engines in a special midyear model, the limited-production Rambler Typhoon. The Typhoon combined the new Rambler Classic 770 two-door hardtop body with a luxurious bucket seat interior, special grille, and Typhoon nameplates. All were painted Solar Yellow combined with a black roof. Under the hood was AMC's hot new 232-cu.-in. inline six-cylinder engine. Using a new lightweight block and seven-main-bearing crankshaft, a top-quality feature, the new six was perhaps the smoothest-running American six on the market and offered a solid 145 horsepower.

Classic

How to pick a new '64 Rambler just for the sport of it.

Following its introduction in 1963, not much changed for the Classic in the next year other than a revised grille and exterior trim. It continued the 550, 660, and 770 trim levels and two- and four-door sedans and a four-door wagon. Added to these was a stylish new two-door pillarless hardtop.

Then, in May 1964, came the announcement of a sporty Typhoon model. This car commemorated the first new six-cylinder engine for AMC since 1956, the Torque-Command 232-cu. in. six. Based on the Classic 770 two-door hardtop, Typhoon featured Solar Yellow paint, a Classic Black roof, and distinctive Typhoon script in place of the usual Classic name. All other options were available—but the real storm was under the hood.

The new straight six was a clean-sheet-of-paper creation, with modern, thin-wall castings and a short-stroke design boasting a 3.75-inch (9.5-centimeter) bore and 3.5-inch (8.9-centimeter) stroke. The stout bottom end featured seven main bearings and a fully counterweighted crankshaft. The previous six, dating to 1956, was an overhead valve adaptation of the Nash L-head engine that had been new in 1941. American Motors sold far more six-cylinder cars than V-8s, so the new Torque-Command was a critically important development for the company.

The special Typhoon edition, powered by the new 145-horsepower six, accounted for 2,520 of the 206,299 Classics sold in 1964. "[It] will go from nothing to 60 miles an hour in 13 seconds, and that's better than a lot of V-8s will do," Abernethy proudly told the *New York Times*.

In early 1964 American Motors unveiled the Tarpon concept car. A sporty compact, the Tarpon was created to solve a longtime problem: how to make more money on compact cars. Stylist Bob Nixon created this design, and the prototype was built on a 1964 Rambler convertible body, with a low fastback roof tacked on. It was shown weeks before Ford's Mustang was announced and was an instant hit. One of the most grievous mistakes that CEO Abernethy made was to reject basing this car on the American body in favor of making it on the larger Classic. It was renamed Marlin.

He continued, "Our greatest problem has been seven years of association with economy. Our image of selling a sensible-sized car and economy is still with us, and we like it. But we're not known yet—as we're going to be known—as offering a sensible-sized car with all the options and luxury you want. . . . If that's what the people want, we'll give it to them."

The Results

AMC was in a real Catch-22 by the end of 1964: it needed new products to survive, but new products for automakers were extraordinarily expensive to develop. Roy Abernethy had spent

MAKE	RAMBLER		
Model	American	Classic	Ambassador
Passengers	5	6	6
Wheelbase (inches/ centimeters)	106/269	112/284	112/284
Engine (Standard)	195.6 cu. in., L-head I-6, 90 hp	195.6 cu. in., OHV I6, 127 hp	327 cu. in., OHV V-8, 250 hp
Engine (Optional)	195.6 cu. in., OHV I6, 125 hp or 138 hp	195.6 cu. in., OHV I6, 138 hp	327 cu. in., OHV V-8, 270 hp
Engine (Optional)	232.0 cu. in., OHV I6, 145 hp	232.0 cu. in., OHV I6, 145 hp	
Engine (Optional)		287 cu. in., OHV V-8, 198 hp	
Production (Model)	2-door hardtop coupe: 34,022 2-door convertible: 8,907 4-door sedan: n/a 4-door station wagon: n/a	2-door hardtop coupe: 23,388 2-door sedan: 13,795 4-door sedan: 96,816 4-door station wagon: 72,300	2-door hardtop coupe: 4,419 4-door sedan: 9,821 4-door station wagon: 4,407
Production (Total)	160,321	206,299	18,647

Total American Motors 1964 Production: 385,267

ROAD TEST: 1964 RAMBLER AMERICAN 440 SEDAN LONG TERM TEST

Publication: *Car Life* April 1964

Author: *Car Life* Staff

There really had been no question but that the Rambler American would turn out to be the most economical of the three long-term test cars in this project. And indeed, it was, operating for 9,002 miles at a cost of $0.0181 per mile running expense.

And the Rambler, more than the other two cars, showed significant improvement in performance with the miles as the various rotating and reciprocating parts settled into wear patterns of least friction. With its long-stroke Six struggling to generate 138 bhp and propel the car's 2,960 lb. test weight, the American's increased sprightliness was evident even without the testing equipment to measure it.

This engine is the most powerful of three available for the American and would appear to be the best choice for the driving conditions encountered by most Americans. It was the three-speed plus overdrive transmission, controlled by Rambler's Twin-Stick shifter arrangement in the console, which actually was at the root of our discontent.

A final drive ratio of 3.78:1 was installed in the test car, with the result that first gear was too low to be of much usefulness. Second gear provided too short a spacing and was itself low enough to serve quite adequately to start from rest. Direct high gear, then, had to do most of the work, with an engine of such small means, obviously not too satisfactory a situation.

There is little point in repeating what was said in the earlier test about the American's body structure except to say that the 9,002 miles had little adverse effect on its strength or well-known durability. Interior appointments, which seemed quite luxurious during the first test continued to hold that appeal, with the added advantage of a demonstrated durability for such things as floor rugs, upholstering materials and door paneling.

The American is such a beautiful example of a stylist's tour de force that such shortcomings are all the more glaring. Staff members without exception, upon seeing the car for the first time and reading its specifications could hardly conceal their enthusiasm. Can an auto enthusiast find happiness behind the wheel of a Rambler American? The answer to that depends, more than anything else, on the transmission selected. . . . The car is parsimonious, peppy and has more than a little pulchritude.

$45 million to increase production capacity at the company's main Kenosha plant, already the highest-capacity auto assembly plant in the world. The company showed a $44 million profit, thought this was challenged by those additional costs, and total production was 385,267 units, down from 1963's record numbers.

Market share was also down, to 5.0 percent.

RIGHT: Another bright star that shone in 1964 was this special-built Rambler American show car. Called the Carrousel, it featured a gorgeous bucket seat interior with full-length floor console, floor-mounted transmission shifter, custom door panels and side trim, and a beautiful metallic blue paint job. We wonder whatever happened to this car: a few of the other specially trimmed Ramblers from this period have survived in the hands of owners who have maintained or restored them.

BELOW: The convertible models of the American, Classic, and Ambassador. In light of the disappointing sales results for 1964, AMC President Roy Abernethy ordered a major restyling of the Rambler Classic and Ambassador series. Retaining the same basic body used in the prior two years, AMC stylists under the direction of Styling VP Dick Teague created a new look for the Ramblers that was longer, heavier, and much more substantial looking.

1965

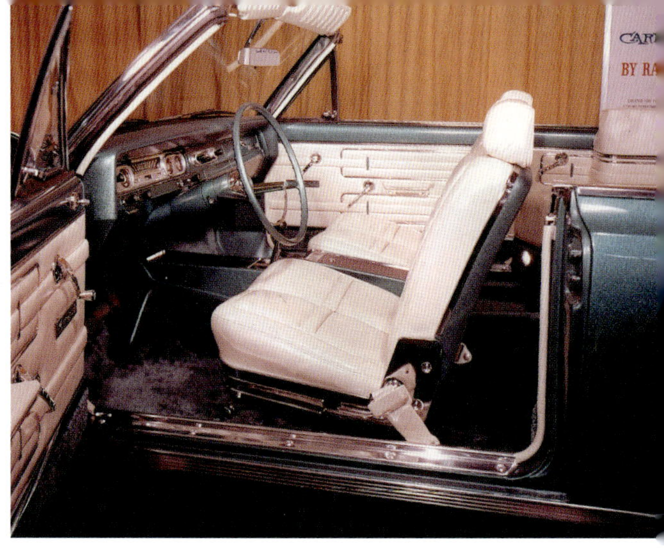

Classic

The space, larger! The look longer! The go, greater!

The 1965 Classic really was larger and longer. Five inches were added to the length of the trunk, with the rear fenders now squared off. Front-end sheet metal was also new, with quad horizontal headlights and a V-shaped grille. The result was more room in the trunk, a larger rear seat area, and a bolder look. A sporty new convertible was offered in 770 trim.

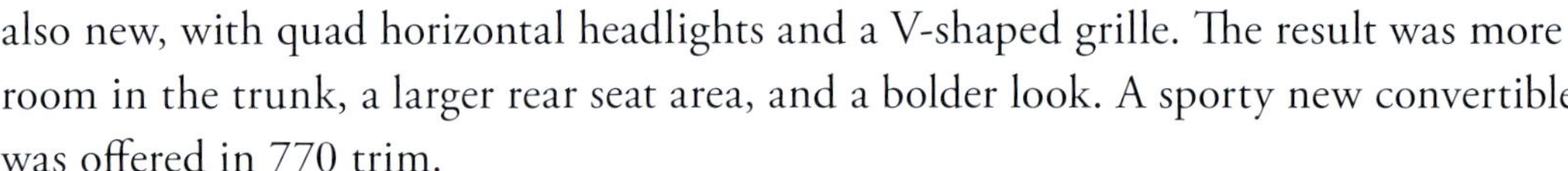

It was a difference in philosophies—George Romney had believed in building products the Big Three would have otherwise ignored in the marketplace, while his successor, Roy Abernethy, wanted to take on the Big Three with full force. The new General Motors intermediate cars, especially the Chevrolet Chevelle and Pontiac Tempest, were eating away at the Classic's market, and the longer Classic was Abernethy's first chance to fight back.

Powertrains this year included a new 199-cu. in. version of AMC's modern lightweight six, standard on Classic 550, with the 232-cu. in. standard on the rest of the Classic line. (The special 232-powered Typhoon model did not return in this year.) AMC called Classic one of its Sensible Spectaculars in trying to promote their exciting new products while not ignoring their longtime market favorites. As it happened, 204,016 Classics were built, 2,283 fewer than the previous year. Considering the intense competition from the Big Three they experienced, it was still a successful year.

Ambassador

A whole new horizon in size, style, stunning performance . . . !

Ambassadors benefited from the increased length of the Classic since they shared the same rear structure. Up front, the Ambassador grew 4 inches (10 centimeters) forward of the cowl, using the same manufacturing trick found on the 1958–1961 Ambassadors. Then Teague and his designers gave it bold new front-end sheet metal to match. The horizontal grille featured a convex V shape surrounded by stacked quad headlights. New tall, vertical taillamps wrapped around the corners, with a fluted horizontal trim between them. A chrome strip ran atop the fenders along the entire body.

The Ambassador no longer looked like a tarted-up Classic, instead now sporting a distinctive look to match its name.

LEFT: The Classic four-door sedan for 1965 looked so much larger than the 1963–1964 models, even though they rode the same 112-inch (284-centimeter) wheelbase as before. Longer rear fenders; a rich-looking, full-width grille; and squarer lines all combined to convey the look of a bigger car. Originally, the 1963–1964 styling was to be only mildly changed for 1965, but Abernethy was trying to recapture the sales momentum he'd inherited. The Chevrolet Chevelle/Malibu and Ford Fairlane products were stealing sales from AMC at a worrisome rate.

MIDDLE LEFT: The Rambler Classic for 1965 added this attractive two-door convertible to the model lineup. Offered in 770 trim, it proved to be a popular halo car that emphasized the Rambler's effort to move its image to a more upscale plateau. The convertible offered a choice of four top colors, two six-cylinder engines, and two V-8s. A power-operated soft top was standard equipment.

BOTTOM: This Ambassador 880 series two-door sedan was the lowest-priced model in the Ambassador range, serving as a popular fleet car for businesses that wanted to project a look of success yet also wanted to hold down fleet costs. With the optional painted roof, full wheel covers, and white sidewall tires, this budget Ambassador was attractive, yet with a six-cylinder engine could deliver excellent fuel economy. Rambler's solid unibody construction assured buyers of top quality and extra safety.

RIGHT: A frontal view of the 1965 Rambler Classic 770H two-door hardtop, with its roof painted a contrasting color for extra eye appeal. This sporty midsize car was an attractive model that offered decent performance even with a six-cylinder engine; with the big V-8 it was a tiger. Rambler dealers should have been encouraged to order more of these models for stock, but with slowing sales the dealers tended to order lower-priced models.

BELOW: The understated elegance of the Ambassador 990 four-door sedan spoke of luxury and comfort without the ostentation so common in American luxury cars. Ambassador's new front-end styling featured stacked quad headlamps in a bright V-shaped convex grille. Chrome moldings sat atop the squared fenders and ran along a character line. Ambassador 990 models included the ribbed rocker panel molding seen here. The long list of standard equipment included full wheel covers; luxurious interior trim; AMC's new 155-horsepower, 232-cu.-in. six-cylinder engine; and a roof rack on station wagon models. This year Ambassadors rode a longer 116-inch (295-centimeter) wheelbase to provide a smoother, quieter ride along with a more substantial appearance.

Two-door sedan, four-door sedan, and station wagon bodies were available in the basic 880 model, while the top-shelf 990 was available in stylish two-door hardtop and new convertible forms, along with the four-door sedan and wagon styles.

Ambassador continued to offer the 327 V-8 in both two-barrel, 250-horsepower or four-barrel, 270-horsepower versions, though the 232 Torque-Command six was now standard equipment—the first time since 1956 Ambassador had a six. Transmissions were the same as the Classic's. Disc brakes were a welcome option.

Dick Teague told author Chris Poole, "Well, we were looking to make a buck, and also make it look sleek and lower and longer. And it really is a handsome car, I think. I know that sounds immodest. I don't mean to sound that way because I had a lot of help. But it was a good-looking car. It stands the test of time."

Buyers thought so: 64,145 were built, four times the number produced in 1964.

LEFT: The big Ambassador 990 station wagon for 1965 offered families luxury and convenience in a high-class automobile built for travel. Its longer wheelbase helped smooth out the roads as the miles passed by in complete comfort. Available in two- and three-seat versions, the Ambassadors maintained Rambler's long tradition of offering the best in family station wagons.

Marlin

Meet America's first man-size sports-fastback!

"Solid Rambler virtues wrapped in an exciting new package with some added safety features" is how *Motor Trend* summed up the new Marlin. For a company that built conservatively styled cars, Marlin was an eye-opener. A big fastback based on the Classic, with new top and rear sheet metal, it was dramatic to say the least. "Early in 1963, management expressed interest in a new car with a sports flair—something consistent with our other models, yet definitely apart and unique," Dick Teague told *Motor Trend*. "We presented our fastback sketches to B. A. Chapman, executive vice president responsible for automotive styling. He approved going to a clay mock-up for further evaluation by Roy Abernethy and our policy committee. It turned out that everyone approved."

RIGHT: Midyear brought a new series of cars from American Motors: the Rambler Marlin sports fastback two-door. A midsize car, based on the Rambler Classic, it mated the styling theme of the Tarpon compact concept with an intermediate body. The popular two-tone paint treatment for Marlin included the roof panel, extending down the trunk lid nearly to the closing line. The Marlin was originally meant to feature a much lower roofline for a sportier look. But President Roy Abernethy ordered Chief Stylist Vince Geraci to raise it several inches, which Geraci felt spoiled the lines. Abernethy was a big man and disliked small cars and low rooflines.

203777A
WISCONSIN

PREVIOUS PAGES: Even with its higher roofline, the Marlin was a sharp-looking car, with styling similar to the Dodge Charger. The special bright trim around the curved window section at the rear of the greenhouse was a nice touch. The only problems with the Marlin were that, 1) it wasn't a compact sporty car, which was where the market was moving, and 2) it didn't address the original problem it was designed for: how to make better profits on compact cars. Placing Marlin on the Classic chassis was a major mistake by Abernethy and proof that executives should stay out of styling decisions. *Tom & Kelly Glatch*

ABOVE: Marlin was a bit of an odd duck: a sporty hardtop, its standard equipment including a six-cylinder engine, three-speed manual transmission, and a bench front seat like any other midsize car. Abernethy felt there must be a big market for a sporty car that could hold six passengers. He was wrong: Marlin sales remained well below expectations.

The original concept car was based on the American and named the Tarpon. "More than 20,000 people saw the car at the 1964 SAE convention in Detroit," Teague said. "The engineers there liked the idea and told us so. Later, at the Chicago Auto Show, this same Tarpon styling exercise got an enthusiastic yes vote from people surveyed at the Rambler exhibit. Over 60% said they'd like to own a model with the Tarpon's fastback styling. Some offered to place orders on the spot."

Designer Bob Nixon recalled, "We took the American convertible and put a new roof and quarter panels on it and made a show car out of it." Was it influenced by Ford's Mustang? "No, we didn't know about the Mustang at the time," said Nixon, "We did a lot of conceptualizing back then, coming up with new car ideas, and one of them was the Tarpon."

But something happened in the translation from concept to show room model. Management wanted a larger 3+3 vehicle, based on the Classic. "If Abernethy didn't like it, nobody liked it—except me." Teague recalled years later. "I was a maverick, I guess. So, they made the Marlin out of the Classic instead of the small American." He worried, though: "Would the longer wheelbase and added length change or ruin the Tarpon's good points? At the same time, a sporty fastback with full six-passenger seating capacity had some interesting possibilities. Not only would we add youth appeal, but we could reach for another important consumer group—the young marrieds and young executives with family plus business requirements in seating space."

After three clay models were built, the final version seen in the show rooms was chosen—well, almost. Abernethy was a large man, standing over six feet tall, and he felt a bit cramped in the rear seat of the Marlin. He ordered 6 inches (15 centimeters) more headroom over the rear seats. If the roofline of the Marlin doesn't seem to flow the way the 1966–1967 Dodge Charger or the 1968–1969 Ford Torino did (both six-passenger fastbacks that followed on the heels of the Marlin), don't blame Dick Teague and his team.

The available powertrains were the same as the Classic. Starting at $3,100 for the base six-cylinder version, first-year Marlin production was 10,327.

MAKE	RAMBLER			
Model	American	Classic	Marlin	Ambassador
Passengers	5	6	6	6
Wheelbase (inches/ centimeters)	106/269	112/284	112/284	116/295
Engine (Standard)	195.6 cu. in., L-head I-6, 90 hp	195.6 cu. in., OHV I6, 127 hp	232 cu. in., OHV I-6, 155 hp	232 cu. in., OHV I-6, 155 hp
Engine (Optional)	195.6 cu. in., OHV I6, 125 hp	195.6 cu. in., OHV I6, 138 hp	327 cu. in., OHV V-8, 250 hp	287 cu. in., OHV V-8, 198 hp
Engine (Optional)	232 cu. in., OHV I-6, 155 hp	287 cu. in., OHV V-8, 198 hp		327 cu. in., OHV V-8, 270 hp
Engine (Optional)		327 cu. in., OHV V-8, 250 hp		
Production (Model)	2-door hardtop coupe: 21,948 2-door sedan: 35,474 2-door convertible: 3,882 4-door sedan: 34,327 4-door station wagon: 17,537	2-door hardtop coupe: 20,484 2-door sedan: 11,643 2-door convertible: 4,953 4-door sedan: 105,110 4-door station wagon: 61,826	2-door fastback coupe: 10,327	2-door hardtop coupe: 11,416 2-door sedan: 1,301 2-door convertible: 3,499 4-door sedan: 35,416 4-door station wagon: 12,513
Production (Total)	113,168	204,016	10,327	64,145

Total American Motors 1965 Production: 391,656

1965 was the 155-horsepower version of the 232-cu.-in. six. A two-barrel carburetor supplied the extra power, which provided faster acceleration at a slight decrease in fuel economy. The durability of the 232-six became legendary, and the engine, along with several variations of it, remained in production far beyond the years when AMC cars were still being built—they were used in Jeeps for decades.

American

The Compact Economy King.

In typical American fashion, changes to the 1965 model were few. The grille received three vertical indentations, and a chrome strip was added to the beltline on all but the basic 220 version. The 440 continued to be the only series offering a two-door hardtop body (440 and 440H), while all series offered two-door sedan, four-door sedan, and four-door wagon bodies.

Car Life magazine, testing a 1965 440H, wrote, "The American, at least in the test version, is well-powered enough to feel frisky, diminutive enough to be nimble, and handsome enough to swell pride. There was nothing, aside from outright limousine service, which the car did not perform and perform well. It seemed so much fun that one staff member, suspected of being something of a heretic anyway, started talking about trading off his Corvair Spyder for one." AMC built 113,168 units that year.

The Rambler American series for 1965 was little changed in appearance. Vertical ribs were added to the grille, and little else. However, mechanical improvements and additions were numerous. The standard engine for the 220 and 330 series remained the old flathead (L-head) 195.6-cu.-in. six, but the new 232-cu.-in. six with 155 horsepower was available as an option, as was the carryover 195.6 OHV six with 125 horsepower. The 440 series got the 125-horsepower six as standard with the 155-horsepower job optional.

The Results

Dick Teague was proud of what his small team of designers had done in recent years, telling *Motor Trend*:

> I feel the AMC team has pulled off at least four triumphs lately. The first was our redesigned American in 1964, which captured the youthful flavor and sold remarkably. Second, we've successfully put large-car dimensions inside our intermediate-sized Classic. Third, we've created a unique and practical big car in the new Ambassador. And finally, we've managed to design what we consider a pleasing fastback hardtop on a large, modern, six-passenger chassis.

It's interesting to note that Raymond Lowey, famed independent industrial designer and creator of Studebaker's 1953 Starliner and 1963 Avanti, reached out to AMC in 1965 looking for work. Roy Abernethy kindly replied that his own styling staff was quite talented and meeting the company's objectives.

Its new products were beginning to improve the company's outlook. *Time* reported in 1965 that "Compacts now account for only 18% of auto sales, and AMC is stranded without the right variety of cars for today's prospering auto market." Notwithstanding the challenges American Motors faced, production was up about 3,000 to 391,656 units, thanks to the popularity of the updated Ambassador and the addition of the Marlin. Market share, however, went from 5.0 percent in 1964 to 4.4 percent in 1965, and profits dropped to just $5.2 million.

1966

Ambassador

Cadillac? No. Imperial? No. Ambassador DPL? Yes!

The Ambassador was no longer branded a Rambler. After the major changes that had taken place the previous year, it received minor exterior trim updates, including four stylish chrome inserts on the front fenders. A new model was added, DPL (short for Diplomat), a logical addition to the Ambassador brand. The DPL stood above the 880 and 990 trims as the ultimate Ambassador, based on the five-passenger, two-door hardtop body with a sumptuous bucket seat interior. Powertrains remained the same. Demand was less than the previous year, unfortunately, with 71,692 produced, including 1,798 convertibles.

ABOVE: The luxurious Ambassador 990 convertible for 1966, the fanciest and most beautiful of the American Motors line of convertibles that year. The new 990 came with unique bright windshield posts, fluted rocker panel moldings, bright trim around the wheel openings, and a gorgeous interior. This particular car is shown with the optional wire wheel covers and whitewall tires, and even appears to have a tinted windshield with a sun band. These convertible Ambassadors remain popular with collectors today.

MIDDLE LEFT: This sporty 1966 ½ Rogue two-door hardtop represented the top of the Rambler American lineup and was introduced midyear in an effort to regain some of the sporty compact business that was going to Ford's insanely popular Mustang. Notice the Rogue emblem on the front fender. The rear fender badge indicates this car is equipped with the new, optional 290 V-8 engine. The Rogue hardtop was fitted with stylish full-wheel covers as standard equipment and also offered sporty wire wheel covers as an option. The Rogue couldn't hope to sell in super-high volume, but it was moderately successful. In the period from 1965 to 1967, American Motors completely missed the pony car market, an error entirely caused by Roy Abernethy.

LEFT: Once again, the Ambassador 880 two-door sedan was the lowest-priced Ambassador in the lineup. Despite its budget pricing, the Ambassador offered comfortable and attractive interior trim, as well as bright trim around the windshield, side, and rear windows. Bright hubcaps were standard equipment, but most buyers ordered the optional full wheel covers for a fancier look. Note the twin bright fluted trim pieces placed at the leading edge of the front fender. It was placed there to lend a wraparound look to the grille.

RIGHT: One big news item in the 1966 American Motors lineup was the availability of V-8 power for the first time in a Rambler American. The Typhoon 290 V-8 was part of a new series of AMC V-8 engines using a lighter, more compact engine block. With 290-cu.-in. displacement, this little mill could deliver up to 225 horsepower in standard form. Here we see AMC engineer Carl Chakmakian (*left*) showing the new engine to *Motor Trend* editor Don McDonald.

BELOW: The senior Rambler two-door hardtops were treated to a sharp new roofline for 1966, replacing the rounder-styled roof seen on previous models. This move eliminated a holdover styling element and greatly improved the overall styling. This 1966 Rebel was the top of the line in the Classic series, a sporty hardtop with great styling as well as a beautiful interior with bucket seats and upgraded trim. The fluted panel fitted between the taillamps is a clever styling touch, as it almost duplicates the bright trim on the taillamps themselves.

Rambler American

Racy! Rambler! Rogue! At the head of the class.

The American remained a Rambler, since it continued in the tradition of offering small size and low cost.

It did receive a mild update to the front-end sheet metal, with a squarer recess around the headlights. Replacing the 440H was the Rogue, based on the same two-door hardtop body but with an upgraded interior, some badge and trim changes, and sharp two-tone paint. The antiquated six-cylinder engines were finally canceled, and the funky Twin-Stick overdrive manual transmission also dropped, with the 199 Torque-Command six now standard and the 232 six an option.

Then came the announcement of a completely new Typhoon V-8 engine, a limited-edition Rogue Typhoon model, at the Chicago Auto Show in February 1966. Power was by the new AMC 290-cu.-in. V-8 that was just ramping up production. This was another completely modern, clean-sheet design, smaller and lighter than the existing engine but with similar displacements. It was also less expensive to manufacture. As *Motor Trend* declared, "some estimate savings as high as 30% overall on engines when the program gets in full swing."

The Rogue Typhoon received a unique Sun Gold and Classic Black paint scheme, black grille, and black pinstripes on the side. Transmissions were the Borg-Warner three-speed automatic or manual four-on-the-floor. All were well equipped with power steering and brakes, radio, reclining bucket seats, and more.

The press loved the $2,961 Rogue Typhoon. "As tested by *Car Life*, the Rogue proved a happy combination of fairly light unit-body construction, a small but healthy V-8 engine, a usable selection of gears in a four-speed case, heavy-duty springs and shock absorbers

MAKE	RAMBLER		AMC	
Model	American	Classic	Marlin	Ambassador
Passengers	5	6	6	6
Wheelbase (inches/ centimeters)	106/269	112/284	116/295	116 /295
Engine (Standard)	199 cu. in., OHV I-6, 128 hp	232 cu. in., OHV I-6, 145 hp	232 cu. in., OHV I-6, 145 hp	232 cu. in., OHV I-6, 155 hp
Engine (Optional)	232 cu. in., OHV I-6, 145 or 155 hp	232 cu. in., OHV I-6, 155 hp	287 cu. in., OHV V-8, 198 hp	287 cu. in., OHV V-8, 198 hp
Engine (Optional)	287 cu. in., OHV V-8, 198 hp	287 cu. in., OHV V-8, 198 hp	327 cu. in., OHV V-8, 250 or 270 hp	327 cu. in., OHV V-8, 250 or 270 hp
Engine (Optional)		327 cu. in., OHV V-8, 250 or 270 hp		
Production (Model)	2-door hardtop coupe: 18,973 2-door sedan: 29,692 2-door convertible: 2,092 4-door sedan: 30,483 4-door station wagon: 12,412	2-door hardtop coupe: 16,248 2-door sedan: 5,505 2-door convertible: 1,806 4-door sedan: 68,529 4-door station wagon: 33,918	2-door fastback coupe: 4,547	2-door hardtop coupe: 14,782 2-door sedan: 1,493 2-door convertible: 1,814 4-door sedan: 39,960 4-door station wagon: 13,643
Production (Total)	93,652	126,006	4,547	71,692

Total American Motors 1966 Production: 295,897

Perhaps Roy Abernethy should have upgraded his cars rather than simply change his brand names. This handsome 1966 Rambler 770 station wagon is certainly a good-looking car that anyone would be proud to own. But too many dealers focused sales efforts on the lowest-priced Ramblers, and those cars were rather stark and lacking in visual appeal, especially the 550 series and, in the American line, the 220 series.

and a disc front/drum rear braking system. And, this combination, though not the quickest, most nimble vehicle on the road, created the sensations that are the rewards of enthusiastic driving." After the initial run of 1,700 Rogue Typhoon models (one for every US dealer), the 290 V-8 was available as an option in two-barrel 200-horsepower or four-barrel 225-horsepower versions on standard Rogues. "It'll take on your Mustang," said the driver in a Rogue TV commercial.

Total production of the Rambler American was just 93,652, including 8,718 of the sporty Rogue and Rogue Typhoon models.

Classic

You made it our hottest seller!

In August 1965, just before the launch of the 1966 model year, the trade publication *Ward's Auto* predicted, "With profits on the skids, American Motors is expected to re-image itself in an attempt to end the perception it is a 1-car automaker. Some AMC

As this press photo shows, American Motors offered a full line of two-door hardtop models, including the sharp new Ambassador DPL (*foreground*), the Rebel in the Classic series just above it, and the Rambler American Rogue (*upper left*). These three cars were competitive offerings that helped keep longtime Rambler owners in the fold. They also served to jazz up showrooms, helping lure new buyers to dealerships.

executives also feel its 'economy image' is hurting sales at a time when model proliferation, luxury, speed and 'heck with the cost' is the prevailing attitude of new-car buyers. Commencing with '66 models, AMC will stop attaching the Rambler moniker and thus its lineup will consist of three distinct models: American, Classic and Ambassador."

Their predictions weren't entirely correct: the Classic continued as a Rambler. It received minor trim changes, new safety features, and the two-door hardtop was now called the Rebel, replacing the 770H. Gone was the midpriced 660 trim, leaving 550, 770, and Rebel to continue. The Torque-Command 232 six and 287 V-8 powerplants remained until February 1966, when the new Typhoon V-8 replaced the aging 287. The 270-horsepower, 327-cu.-in. V-8 engine was also optional.

Total production was down to 126,006 Classics.

In 1966 American Motors management, namely Roy Abernethy, began to deemphasize the Rambler brand name, retitling the Ambassador and Marlin as separate brands, in an attempt to increase sales of the higher line models by divorcing them from what Abernethy referred to as "This Romney image." The effort was mostly in vain, as the Rambler name was so strongly settled in people's minds that many still referred to the cars as Rambler Ambassador and Rambler Marlin. Complicating the move was the fact that Rebels and Americans were still sold under the Rambler brand name, which meant dealers still had Rambler signs on their buildings.

Marlin

How does a guy get the most out of a Marlin?

Ward's Auto forgot to mention the Marlin, maybe because of its Classic underpinnings. While not a huge success in its first year, it was well received. For 1966, Marlin was given the new trim and safety benefits of the Classic. The base price also dropped by $499. Only 4,547 Marlins were produced, however, less than half than in its first year.

The Results

American Motors reported a loss of $12,648,170 for fiscal-year 1966. *Time* foretold the company's future by profiling a new key investor: "Until he invested more than $2,000,000 in ailing American Motors Corp. to become its No. 1 stockholder, Robert Beverley Evans of Grosse Pointe, Mich., cut a bigger figure as a socialite and sportsman than as an industrialist. Though he owns a dozen companies with combined sales of $20 million a year, Evans has left their affairs mostly to underlings, concentrated on such hobbies as golf, quail hunting, and designing and racing a 300-mph jet-powered hydroplane."

Now that Studebaker had ended automobile production on March 5, 1966, American Motors was the last independent automaker in the country. Total production was down to 295,897 vehicles with 3.3 percent market share.

Robert Evans was going to bring changes, but would they come quickly enough?

1967

Ambassador

The Now Cars—Ambassador.

The message on AMC's advertising was simple, "The now cars from the 1967 American Motors." AMC's new chairman, Robert Evans, told *Time* magazine, "We're going after the youth market. That means a different styling. Our job is to get the confidence of the public back."

ABOVE: The United States Postal Service lent American Motors a helping hand by purchasing thousands of Ambassador four-door fleet models for use in delivering the mail. This may have been one of the most unusual postal delivery vehicles of all time, because the idea of using a full-size, upper-medium car for delivery work seems off even today. Nearly all the Ambassador delivery cars featured steering on the right, which was a simple matter for AMC since the RHD configuration had already been developed for export markets. The RHD export Ambassadors were especially popular in the United Kingdom.

That also required new leadership. In January 1967, Roy Abernethy was "invited" to step down as CEO, replaced by Roy D. Chapin Jr.; at the same time, William V. Luneburg was promoted as the a new president. The son of Hudson Motors' founder, Roy D. Chapin Sr., Chapin had joined AMC in 1954. At the time of his promotion, Chapin was executive vice president in charge of international operations. The *New York Times* noted that Abernethy "took the action in good spirit, recalling past success and commenting, 'The market changed swiftly. We could not move rapidly enough to avoid a period of loss, but I believe the basis has now been laid for recovery.'"

Other changes were equally swift. Building the company's confidence again required new power: the V-8 that American Motors introduced in 1956 had been a fine powerplant for the time, but engine design had advanced quickly and by March 1963 engineers began developing a completely new V-8.

Some of the improvements included a thin wall cast iron block that saved 80 pounds in weight yet remained as strong and durable as the first-generation engine. That first V-8 required eleven sand cores to cast the iron block; now just four cores were needed, reducing complexity, while ensuring dimensional accuracy. The cylinder heads were also a modern

BELOW: American Motors needed to increase sales of its larger cars dramatically because they were much more profitable than the Rambler American series. This top-line 1967 Ambassador DPL hardtop two-door has a surprising amount of brightwork and standard features, in an effort to outshine its Big Three competitors. Its all-new body and chassis should have ensured a much higher level of retail sales, but AMC's financial troubles scared off many potential buyers. Rival Studebaker Corporation had ended production midway during the 1966 model year, and many buyers were afraid that AMC, the last of the big independent car companies, would soon follow suit.

LEFT: The Ambassador convertible for 1967 was offered only in the highest-priced DPL series, and less than 1,300 were produced for the year. American Motors probably should have offered the Ambassador soft top in the 990 series as well, if only to boost sales. The six-passenger Ambassador convertible is highly sought after by collectors today as it offers great styling and comfort and, with its long wheelbase and V-8 engine, is a terrific highway cruiser.

BELOW: Another well-loved model in the Ambassador lineup for 1967 was the 990 series station wagon, seen here with distinctive woodgrain side trim and roof rack. American Motors produced more than 11,000 Ambassador station wagons during the 1967 model year. The 1967 fiscal year proved to be one of the worst in AMC history. It was plain that the company's management had to move quickly if they were to save the firm from going under. After management sold off its Kelvinator division, automobiles came to represent nearly 100% of AMC's business.

"wedge" design providing not only improved performance but reduced emissions, and the automakers all knew emissions would soon be a big deal. Overall dimensions were smaller, but there was room to expand the displacement over the 290- and 343-cu.-in. (4.75- and 5.6-liter) versions initially offered on all of AMC's vehicles that year.

What did it take to finalize this new engine design? Engineers at Kenosha and the company headquarters in Detroit conducted twenty-three-thousand dynamometer hours and 2.5 million vehicle miles (4 million kilometers) on 125 engines. Test engineers then drove fourteen engines for a total of 750,000 miles near San Antonio, Texas, on a route to cover a variety of conditions and speeds. Component failure and oil consumption were critical factors, and these new V-8s proved to be superior to the already fine AMC powerplants. Public confidence in these new engines came from an industry-leading five-year or 50,000-mile (80,470-kilometer) warranty on all AMC drivetrains.

The base 880 model started at $2,619 for the two-door sedan, along with a four-door sedan and wagon. The upscale 990 started at $2,776 for the four-door sedan and $3,083 for the station wagon, while the stylish two-door hardtop coupe started at $2,803. The flagship DPL was also available in striking two-door hardtop coupe or convertible models. Even with the power of a Typhoon, just 62,839 Ambassadors were built, 8,853 less than the previous year.

We're going to guess that the advertising tagline, "The Now Cars from American Motors," was created by the ad agency in place before Wells, Rich, and Greene signed on—it has a generic, "let's-phone-it-in" feel, like something from a team that has run out of ideas. That was unfortunate because the 1967 Marlin, based now on the big Ambassador chassis, was an attractive car unique in the full-size market.

Rebel

The Now Cars—Rebel.

"Wind up Rebel's 343 cube 4-bbl. Typhoon V-8—and you'll wind up owning the first Excitement Machine in the intermediate class!" That's how AMC described the Rebel series, which replaced the Classic.

And with the new optional Typhoon engines under the hood, going up to 280 horsepower, they certainly didn't feel boring. With "a road-gripping wide stance" and "optional handling hardware like heavy-duty shocks and springs," a Rebel could be equipped for an exciting experience.

Rebel was also given a major upgrade, with a longer wheelbase and striking, shapely new skin designed by Vince Geraci and Miller Johnson. For once the team had the budget to do it right. "The company invested a lot of money in the new Rebels," said Geraci. "The prior Classics had been overly square, so we decided on a more curvaceous, sensuous design for the new Rebel."

Part of the design was a venturi-style grille treatment that would be used on other AMC cars in the future. Compared with the boxy Ford Fairlane, Mercury Comet, Plymouth GTX, and Dodge Coronet, the new Rebel was almost Italian in its gracefulness. The basic 550 model remained in two-door sedan, four-door sedan, and wagon versions. The upscale 770 came in a four-door sedan, station wagon, or sleek two-door hardtop coupe. The real confidence-builder was the SST, in two-door hardtop or convertible models.

"There isn't a better intermediate-size car sold in the United States than the 1967 Rambler Rebel," said esteemed road tester Tom McCahill in *Mechanix Illustrated*. And yet a mere 100,627 of the sensuous new Rebels were built, less than the previous year's Classic.

Marlin

The Now Cars–Marlin.

Ward's Auto declared in July 1967: "Despite a more stylish look, dwindling sales have trimmed production of the AMC Marlin to just 2,500 units in '67, a second consecutive decline from first-year output of 10,000 in '65." They were right, and only 2,545 would be built in this final year for the model.

It's a shame, really: the Marlin for 1967 was now based on the Ambassador and filled with all the appointments available in AMC's top model. It was a simple update for engineering, since Rebel and Ambassador shared the same rear unibody structure. With the new Typhoon V-8 engines under the hood, performance was enhanced, and the 1967 Marlin was impressive, as Dick Teague noted: "I wanted that to be on the longer wheelbase. I thought we'd roll one year with a Classic-based Marlin, then go the next year with an Ambassador Marlin. I won that battle, but it was too late. The damage had already been done. But looking back on all these cars now, they don't look all that bad to me."

Rambler American

The Now Cars–Rambler American.

While the Rambler American was little changed from the previous year, what was now available under the hood was even more exciting—the Typhoon 343 V-8, now an option for the Rogue.

A 343-cu.-in. engine in America's smallest compact? Both the 290 and 343 versions of the engine have the same exterior dimensions, so why not? A mere seventy-one Rogues were built with the 343, including seven convertibles. This was the last year AMC offered an American convertible.

AMC's print ad for the Rogue stated, "So you see, we don't build them like we used to. That's our message." Loud and clear!

The Results

To help build their new image, AMC retained the hottest Madison Avenue advertising agency at the time, Wells, Rich, and Greene, Inc., the firm that later created the memorable "Plop, Plop, Fizz, Fizz!" ads for Alka-Seltzer and Ford's "Quality Is Job One" campaign.

All these new products cost huge amounts of money to develop, and the company recorded a loss of $75 million. Total production was down from the previous year, with 235,923 cars completed, but the company's new image was growing. And image, as they say, is everything.

The 1967 Rambler station wagon remained a popular model, but overall AMC sales were down sharply for the year. Chapin slashed the price on the Rambler American two-door sedan to $1,839 to make it more competitive with the VW Beetle, while undercutting all its domestic competition. The rest of the American line was also sharply reduced in price, spurring a huge increase in sales.

MAKE	RAMBLER	AMC		
Model	American	Rebel	Marlin	Ambassador
Passengers	5	6	6	6
Wheelbase (inches/centimeters)	106/269	114/290	118/300	118/300
Engine (Standard)	199 cu. in., OHV I-6, 128 hp	232 cu. in., OHV I-6, 145 hp	232 cu. in., OHV I-6, 145 hp	232 cu. in., OHV I-6, 155 hp
Engine (Optional)	232 cu. in., OHV I-6, 145 or 155 hp	232 cu. in., OHV I-6, 155 hp	232 cu. in., OHV I-6, 155 hp	290 cu. in., OHV V-8, 200 hp
Engine (Optional)	290 cu. in., OHV V-8, 200 hp	290 cu. in., OHV V-8, 200 or 225 hp	290 cu. in., OHV V-8, 200 hp	343 cu. in., OHV V-8, 235 or 280 hp
Engine (Optional)		343 cu. in., OHV V-8, 235 or 280 hp	343 cu. in., OHV V-8, 235 or 280 hp	
Production (Model)	2-door hardtop coupe: 9,243 2-door sedan: 29,513 2-door convertible: 921 4-door sedan: 22,161 4-door station wagon: 8,074	2-door hardtop coupe: 26,384 2-door sedan: 9,121 2-door convertible: 1,686 4-door sedan: 38,039 4-door station wagon: 25,397	2-door fastback coupe: 2,545	2-door coupe: 3,623 2-door hardtop coupe: 18,692 2-door convertible: 1,260 4-door sedan: 27,805 4-door station wagon: 11,459
Production (Total)	69,912	100,627	2,545	62,839

Total American Motors 1967 Production: 235,923

1968

Javelin

Hey Javelin!

The press release for August 22, 1967, told the story: "A twin Venturi grille, long hood, and massive bumper fully integrated with body contours highlight the distinctive front styling of American Motors' new two-door sports hardtop, the Javelin. The all-new entry in the U.S. sporty car field will carry four passengers in full comfort." The once-stodgy Rambler now had a pony car—and it was hot!

The Javelin was created by modifying the American's platform, stretching the wheelbase from 106 to 109 inches (269 to 277 centimeters). If that sounds like a humble beginning for a performance car, keep in mind that the Ford Mustang and Mercury Cougar were based on the compact Falcon, the Chevy Camaro and Pontiac Firebird on the Nova, and the Plymouth Barracuda on the Valiant. The American's coil-spring front suspension and leaf-spring rear were retained, though well modified for the job

TOP: After finally dropping the slow-selling Marlin hardtop line, American Motors made its belated entry into the pony car market with its brilliantly designed Javelin. Roy Chapin Jr. and board member Roy Evans, AMC's largest single shareholder, pushed the Javelin program hard, believing it was essential to help change the image of American Motors from purveyors of "old people's cars" to a company catering to hip, young clientele. The new Javelin was roomier and much more comfortable than the Chevy Camaro and Ford Mustang, offered new style, and was less costly, as well. The Javelin name had been suggested by AMC sales executive Guy Hadsall Jr., who in later years came to be known as "Mister Javelin."

ABOVE: The new Javelin could be ordered with a stylish vinyl top, as seen here, as well as a wide variety of six and V-8 engines, three transmissions, three- and four-speed manual or three-speed automatic, a wide range of exterior color and interior trim, air conditioning, power steering and brakes, and a host of other features and equipment options to make the car feel more personalized.

ROAD TEST: AMC JAVELIN 390 SST
Publication: ***Car and Driver***
Author: ***Car and Driver*** **Staff**

Latest entrant in the sporty car sweepstakes, the Javelin, has the benefit of time working for it in its design. It's a third-generation car. It also has the disadvantages of AMC's less-than-glamorous image, and AMC's previous track record in the enthusiast market to contend with.

Our Javelin was the first 390 ever built—but its long suit was its handling. It felt very much like a British sports car—with the same advantages as well as the same disadvantages. The Javelin is nearly neutral when pushed through a hard corner and a controllable, power-induced oversteer can be obtained whenever desired. . . . On the tight handling course the SST was everyone's favorite because of its versatility and predictability.

The Javelin's styling was another area that received unanimous approval. It has a clean understated appearance that is not marred by phony vents, power bulges, mounds or bizarre sculpturing of whatever variety. The Javelin is an honest-looking car with a dramatic flair.

AMC hasn't had any time to play with the 390, at least officially, and so we didn't expect the car to tear up the pavement. We weren't disappointed. It didn't. It was the slowest in the quarter-mile (15.2 seconds at 92 mph), and the engine felt like a lump in the midst of rebellion.

The Javelin, because of its handling, turned out to be the most fun to drive of any of the sporty cars. But its performance was not spectacular and AMC is going to have to make it spectacular if they're going to do well in the enthusiast market.

at hand. "A rude awakening waited for us in the handling test," wrote *Motor Trend* in January 1968. "In SST form with the 343 V-8 which includes a stout handling package, the car turned and cornered as if it were nailed to the road."

All that was wrapped in a body that, in typical AMC fashion, was clean and crisp. Though it carried the long-hood/short-deck look, the rear seat was actually useable for more than a few minutes. "You only need a moment inside a Javelin to discover the abundance of space," commented *Motor Trend*. "Nearly every interior dimension is larger than its competitors, and three in the full-width back seat is a reality." Javelin's look was unique at the time, with the sweeping roof blending seamlessly into the rear quarter panels. This year all AMC cars except the Rambler American received unique recessed door handles, which the press mostly praised.

ABOVE: Midway through the 1968 model year, American Motors sprang a surprise new model on an unsuspecting public: the all-new AMX, a two-seat sports car with fantastic styling and a standard V-8 engine. CEO Roy D. Chapin Jr. later called the AMX a car that was "created to inspire and lift the spirits of American Motors employees and enthusiasts." By cutting a midsection from the AMC Javelin pony car and then adding a new rear section and restyled front end, the company developed the AMX as the only American sports car on the market other than Chevrolet's Corvette. To offer a sports car when even Ford and Chrysler had pulled theirs out of the running was a remarkable accomplishment for the small company, something that greatly enhanced its image.

Power for the base Javelin was the 232-cu.-in. six, a decent performer in the 2,826-pound (1,282-kilogram) coupe. *Motor Trend* reported, "Rated at 145 hp, it is of a recent design, and delivers surprisingly good performance and at least 22 mpg on regular fuel." Next up was the 290-cu.-in. V-8, equipped with two-barrel carburetor and producing 200 horsepower, again on regular gasoline. Three-speed manual was standard on these engines, Shift-Command three-speed automatic optional, both with column shift.

The good stuff started with the 225-horsepower 290 four-barrel with four-speed on the floor, then the performance 343-cu.-in. V-8 with two- or four-barrel carbs and 280 horsepower, of which *Motor Trend* said, "It performed smoothly, quietly, yet 'got on with the program' when pushed. . . . Performance of our test car was just short of surprising." They recorded a quarter-mile time of 15.12 seconds at 93.26 miles per hour (150 kilometers per hour) at Irwindale Raceway.

AMC's manager of shows and exhibits, Guy Hadsall Jr., had suggested the name, and it seemed right for the company's new performance weapon. A major promotion was the famous "Hey Javelin!" TV spot with actor Herb Edelman, created by Wells, Rich, and Greene, Inc. As the voiceover declares: "We at American Motors never had the reputation of building hot, sporty cars. Then we built the Javelin."

"There's a look of success about the Javelin, even though it's entering the game late," concluded *Motor Trend*. The Javelin went on sale in September 1967,

BELOW: A styling mockup of the new Javelin's instrument panel. The sporty steering wheel and cockpit-like sectioning of the driver's and passenger's sides emphasized that this was a car for people who like to drive—and drive fast. Important elements behind Javelin's image included standard bucket seats and a manual transmission floorshift. Some early models apparently came with a column-mounted three-speed gearshift for the manual transmission, and the optional three-speed automatic transmission could be ordered with either a column shifter or a floor-/console-mounted shifter.

American Motors created a new Performance Department during 1968 and put longtime employee Carl Chakmakian, a talented engineer, in charge. Chakmakian was a rare individual, a man who burned with energy and enthusiasm, full of ideas on how to improve the company's products and ready to work relentlessly to do so. AMC stylist Jim Alexander once stated that, "if American Motors had 100 more guys like Carl Chakmakian, we would have been invincible." Chakmakian, seen here standing next to a specially prepared AMX, hired Craig and Lee Breedlove to set a large number of new performance records with the AMX. Craig Breedlove is sitting in Lee's car.

and by January of the next year 12,390 had been sold. At the end of the model year, some 55,124 had been produced, including 26,027 of the hot SST versions.

Success indeed!

AMX

Mr. and Mrs. Breedlove went for a nice, long, Sunday drive in an AMX.

The new AMX was billed as "the hairy little brother of the Javelin." By the time it made its debut at the Chicago Auto Show in February 1968, it was already a record breaker. AMC hired the two standing land speed record holders, Craig Breedlove and his wife Lee, to see what they could get out of the car. They ultimately set over one hundred speed records with the AMX, as certified by the United States Auto Club, on Goodyear's test oval in West Texas. The AMX magazine ad reported: "That's every record in the book from 25 kilometers to 5,000 kilometers. From 1 hour to 24 hours. From standing starts and flying starts."

Development of the AMX began in the fall of 1965, in parallel with the Javelin. Inside and out, the car shared much with the Javelin, but with 12 inches (30 centimeters) of wheelbase removed behind the front seats. A unique hood, top stamping, rear sheet metal, and grille separated the AMX from its bigger brother. *Sports Car Graphic* magazine wrote,

> The Javelin and AMX body/chassis structures were designed almost simultaneously with the intention of utilizing the maximum number of common components and effecting the required wheelbase and overall reduction of 12 inches for the AMX by cutting Javelins pressings at convenient points and using a minimum of additional panel work. The two-in-one end product is the result of some highly skilled body engineering, for the whole thing looks so deceptively simple. . . . The more compact body has trimmed 112 pounds off the weight of the AMX compared with the Javelin, the bare-metal weight of the two car bodies being 755 and 867 pounds.

“I believe this is the most notable achievement of 1968 in the auto industry—two new cars in one year,” said Roy Chapin Jr. “The AMX has a completely different character from the Javelin. As a two-passenger car it doesn’t have universal appeal. It’s aimed at a specialized market.”

The two-seat concept car AMC showed in 1966 was dubbed an “American Motors Experimental” car. “Everybody’s been calling it that, so we decided to officially name it AMX,” Chapin told *Motor Trend*. Considering that the AMX didn’t arrive in show rooms until March 1968, the 6,725 produced made it another winner.

The Ambassador DPL

ABOVE: American Motors was pushing the luxury aspects of the Ambassador DPL and new SST models for 1968. The rich new grille design, bright trim, plus interior trim all pointed to the fact that, although physically smaller than the Big Three’s full-size cars, the Ambassador was a cut above them in luxury appointments and class. The midrange DPL hardtop shown here is stunning in its deep maroon paint.

Ambassador

An unfair comparison between the Rolls-Royce and the Ambassador.

Ambassador was mostly unchanged for 1968, though the grille and taillights were new. Now, though, all Ambassadors boasted air conditioning as standard equipment.

The Ambassador’s many standard features begged the comparison with the Rolls-Royce. “Because air conditioning is standard on the Ambassador,” stated one magazine ad, “we thought it much too unfair to compare it to the Chevrolet Impala or the Ford Galaxie, which list for about the same price. So, we chose the renowned Rolls-Royce Silver Shadow 4-door Saloon for our comparison.” With the Rolls listing at $19,000,

The Ambassador series for 1968 included a new base model known simply as the Ambassador. It was offered in two-door hardtop and four-door sedan versions. The DPL series was now the midpriced Ambassador. At the top of the American Motors lineup was the new Ambassador SST. The DPL and SST Ambassadors were offered in four-door sedan and station wagon versions, plus a two-door hardtop. The Ambassador convertible was dropped from the line due to slow sales. The Ambassador SST hardtop seen here displays the car’s unique side trim plus optional wire wheel covers.

MAKE	RAMBLER	AMC			
Model	American	AMX	Javelin	Rebel	Ambassador
Passengers	5	2	4	6	6
Wheelbase (inches/ centimeters)	106/269	97/246	109/277	114/290	118/300
Engine (Standard)	199 cu. in., OHV I-6, 128 hp	290 cu. in., OHV V-8, 225 hp	232 cu. in., OHV I-6, 145 hp	232 cu. in., OHV I6, 145 hp	290 cu. in., OHV V-8, 200 hp
Engine (Optional)	232 cu. in., OHV I-6, 145 or 155 hp	343 cu. in., OHV V-8, 280 hp	290 cu. in., OHV V-8, 200 hp	232 cu. in., OHV I6, 155 hp	343 cu. in., OHV V-8, 235 or 280 hp
Engine (Optional)	290 cu. in., OHV V-8, 200 or 225 hp	390 cu. in., OHV V-8, 315 hp	343 cu. in., OHV V-8, 235 or 280 hp	290 cu. in., OHV V-8, 200 or 225 hp	390 cu. in., OHV V-8, 315 hp
Engine (Optional)			390 cu. in., OHV V-8, 315 hp	343 cu. in., OHV V-8, 235 or 280 hp	
Production (Model)	2-door hardtop coupe: 4,765 2-door sedan: 39,480 4-door sedan: 26,323 4-door station wagon: 10,414	2-door coupe: 6,725	2-door coupe: 56,444	2-door hardtop coupe: 23,329 2-door convertible: 1,200 4-door sedan: 30,969 4-door station wagon: 18,397	2-door hardtop coupe: 14,932 4-door sedan: 29,021 4-door station wagon: 10,698
Production (Total)	80,982	6,725	56,444	73,895	54,651

Total American Motors 1968 Production: 272,697

The 1968 Rebel was no longer badged as a Rambler, leaving the compact American as the sole Rambler-branded car in the US American Motors lineup. Once again, only the 550 and 770 trim series were offered, meaning buyers had to choose between a stripped, low-line car or a fancy one: there was no midrange choice, a questionable practice by AMC. The Rebel 770s were treated to a bright new grille with richer looks.

RIGHT: Beginning in 1968, the Rambler American line no longer offered a convertible model. Sales of convertibles had been falling throughout the industry as hardtops grew in favor, and air conditioning began to be purchased by more and more buyers. Women especially seemed to prefer an air-conditioned car over a soft top because their hair wouldn't get blown into tangles in the hardtop. This sharp Rambler Rogue boasts optional wire wheel covers and redline tires, which were a fad at the time.

AMC made a convincing argument—whether in standard Ambassador trim, the luxury DPL, or the new SST model, these were big, beautiful automobiles equipped with more than their Big Three rivals offered at comparable prices.

Buyers thought so, too, purchasing 60,872 units.

Rebel

Some people have a love affair with the Javelin but then marry the Rebel.

It was hard not to fall for the new Javelin, but then, as with many relationships, reality hits. That's where the Rebel came in. It had many of the same powertrains as the Javelin but with room for the family. The Javelin only came in the 2+2 coupe, but the Rebel 550 line offered four-door sedan and station wagon versions, as well as a new hardtop—and a new convertible! The midrange 770 came in a four-door sedan, station wagon, or sleek two-door hardtop coupe. And if you really wanted Javelin-like performance the wife and kids could enjoy, there was the SST in its compelling two-door hardtop coupe or convertible models. The Rebel really was the best of both worlds, and 79,325 were built.

ABOVE: The prosaic Rambler four-door sedan was offered in base 220 and highline 440 series for 1968. This Rambler American four-door shows off its rich-looking side and rear trim, sporty wheel covers, and optional whitewall tires. The 440 emblem can be seen on the roof sail panel. These were popular with buyers who desired a small, economical sedan with room for six and plenty of style. The standard six-cylinder engines were renown for durability and excellent fuel economy.

Rambler American

An unfair comparison with the VW and the Rambler American.

The American didn't change much for 1968, and it didn't need to. It was still America's lowest-priced car, and a compelling challenger to the imports arriving in growing numbers. Wells, Rich, and Greene's ads made a strong point: "The Volkswagen on the left gives you the advantages of a little economy car. The Rambler American on the right gives you the advantages of a little economy car without being little. It lists for $1,946, scrimps on gas, and doesn't change styles from year to year. Yet it seats six comfortably and gives you more than twice the horsepower and trunk space of the VW."

The American also had a heater that worked and the option of air conditioning, plus many more amenities the imports did not. Apparently many readers agreed, as 94,369 Americans were built.

ABOVE: In May 1968 workers on the final assembly line in Kenosha celebrate production of the year's 50,000th Javelin. This marked a level that some worried might not be reached at all, but the Javelin was warmly greeted by buyers, especially young ones. Many AMC dealers reported seeing a class of people they had never before seen in their showrooms. The Javelin was bringing new people in to American Motors.

RIGHT: The 1968 Rambler American 440 series station wagon was likewise a popular model with young families looking for a comfortable car at a low price, some luxury touches, and top fuel economy. This particular Rambler American is equipped with the optional American Motors-designed-and-built 290-cu.-in. V-8 engine for effortless highway cruising combined with superior V-8 economy.

The Results

Change in the auto industry is expensive, a point the *New York Times* drove home: "American Motors earned $11.8-million or 61 cents a share in fiscal 1968 ended Sept. 30, but only $4.8 million of that came from automotive operations, and the remainder from tax credits."

Cutting costs in other areas was critical, and in 1968 AMC sold its Kelvinator appliance operation to make ends meet.

AMC produced 272,697 units and held 3.2 percent market share in this year, more than Chrysler, Cadillac, or Lincoln.

1969

Javelin

Big Bad Javelin.

The big news for 1969 was the introduction of the Big Bad colors. Buyers could choose one of three Big Bad paint options: Big Bad Orange, Big Bad Blue, or Big Bad Green. On Javelin and AMX models this included painted bumpers. The race-developed, roof-mounted Breedlove spoiler was a new option. In the 1969 American Motors Salesmen's News Flash, sales professionals were told that the colors would "give you an 'In' with the performance crowd." The Big Bad cars certainly drew attention!

A 390-cu.-in. AMX V-8 version of the AMC V-8 was also rolled out later in the model year. Now in its second year, Javelin attracted plenty of "in-crowd" buyers, 40,675 of them.

AMX

The first American sports car for under $3,500 since 1957.

You had to go back to the 1957 Corvette to buy a new two-seater for less than $3,500. The AMX was quite a bargain, and for just $123 more you could now order the new 390-cu.-in. engine. *Sports Car Graphic* took a 390-equipped AMX for a spin, afterward posting this assessment: "The 390 CID V-8, though quite modestly tuned, feels smooth and lively and suggests that American Motors power figures are more realistic than most.

The AMC Javelin offered new colors, new sports stripes, and new appearance items for 1969, along with the optional new 390-cu.-in. V-8. Hot new options for the 1969 Javelin are showcased in this press release photo from American Motors. The Big Bad colors—red, green, and blue—included painted bumpers as seen here, along with a lower grille area with bright molding. Also new was an optional roof-mounted rear spoiler, rocker panel trim that mimicked side exhaust pipes. Note the twin flat black hood scoops that replaced the stripe on the optional Go package. A new standard battery, the transparent Clear Power 24, made it easy to check fluid levels without taking off the battery caps.

RIGHT: The Ambassador series stood out from every other American car because air conditioning had become standard equipment. In addition, Ambassadors were completely restyled on a longer 122-inch (310-centimeter) wheelbase for 1969, the longest wheelbase ever offered by American Motors. Ambassadors received bold new front-end styling, along with interior refinements and mechanical improvements. This DPL four-door sedan was equipped with the optional velour upholstery, indicated by the bright panel between the two lower-body bright moldings (with standard upholstery, this area would have been body color). The extra body and wheelbase length give this car a feeling of great substance and solidity.

BELOW: The top-of-the-line Ambassador SST series featured woodgrain side trim on all models, as we see on this sharp two-door hardtop. The area between the two lower-body bright moldings is filled with wood-look vinyl trim, a distinctive feature in the full-size market. It's indicative of the approach AMC was using, trying to differentiate its offerings from what the Big Three was producing.

That 5000 RPM red line felt to us like a conservative guess rather than an accurate measure of valve gear efficiency. The 390 CID engine doesn't impose as much of a nose heavy problem as was anticipated."

Of the AMX they concluded, "It is aimed at the high-performance enthusiast, call him the sports car enthusiast if you will. We would sum up our appraisal of the AMX by saying that, in our view, it is a very good sports car indeed!" This summation was echoed by 8,293 buyers.

Ambassador

Test ride the 1969 Ambassador. Our chauffeur will pick you up.

The Ambassador was no longer the smallest of the big cars, once AMC added four more inches (10 centimeters) to its length. The now-122-inch (310-centimeter) wheelbase of the biggest AMC was the same as the Dodge Monaco, and an inch (2.5 centimeters) longer than the Ford LTD.

The 1969 American Motors Rebel line was trimmed to two series and six models. The base Rebel series and the Rebel SST series both included two-door hardtops, plus four-door sedans and station wagons. A revised grille debuted along with new headlamp bezels and new taillamp assemblies for a modest but appreciated appearance update. The convertible models were dropped. Rebels also got all-new instrument panels and new door trim panels, while station wagon models now got the dual-swing tailgate as standard equipment.

The press was always amazed when they pitted an AMC product against its Big Three competition. *Motor Trend* in November 1968 compared an Ambassador SST two-door coupe against similar family cars, writing, "Front end treatment gives the Ambassador an unfettered, bold continental look that puts down the Nash Kelvinator image once and for all. The '69 Ambassador is also wider, and four inches longer than it was in '68, which definitely puts it in the same class as the other cars tested."

With AMC's 343 V-8 under the hood, the Ambassador SST had the lowest horsepower of the four cars tested. "Even so, performance was still brisk for a family car, with a 4-bbl Carter carburetor and 10.2:1 compression," wrote *Motor Trend*. "Suspension is fluid and supple, but we did have a slight surprise when it came to handling. AMC has come up with a new rear suspension geometry on the '69 Ambassador, for a more stabilized ride and reduced vibration."

"This is where the Ambassador really shows star quality and class in the family car race," they concluded. "Standard features like air conditioning and fully reclining seatbacks make the Ambassador a real family wagon. . . . And it looks great besides. . . . The Ambassador, being the only car with air conditioning as a standard item, will probably influence a lot of mothers, who in turn will influence the old man." The old man must have listened: 76,194 were produced.

Rebel

An intermediate-sized car with the price of a compact.

Motor Trend was again surprised, this time by the latest AMC Rebel. In their June 1969 issue they gushed: "The Rebel front seats afforded the most comfort by far. . . . Rear seats in the Rebel were also softly padded and adequately comfortable. Seating room-like comfort is

MAKE	RAMBLER	AMC			
Model	Rambler	AMX	Javelin	Rebel	Ambassador
Passengers	5	2	4	6	6
Wheelbase (inches/ centimeters)	106/269	97/246	109/277	114/290	122/310
Engine (Standard)	199 cu. in., OHV I-6, 128 hp	290 cu. in., OHV V-8, 225 hp	232 cu. in., OHV I-6, 145 hp	232 cu. in., OHV I-6, 145 hp	290 cu. in., OHV V-8, 200 hp
Engine (Optional)	232 cu. in., OHV I-6, 145 or 155 hp	343 cu. in., OHV V-8, 280 hp	290 cu. in., OHV V-8, 200 hp	232 cu. in., OHV I-6, 155 hp	343 cu. in., OHV V-8, 235 or 280 hp
Engine (Optional)	290 cu. in., OHV V-8, 200 or 225 hp	390 cu. in., OHV V-8, 315 hp	343 cu. in., OHV V-8, 235 or 280 hp	290 cu. in., OHV V-8, 200 or 225 hp	390 cu. in., OHV V-8, 315 hp
Engine (Optional)			390 cu. in., OHV V-8, 315 hp	343 cu. in., OHV V-8, 235 or 280 hp	
Production (Model)	2-door hardtop coupe: 5,055 2-door sedan: 51,062 4-door sedan: 28,191 4-door station wagon: 13,233	2-door coupe: 8,293	2-door coupe: 40,675	2-door hardtop coupe: 10,801 4-door sedan: 31,480 4-door station wagon: 17,825	2-door hardtop coupe: 13,502 4-door sedan: 46,001 4-door station wagon: 16,691
Production (Total)	97,541	8,293	40,675	60,106	76,194

Total American Motors 1969 Production: 282,809

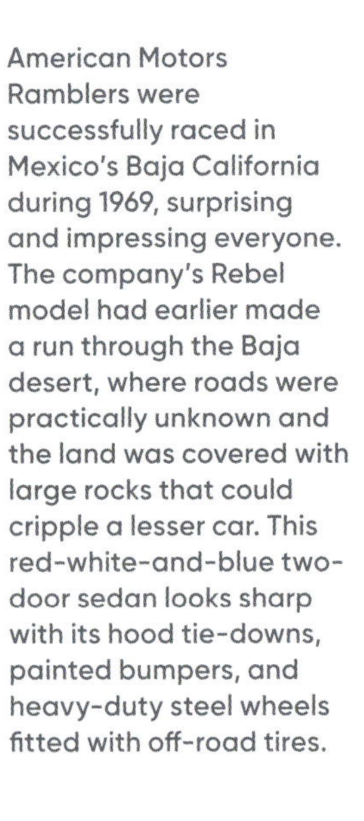
American Motors Ramblers were successfully raced in Mexico's Baja California during 1969, surprising and impressing everyone. The company's Rebel model had earlier made a run through the Baja desert, where roads were practically unknown and the land was covered with large rocks that could cripple a lesser car. This red-white-and-blue two-door sedan looks sharp with its hood tie-downs, painted bumpers, and heavy-duty steel wheels fitted with off-road tires.

LEFT AND FOLLOWING PAGES: In addition to the regular models for 1969, the Rambler series also offered the limited-production SC/Rambler Hurst two-door hardtop, of which a reported 1,512 units were produced in two color schemes. These hot machines were powered by the 315-horsepower AMX 390 V-8 hooked up to a standard four-speed manual transmission. Known as the Hurst Scrambler, this model is perhaps the most collectible AMC car there is. Its distinctive paint colors and amazing performance have broad appeal. AMC's Mexican affiliate was said to have offered a similar car powered by a hotted-up six-cylinder engine, since they didn't produce a V-8 of their own. *Tom & Kelly Glatch*

a success in the Rebel. Convenient features abound on the Rebel, and AMC designers have given people the little extra touches that loom large when needed."

The suspension updates of the Ambassador were shared with the Rebel, as *Motor Trend* noted: "With the Rebel's track increased to 60 inches, the front and rear suspensions were redesigned in '69 to improve ride more in line with a heavier car. Front shocks are now equipped with a dirt shield to help keep out dirt, grime and small stones. The Rebel ride is extremely comfortable for a family sedan."

Look out Chevrolet, Ford, and Plymouth, the AMC Rebel "was the most comfortable in any driving situation though, and with a plurality of comfort and convenience features, goes a long way toward being all things to all people in a family car." AMC built 78,894 Rebels for this model year.

Rambler

It Only Hurts Them for 14 Seconds.

The Rambler American was now just the Rambler. Rumors were already circulating that this would be its last year, whatever it was called. It was to be a grand finale for one of AMC's great models.

Hurst Performance, Inc. had expanded from making aftermarket shifters and wheels to helping create low-volume vehicles that automakers didn't have the resources

AMC
390
AMC

BFGoodrich

The handsome Rambler 440 four-door sedan for 1969. This year—the final year for this body in America—the "American" name was dropped from the car badges, leaving only "Rambler." The model lineup for 1969 was the same as in the previous year: the base 220 series in two- and four-door sedans, the 440 series in four-door sedans and station wagons, and a single Rogue two-door hardtop.

or expertise to produce. Now they focused their magic on the little Rambler with the amazing Hurst SC/Rambler.

Based on the previous Rogue, the SC/Hurst included AMC's 315-horsepower, 390-cu.-in. engine, Borg-Warner four-speed, and 3:54:1 Twin Grip differential. To this Hurst added a large functional fiberglass hood scoop, Sun 8,000-rpm tach, adjustable Gabriel Air Shocks, glass-pack mufflers, and, of course, a Hurst shifter. The SC/Hurst featured a bold red-white-and-blue paint scheme that was impossible to ignore. As planned, five hundred cars were built, but overwhelming demand called for additional cars. The only difference in the second, B-series cars was a toned-down paint scheme. Apparently the A-series attracted too much attention—perhaps from the law—so the B cars had smaller red-and-blue side stripes on a white body. A third lot was built, with most using the A's paint scheme. In the end, 1,512 were sold.

The bold, brash little SC/Ramblers generated a lot of other attention. An A-series SC/Rambler was featured as the cover story in the May 1969 issue of *Super Stock & Drag Illustrated* magazine. AMC's marketing also cranked up the spin machine, with ads shouting "A Rambler that does the quarter mile in 14.3" in *Car and Driver* magazine. This was one quick little compact, with *Road Test* magazine recording quarter-mile times at 14.14 seconds at a speed of 100.44 miles per hour (161.64 kilometers per hour), while *Super Stock & Drag*

Illustrated got an SC/Rambler to deliver 12.6 seconds with a little work, a stunning supercar number at the time.

Power-to-weight ratio was the heart of performance, and at 3,160 pounds (1,433 kilograms), the bantamweight Hurst SC/Rambler could humble heavier cars with much more power under their hoods. Or, as AMC declared, "you could make life miserable for any GTO, Road Runner, Cobra Jet or Mach 1." All for a bargain $2,998.

Production of all Ramblers remained a respectable 97,541, a nice increase from 1968.

The Results

The new products that began as Robert Evans's suggestions were quickly brought to market during Roy Chapin Jr.'s tenure. New products take time in the auto industry—they also take millions of dollars to develop. The *New York Times* broke it down: "In all the 1969 fiscal year net income was $4.9-million, or 26 cents a share." Total production was up nicely at 282,809 units with 3.5 percent market share.

At the close of the 1960s, AMC adopted the now famous red-white-and-blue logo, dubbed the A-Mark, which was created by Walter P. Margulies. Even in the smallest details, AMC was boldly moving into the 1970s.

VEHICLE: 1969 AMC HURST SC/RAMBLER

Owner: Ted Hinkle, Mt. Pleasant, Wisconsin

In college, my roommate was a real car nut, and we saw this car in the back of *Motor Trend* magazine. And you say, hey, yeah, I need something like that. But I was a poor college student. When we got back on Christmas break, I called Young Motors in Tipton, Indiana, and he didn't even know what I was talking about. Two weeks later he calls and says, "I could get you a SC/Rambler" and I said go ahead and order it. Of course, I didn't have a job and had no money, so I joined the Army. My brother was a lieutenant in the infantry, and I learned to fly "Huey" (Bell UH-1) helicopters.

So, I'm making 160 bucks a month, payments were 103 bucks a month, so I'm ahead. I took delivery April 25, 1969, when I was on break, paying $3,052,94, and I drove it down to Fort Polk, Louisiana. I have driven it to Texas when I was transferred for primary flight school, and to Fort Rucker in Alabama. It was my driver for a year, and then the second year it was in storage while I was in Vietnam. My best time at Bunker Hill Drag Strip was 12:00 even, on slicks and 4.44:1 gears. It was also in our wedding in 1982. It has 42,259 miles on it, and it's still fun!

1970–1974

CHAPTER

4

THE NEW-GENERATION CARS

One of the greatest challenges in the automotive business is planning for the future. Concepting the new approach to refresh an existing vehicle can take a year, followed by three or more years of development and, then, manufacturing. It may take close to a half decade before an entirely new automobile can roll out of the plant—costing a huge amount of time and money along the way. Get it right, and a new vehicle can provide years of enjoyment for owners and strong profits to the automaker—look at AMC's 1956 Rambler or the first Ford Mustang. Get it wrong, and the impact to the company can be devastating—consider Ford's Edsel or Chevy's Vega debacle. The stakes are enormous.

ABOVE: One of the most exciting products ever conceived by American Motors was the Gremlin, introduced on April Fools' Day 1970 as a midyear product. The new Gremlin was the first subcompact car from a major US automaker. The fact that AMC was able to beat GM, Ford, and Chrysler to market with a product going up against VW was nothing short of amazing. Gremlin's rapid development was possible because it was based on a cut-down Hornet chassis and body. The only changes required once the wheelbase was shortened to 96 inches (244 centimeters)—a full foot shorter than Hornet—was to design a new rear section, new grille, and slightly different hood stamping.

OPPOSITE TOP: The all-new 1970 AMC Hornet line of compact automobiles was introduced in the fall of 1969 to excellent reviews. Hornet was much different from the Rambler, which it replaced in the US market. Seen here in basic two-door form, the new Hornet was also offered in a handsome four-door sedan model, both on a longer 108-inch (274-centimeter) wheelbase, for increased interior room and comfort. Two trim levels were available: base and fancier SST. The large, flared wheel openings and long-hood, short-deck design gave Hornet more than a bit of pony car sportiness. Various six- and eight-cylinder engines were offered.

OPPOSITE BOTTOM: In anticipation of higher levels of car production resulting from the new Hornet and an upcoming subcompact, American Motors management authorized the purchase of four new metal stamping presses for the Milwaukee Body Plant. Sadly, the late 1969 union strike crippled production for weeks, which in turn meant that not enough Hornets could be built to meet demand; it would be months before AMC dealer stocks could adequately meet demand. By that point a great deal of momentum had been lost and Hornet sales were lower than anticipated. Despite introducing compelling new products that year, AMC reported a sizable loss for fiscal 1970.

The 1970 Gremlin was offered in two distinct models: a two-passenger car with no rear seat and a fixed rear window, and a four-passenger model with a flip-open rear hatch window and a fold-down rear seat. Gremlin's overall design was clever: the 22-gallon (83-liter) gas tank had a center-mounted filler at the rear of the car, so it didn't matter on which side of the fuel pump you parked. The hood was counterbalanced, so it held itself open, unlike the Ford Maverick, which needed a hood prop to stay open. And Gremlin's optional roof rack actually looked sporty on the short-wheelbase car, while increasing cargo capacity.

Then there was the increased burden of government mandates. Legislation like the Clean Air Act of 1963 and the National Traffic and Motor Vehicle Safety Act of 1966 established two new federal agencies, the Environmental Protection Agency (EPA) and the National Highway Traffic Safety Administration (NHTSA). All of these functioned with the admirable goals of reducing pollution while increasing fuel economy and automobile safety. But how the new regulations would shape the future of the automobile industry was unknown.

America was also entering the new decade in a profound funk, carrying over the effects of the ongoing, unpopular war in Southeast Asia along with mounting inflation and economic concerns.

In 1970 AMC bought the Kaiser Jeep Corporation. This purchase was intended to augment the company's revenue stream and help cushion the rollercoaster effects of the auto business on the company's bottom line. The storied Jeep brand had been struggling under Kaiser's ownership; AMC's first job would be to revive Jeep's US sales.

As part of the purchase, AMC also acquired a division that built vehicles for military and government agencies, which they spun off as AM General. Ironically, much of that division's business had begun under the old Studebaker Corporation.

Gerald Meyers was vice president of American Motors' product group at the time of the Jeep purchase. His job was to peer into the future and predict what buyers would want in their next new car, then create a strategic plan for the next generation of AMC cars to meet that demand. Not an easy task in the best of times, but unforeseen events made Meyers's job doubly challenging.

American Motors was moving forward into the new decade, and Chairman Roy Chapin Jr. was promoting the company's "philosophy of difference" and promising a new product every six months. How effective would Meyers' crystal ball be under that kind of pressure?

1970

Hornet

The little rich car for people who aren't rich.

Work on a new strategy for AMC cars began in earnest during 1967 as plans were being drafted for the Rambler American's replacement. Inspiration for the next-generation compact came from two concept cars created in 1966, part of Dick Teague's Project IV program:

- The Cavalier concept championed interchangeability: fenders could be swapped left-front to right-rear, and right-front to left-rear, while the four doors were equally interchangeable. The hood and trunk lid were also identical, as were the front and rear bumpers. If implemented, the design was estimated to reduce the cost of tooling and production by as much as 30 percent.
- The other sedan concept, the Vixen, featured a unique semi-fastback roofline and deeply recessed rear window.

Using ideas from both concepts, designers created the stylish new Hornet series. Riding a 108-inch (274-centimeter) wheelbase, the Hornet had more interior room and a smoother ride than the American's 106-inch (269-centimeter) wheelbase offered. *Car Life* magazine was impressed: "This Hornet interior was designed to not look cheap, and it doesn't. There are carpets, and the seats and panels are styled, that is, they have panels, trim lines, etc., to break

Famed puppeteer and ventriloquist Shari Lewis was hired by American Motors to help introduce the new Gremlin to dealers. Here we see Lewis with a Gremlin puppet/doll, seated in an early Gremlin car. The entire Gremlin marketing program was lighthearted and tongue-in-cheek, to emphasize that the new AMC car was meant to be fun. And it was: inexpensive to buy, fun to drive, and very, very counterculture, which was young people's mood at the time.

ROAD TEST: 1970 AMC HORNET

Publication: *Popular Science*, January 1970
Authors: Jan P. Norbye and Jim Dunne

Need all around transportation? Then come with us as we test the four lowest priced US cars. The fantastic success of Ford's Maverick has convinced the auto industry that the economy car market is where the action is going to be in 1970. Pending the arrival of the mini-compacts next fall, American Motors, Chrysler, and GM are competing for a piece of the action with respectively: a) an all-new vehicle; B) an old car with a jazzy roof line; and C) an old car with a special price.

The Maverick and the Hornet are true economy cars, with basic price tags just under the magic $2000 mark. The Duster is a new version of the Valiant, some $200 more expensive. The least expensive Chevy lists for more than $400 above the Hornet.

We tested the cars with comparable 6-cylinder engines, automatic transmissions, manual steering, and brakes. While we were not surprised that the bigger and heavier Nova burned more gasoline than the Ford and AMC cars, it was surprising that the Hornet had a 2 miles-per-gallon advantage over the Maverick.

HORNET. It offers more interior space. And better trunk room than the Maverick but suffers from the same lack of quality in the seats. Hornet has huge glass area and excellent visibility in all directions. The steering is lighter than the Maverick's—but even slower! The Hornet had the poorest brake performance of all four. If you're considering a Hornet, get the optional disc brakes! The Hornet proved to have outstanding fuel economy and modest performance in the manner of a true economy car.

CONCLUSIONS. *Dunne:* My choice is the Hornet. It's a practical family car and I like the styling. I think it's better value than any of the others.

NORBYE: I enjoyed driving the Nova. And I am impressed with its brakes. But how could they justify that price for an economy car? I'd have to settle for the Hornet. And pay extra for the optional disc brakes.

up the expanses of fabric. Nicely done." Ten paint colors were available. For an extra $39.40 there were color choices that included Big Bad Blue, Big Bad Green, or Big Bad Orange.

The standard engine was AMC's fine 199-cu.-in. straight six, perfect for this car, with the 232 six available as an upgrade. There was also a transformative option, a new 304-cu.-in. V-8. *Car Life* commented, "The Hornet proper is AMC's replacement for the Rambler, for those who like the size, but not the sensible image, of the original Compact. The Hornet V-8 is for buyers who feel the same way but wants more power and is willing to pay the price for more gasoline."

The 304 V-8 was the first AMC engine to respond to the growing demands of emissions regulations. Raising the deck height of AMC's V-8 engines by .16 inch (.4 centimeter) bumped the 290 to 304-cubic-inches. "The intent is to offer more torque, through sheer displacement, and to use that torque by gearing the V-8 to revolve more slowly—and more quietly—than the six," said *Car Life*. "And it plays David, too. The times are closer, but it has as much performance . . . as the larger Intermediates with bigger engines, like the 350 Tempest and Skylark tested last year."

It's unclear why American Motors management chose to commemorate production of the 2,400th Gremlin built. The two older men in the photo aren't identified, but we recognize the younger is the late George Maddox, a production man who rose to become a senior vice president at AMC, and president of its AM General subsidiary. Maddox was a well-liked, well-respected manager.

Typical of AMC products, there was plenty of innovation in the Hornet. "The doors were very thin in cross section," said Meyers, "which in turn provided greater interior roominess. I knew we were on to something when a top-rank GM executive looking over a Hornet at an auto show asked one of his designers why GM hadn't been able to come up with a compact door design like that. Besides that, the Hornet had bumpers that interchanged front and rear, plus a roof panel that fit both the two- and four-door sedans. That was all Teague's doing, along with designer Bob Nixon." The Hornet also featured an all-new front suspension with anti-dive geometry, and all 1970 AMCs benefited from this competition-bred design.

The Hornet name may have been a throwback to the Fabulous Hudson Hornets of the early 1950s, but just as likely it was a catchy name for a slick compact that was creating a buzz in the marketplace. Available in base or upscale SST trim, the cars gave buyers options. "If [a buyer] wants economy, he can have it. If he wants performance, he can have that," Chairman Roy Chapin Jr. told reporters. With fresh style, impressive room, and plenty of standard features, the Hornet represented great value for its $1,994 starting price (one dollar less than Ford's new Maverick, a smaller, more spartan rival). It had taken an investment of forty million dollars and a million man-hours, but Hornet was a hit in the show rooms—73,572 were sold the first year, despite a five-week-long labor stoppage that reduced AMC's production.

Gremlin

The New American Car.

Popular Science's Michael Lamm commented, "If this car catches on with the kids the way the VW did, look out VW!"

New, different, with a spunky, attention-grabbing look, this was no ordinary small car—it was the first American-built subcompact, appearing a model year ahead of the new small cars coming from Ford and Chevrolet. *Car and Driver* magazine said of the Gremlin, "For the record, American Motors claims to have singled out Volkswagen as the adversary, but it hasn't countered with a VW kind of car. Instead, it has tried, by way of market surveys, to

Like its Ambassador stablemate, the 1970 AMC Rebel was treated to new quarter panels and a revised roofline. This basic-looking two-door hardtop would have been so much more exciting had it been ordered with a white vinyl top and a set of full wheel covers, which would not have cost all that much extra. The Rebel was available with three different wheel cover styles this year.

distill the qualities that make VWs and other small imports desirable to Americans and then build from that foundation."

Car Life showed a drawing of the Gremlin overlayed on the VW Beetle: 2 inches (5 centimeters) longer, 7 inches (18 centimeters) lower, and 9 inches (23 centimeters) wider. It was also 700 pounds (318 kilograms) heavier, which made the Gremlin safer and more stable in high winds. They also praised its design: "There is no tailgate to flop down or swing open as in most wagons, but the rear window springs up to allow luggage to be placed in the rear compartment."

Using much of the manufacturing techniques and components of the Javelin/AMX siblings, Gremlin was launched midyear on April 1, 1970, as America's first subcompact and first hatchback. Like the AMX, the Gremlin was 12 inches (30 centimeters) shorter and shared Hornet's sheet metal from the B-pillar forward.

The basic design was created by Bob Nixon and his team, though Nixon handed over completion of the design to Vince Geraci's Senior Car Studio when he found his team had too many projects. Stylist Dick Jones did the superb surface development, while Wade O'Connell created the catchy Gremlin Man emblem that graced the front fenders. Meyers remembered, "When Teague's people were working on the body design for the new Hornet, he had them design in a 12-inch section in toward the middle that could be cut out to shorten the wheelbase. The [Gremlin's] tooling bill was ridiculously small, just $6 million."

The base-price Gremlin, tagged at $1,879, was for a stark two-passenger job equipped with just a front bench seat, no back seat, and a non-opening rear window. The more popular four-seat model, priced at $1,959, included a fold-down rear seat and a hatchback-style swing-up rear window. The public appreciated options like the Interior Appointment Package, which featured an underdash shelf, glovebox door with lock and light, and a cigarette lighter—all for just $19.95. A Custom Interior trim package included carpeting, better door and seat trim, and a custom steering wheel for $49.95 with bench seat, $89.90 with buckets.

Gremlin offered the same powertrains as the Hornet, except the 304 V-8. "The Gremlin is very good competition for the VW and other imports," *Car Life* concluded. Despite the Gremlin coming to the market late in a model year marred by a strike, some 25,300 buyers agreed.

Rebel

Introducing the Rebel "Machine."

Motorcade magazine called the 1970 Rebel "a catch-up car" trying to reverse its fortunes in the midsize class. "Part of the effort is apparent in American Motors' 1970 Rebel SST, a vehicle designed to compete in the marketplace with the letter-designated, paint-striped, peculiarly numbered, widely-advertised power image products of No. 1, No. 2 and No. 3."

The restyled Rebel boasted new rear quarter panels, a more squared-off roofline on sedans, and a large rear bumper with long integrated taillights, while up front was a new venturi-like grille. Hardtops also received a new roof with a reverse C-pillar motif. The standard engine was now the 232 six or optional 304 and 360 (the latter replacing the former 343) V-8s. Of the 360 two-barrel Rebel SST, *Motorcade* magazine said, "The 1970 Rebel SST, all-'round, is equal in interior styling and comfort, is more than equal in braking efficiency and outward detail, but still has the catch-up game to play in performance." They should have driven "the Machine!"

Buoyed by the unexpected success of the Hurst SC/Rambler, Hurst Performance and AMC again joined forces for another limited-production offering, the Rebel Machine. The $3,450 Machine exclusively got the Go Package—a 340-horsepower 390 V-8 from the Javelin and AMX—plus a Hurst-shifted four-speed manual (or optional automatic). The Machine featured a unique fiberglass hood scoop containing a built-in tachometer located in the driver's line of sight. Heavy-duty suspension, standard front disc brakes, and special Kelsey-Hayes steel wheels completed the package.

In keeping with its ongoing program to change the company's image, American Motors offered a special Machine package for the 1970 Matador hardtop. The package included a special 340-horsepower version of the 390-V-8, four-speed manual transmission, Ram-Air hood scoop with a unique scoop-mounted tachometer, power disc brakes, mag-style wheels, and a lot more. A separate Machine Red, White, and Blue package added AMC's special paint scheme, plus trim decals on the exterior and upgraded interior trim.

The Ambassador's styling was given some important updates for 1970, including a revised grille, new quarter panels, revised roof, and upgraded interior trim. This Ambassador hardtop, in black paint with a white vinyl top, is equipped with AMC's potent 390-cu.-in. V-8 as identified by the red engine numbers badge on the front fender. The subtle white body stripe and wire wheel covers add a lot of class to an already classy car. Think of this as a gentleman's muscle car or a high-speed grand tourer.

The director of marketing for Hurst Performance at the time was Jim Wangers, who six years earlier had worked with John DeLorean to create the legendary Pontiac GTO. Many consider the GTO the industry's first muscle car, though the original Rebel, the limited-issue 1957 model, was actually first.

Most Machines were painted white with Electric Blue hood and lower body stripes (paint code 25A), along with a bold, reflective red-white-blue horizontal stripe made by 3M along the beltline. The Machine could be ordered in other colors with the hood sprayed matte black (one source claims that 595 units were built this way). Either way, the Machine had no Hurst branding.

All well and good, but it was no longer 1964, and the era of muscle cars was ending quickly. Even with Jim Wangers's legendary magic, total production of the Machine was either 1,936 units or, more likely, 2,326, depending on the source. *Super Stock & Drag Illustrated* magazine said of the Machine, "This moderately quick five-seater has what the youth market has been after; style, power, looks, handling, and insurability." They recorded a very respectable 14.3 seconds at 99 miles per hour (159 kilometers per hour) in the quarter mile in a bone-stock Machine, but were able to turn 12.81 seconds at 107.35 time with minor modifications. Wangers, more familiar with General Motors–like sales numbers, deemed the Machine "a flop," but it did wonders for AMC's image. Overall, 1970 Rebel builds were 49,701, down 10,405 from the previous year.

Ambassador

If you had to compete with GM, Ford, and Chrysler, what would you do?

After the major updates of 1969, the 1970 Ambassador remained much the same, though it was treated to the revised rooflines and rear-quarter updates of the Rebel. Standard air conditioning continued to be unique among full-size American cars, something no other car in its class could claim. The base Ambassador still came with the 232 six and three-speed manual transmission, but the upscale SST and DPL models had the new 304 V-8 with automatic transmission as standard equipment, plus the new 360 V-8 option. For even more performance, the mighty AMX 390 V-8 could be ordered on SST and DPL models.

Sadly, production dropped 21.3 percent from 1969, at least partly due to the United Auto Workers' strike of 1970.

Javelin

Mark Donohue puts his mark on the Javelin.

There was shocking news for 1970: Roger Penske would campaign the Javelin in the super-competitive Sports Car Club of America (SCCA) Trans-Am series. This meant that one of the most successful racing teams in the world, headed by brilliant driver/engineer Mark Donohue, would be competing in AMC cars during the coming season. (Donohue had actually left Chevrolet for AMC.) The street cred built by the Javelin's racing success would prove invaluable.

An updated twin venturi grille and longer hood on the 1970 Javelin updated the look nicely, while the new 304 and 360 V-8s gave it more pop. In back was a new rear panel design with full-width taillamps and a single center-mounted backup light. But racing exists to improve the breed, a dictum Donohue took to heart: applying the knowledge he'd gained with a degree in mechanical engineering from Brown University, he worked

BELOW LEFT AND RIGHT: American Motors was still heavily involved in racing activities this year. This two-page ad highlights the run of a specially modified Javelin in the Trans-American Championship series. It was capable of reaching speeds over 175 miles per hour (282 kilometers per hour). To commemorate its successes, AMC built a limited number of production Javelins for the street that featured the 390 V-8 engine and four-speed transmission, along with AMC's trademark red-white-and-blue racing colors scheme.

A Javelin for the road.

4-speed close-ratio gear box with Hurst shifter. Power disc brakes in front. Heavy-duty springs and shocks. Front and rear spoilers. F70 x 14 tires with raised letters. 140 mph speedometer and tachometer.

Now, if the racer's a little too much for you, there's the Javelin that started our sports car craze in the first place.

We've put in standard highback bucket seats and redesigned the instrument panel.

We've also added a lot of new options. Like corduroy upholstery trim in five colors, leather trim in three. Landau-style vinyl roof. New style rally and accent stripes.

And a lot of other things that can make the Javelin look and act just as racy as you want it to.

American Motors

A Javelin for the track.

On this page you see a basic Javelin specially-prepared and modified for Trans-American Road Racing.

It's been clocked at 175 mph, goes from 0 to 60 in under 5 seconds, does the quarter-mile in under 11 seconds.

One of the country's top performance writers, Karl Ludvigsen, said in a recent article: "Hopefully, American Motors will see fit to sell an exact street equivalent of its Trans-Am Javelin, because it could be one of the nicest in a nice class of cars."

Which brings us to the Javelin on the opposite page.

This year, we're producing a limited number of Javelins in racing red-white-and-blue.

We couldn't make it an *exact* street equivalent. That's illegal.

We have, however, put in standard equipment that's optional in most other cars.

It has a 390 engine. Ram-air hood. Dual exhaust system. Heavy-duty engine cooling. Twin-grip differential.

with AMC to develop more upgrades. Between January and April 1970, the Mark Donohue Edition Javelins were built.

The most visible change was a fiberglass ducktail spoiler created to increase downforce on the Penske racers, reported at about 100 pounds (45 kilograms) at racing speed—"Starting now you can buy a Javelin with a spoiler designed by Mark Donohue," the print ad read. New cylinder heads with superior breathing were also introduced (these were the famous "dogleg" heads), proven to flow 20 percent better on the exhaust side than the 1966–1969 rectangle port heads.

The $1,100 Mark Donohue Edition cost included the 360 Go Package, with the AMX Ram Air hood and the upscale SST exterior and interior decor group as standard equipment.

AMC also built one hundred special Trans-Am Edition Javelins. You couldn't miss them: they had the same red-white-blue paint scheme and adjustable rear spoiler used by Ronnie Kaplan's Trans-Am team prior to 1970. Based on the Javelin SST, the Trans-Am Edition cost $4,078 and there were no other options available. AMC's Marketing Vice President William McNealy said, "The idea for that car was actually Dick Teague and the boys in styling. Dealers really liked those cars. They were able to display them like a trophy in their show rooms."

Total Javelin production for 1970 was 28,210.

AMX

A Sports Car for the Price of a Sporty Car.

Inspiration comes from many places. For Dick Teague, one of those places was driving his white AMX late at night on Woodward Avenue in the Detroit suburbs. He wasn't there to street race, like some were, but to observe what the youth movement was into. Those observations affected all AMC products.

The AMX received a bold new grille treatment and a Ram-Air hood that added 2 inches (5 centimeters) to the overall length. The new 304 V-8 was now the base engine. *Motor Trend* called the 1970 AMX "the best version yet of this blend of muscle car and sports car." The $3,395 AMX was still quite a performance bargain, and 4,116 were built this year.

The Results

Across Detroit the numbers were clear: the muscle car era was over. Sales of performance cars were half the peak of 1969, and the future looked even more grim. The demographics had changed: Baby Boomers were getting married and leaving their "toys" behind for more practical vehicles that still had a measure of fun and flash. Plus, insurance rates for muscle cars producing more than one horsepower for ten pounds of weight were now astronomical, the insurance companies' reaction to the explosion of claims caused by these mega-horsepower cars.

The *New York Times* put AMC's situation in stark terms: "The American Motors Corporation reported today a loss of $56.2-million for the fiscal year ended Sept. 30." The loss had been expected: the strike in the fall of 1969, the economic downturn, rising costs, and the cost of acquiring Kaiser Jeep were all contributors to the red ink in AMC's ledgers.

1971

Javelin

All sporty cars look pretty much the same. . . . Except for the 1980 looking Javelin. Dick Teague said of the 1971 Javelin, "It was just basically a heavy facelift. . . . We never had a lot of money to do really dramatic things." Still, compared with the 1970 model, its wheelbase was 1 inch longer at 110 inches (279 centimeters, height was reduced by 1.08 inches (2.74 centimeters), while overall length was up just .73 inches (1.9 centimeters), yet it sure looked longer.

It looked wider too, 3.31 inches (8.4 centimeters) wider, with the tires pushed out 3 inches (7.6 centimeters) to fill the wheelwells. Chuck Mashigan's Advanced Styling Studio did an amazing job on a limited budget. The roof panel had twin cockpit-like indents and a spoiler lip, while the roofline was more of a semi-notchback. Most notable were the raised fender blisters front and rear. Eric Kugler in Advanced Styling said he designed the bulges to mimic the fenders of contemporary Trans-Am cars. "They were raising the fenders for tire clearance, so they could lower the front ends of the cars," Kugler told *Hemmings*. "I liked how, in profile, it had a real Coke-bottle effect."

Inside was a new "curved cockpit" instrument panel, focused on the driver with minimal distractions. The 232 six remained the standard powertrain, the 258 six and V-8s in 304 and 360 displacements optional. Better yet was the new 401 V-8 (replacing the former 390).

If you wanted the best of everything, the new Javelin AMX model was the way to go. The original two-seat sports car was gone, replaced by a performance-oriented upgrade of

BELOW: Dick Teague had hoped the two-seat AMX would be continued after 1970. To attempt to sell management on the concept, Teague created an updated two-seater out of his personal 1968 AMX company car by grafting the fenders and front end from the upcoming 1971 Javelin. Though it would ultimately be denied, the 1971 prototype he created left us with a glimpse of what could have been. Though the two-seat AMX shared most of the components of the Javelin, AMC President Bill Luneburg rejected the proposal in his relentless pursuit of increasing manufacturing efficiency. *Tom & Kelly Glatch*

FOLLOWING PAGES: The raised fender arches over the front wheels were created by Small-Car Studio manager Chuck Mashigan, who wanted to give some of the feel of exotic European sports cars to the new Javelin series. Dick Teague simply added this new look to his personal 1968 AMX, while the adjustable spoiler from the 1970 Javelin Trans-Am model was a nice touch. The special fiberglass hood and unique grille gave Teague's "197X AMX" prototype an aggressive appearance, differentiating it from the Javelin. Sadly, it was not to be.

AMX
AMC

AMX
POLYGLAS - E70-14
GOODYEAR
POLYGLAS - E70-14

RIGHT: The Hornet returned for 1971 with a larger 232-cu.-in., 135-horsepower, six-cylinder engine as standard equipment, and a new 258-cu.-in., 150-horsepower six available as an option. The 304-cu.-in., 210-horsepower V-8 was optional on Hornet SST models. Exterior appearance changes were minimal: the grille now included bright trim on all models and turn signal/running lamps were given amber lenses. Under the skin, however, were a host of small mechanical improvements.

BELOW: The Hornet lineup was expanded to three series for 1971: Hornet (base), Hornet SST, and the new Hornet SC-360 sporty compact. Offered in a single two-door sedan model, the new SC-360 was designed to fly under the insurance industry's radar. The cost of insurance coverage for young drivers had soared over the previous five years, especially on high-performance and pony cars, which was strangling sales. The Hornet SC-360 came standard with a relatively mild 360-cu.-in. V-8 with two-barrel carburetor rated at 245 horsepower. A four-barrel version of the 360 mill, belting out 285 horsepower, was optional. With either engine, the lightweight Hornet two-door delivered exciting performance. And, of course, further horsepower could be wrung from these engines with fairly minor modifications.

the basic Javelin. It wasn't like Dick Teague didn't try: he took a 1968 AMX engineering car and added the new Javelin's front clip to show management what the next-generation AMX could be. But the men at the top saw value in freeing up extra manufacturing capacity by eliminating the low-volume AMX, so the two-seater was dropped. Javelin production also shifted to the Milwaukee Body Plant, where the large cars were also partially manufactured as "a matter of cost savings," William Luneberg told the *Kenosha News*.

Outside, the biggest difference on the AMX was a handsome, fine-mesh, stainless-steel grill, like that used on the Penske Trans-Am racers (an old aerodynamics trick used to reduce drag). The

grille was actually an insert placed over the stock Javelin grille. Red-white-and-blue block letters spelling AMX were placed on the grille, rear spoiler, and C-pillars, along with a cowl-induction hood with T-stripe. Other standard goodies included Twin-Grip, limited-slip differential; heavy-duty cooling; power-assisted disc brakes; and a blacked-out rear taillight panel. The AMX rode on the same 15 x 7-inch styled steel wheels as on the '70 Rebel Machine with white-letter E60x15 Goodyear Polyglas tires, and engine options were limited to the top 360 and 401 V-8s.

The new Javelin and AMX sold well with 24,812 and 2,054 produced, respectively.

Hornet

It's not so much a station wagon as it is a sporty car with cargo space.

AMC's stylists felt that trying to sell maturing Baby Boomers a boring station wagon just wouldn't cut it. Instead, they created the new Hornet Sportabout, a four-door wagon with as much sport as space. Forget the wagon's traditional rear doors: the Sportabout had a one-piece sloping hatchback instead, which "combines fun with function." You couldn't get Ford's new Maverick or Chevy's updated Nova in a wagon. Gerald Meyers recalled, "That was unique at the time. There was nothing else like it here in the U.S. The only place where four-door hatchbacks were popular was Europe." William McNealy's team came up with the catchy Sportabout name. Available only in upscale SST trim, the Sportabout added more sting to the Hornet lineup and greater profits to AMC's bottom line.

AMC also introduced a performance car for the times, the Hornet SC/360. Available only as a two-door sedan, the SC/360 delivered 0-to-60-mile-per-hour (0-to-97-kilometer-

Perhaps the biggest news for 1971 was the introduction of a station wagon model in the Hornet line. Dubbed the Sportabout, its low, sporty roofline was a breath of fresh air in the station wagon market, and AMC advertising emphasized its uniqueness. Ads proclaimed that the new Sportabout was the first station wagon that doesn't make a woman look like a teamster. Demand for the new wagon exceeded expectations.

per-hour) times of 6.7 seconds and could do the quarter mile in 14.9 seconds at 95 miles per hour (153 kilometers per hour)—all for $2,663. Lots of flash for not much cash.

Hot Rod Magazine said of the SC/360, "The Hornet, like Ford's Maverick, belongs in the 'midi-small-car' class. But where the Maverick Grabber, with its top-option 250-cu.-in. six grabs you everywhere but in the driver's seat, AMC reaches into the parts bin for a 360-cube V-8 that'll flatten eyeballs right back into the ol' head when punched." But the best feature, they noted, was that "AMC product planners aimed for an attractively priced car with a decent amount of performance without tripping the insurance company's paranoia-induced weight-to-horsepower guidelines." Out of a total of 123,304 Hornets produced that model year, only 784 SC/360s were built, making it a rare and desirable collectors' car.

One of Detroit's marketing geniuses was this man, R. William McNealy Jr. As Vice President of Marketing, McNealy was responsible for all advertising and marketing functions for AMC cars and Jeep vehicles, along with AM General and AMC's subsidiary companies. He's shown here in a new 1971 Gremlin in front of American Motors headquarters in Detroit.

Gremlin

Why is it when other car companies come out with sporty little cars, the cars come out looking the same?

After a late start in 1970, AMC's popular subcompact was back, and with a new model added: Gremlin X. It featured bold exterior graphics, body color front fascia with black grille insert, slotted road wheels with D70x14 Goodyear Polyglas tires, and "the same bucket seats we put in our Javelin." The 199 six cylinder was dropped, the 232 was now standard equipment, and an optional 258 six was available.

Bud Lindemann on his *Car and Track* TV show reported, "For power our tester had the 258 cubic inch six delivering 150 horsepower. . . . In the acceleration runs it took 4.1 seconds to make 30 miles an hour; on the way to 45 miles an hour the clock ate up six seconds. Without any wheel spin or excessive tire wear we made 60 miles an hour in 10.4 seconds. While this may not be newsworthy enough to write home about it, it is better than the times of the other domestic minions." All for just $300 over the four-seater's base price of $1,999. Gremlin production doubled from 1970, with 53,480 built.

Matador

What's a Matador?

The Rebel was gone, replaced by the Matador. Mostly a restyled Rebel, you can see the Matador's heritage in the roof, although the 4-inch (10-centimeter) longer wheelbase and wraparound chrome front bumper and grille really changed things up. The emphasis was now on family transportation with style, and, with civil unrest throughout the country, "the word 'rebel' in headlines carried an unsettling connotation," said *Popular Mechanics* magazine.

With the same powertrain options as the rest of the AMC lineup (Gremlin excepted), including the two-barrel 360 V-8, a Matador could be mildly quick. If you still had the need for speed, the $373 Machine Go package added a four-barrel carb, dual exhausts, heavy-duty handling package, power front disc brakes, and more with either 360 or 401 V-8 power, though with 10 less horsepower the 401 couldn't match the performance of the 1970 Machine. Only around fifty-five versions of the Machine Go edition (AKA Matador Machines) were built, while total Matador production was 54,813, a disappointingly weak increase from the prior year.

RIGHT: One of the new options offered for the 1971 Gremlin by American Motors was a fold-back fabric sunroof, as seen here with pretty model Paulette Lindberg. The sunroof, the first offered on an American subcompact, became available on April 1, 1971, and debuted at that year's Chicago Auto Show. Meant to lend some European flair to AMC's cars, it was also offered on Hornet two-door sedans and the Sportabout wagon.

BELOW: The new Matador line for 1971 replaced the Rebel. It utilized the same basic body as the Rebel, but with a longer 118-inch wheelbase, and all-new front sheet metal and grille with a richer, more contemporary look. Matador was unique in the midsize segment because it had no base-level trim; there was only one trim level and it included color-keyed carpeting, expensive seat upholstery and door panels, custom steering wheel, and all the little doodads that everyone else charged extra for. It was larger than the other midsized cars as well and represented tremendous value in a family car.

The Ambassador series for 1971 consisted of three trim levels: base DPL, upscale SST, and the top-line Brougham seen here. The DPL, a single four-door sedan series aimed mainly at fleets, came standard with a 150-hp six-cylinder engine. The SST and Brougham models were equipped with a standard 304-V-8 engine. All Ambassadors came with factory-installed air conditioning as standard equipment, along with a column-shifted "Shift-Command" three-speed automatic transmission.

Ambassador

Is purely and simply the only 1971 station wagon in the world with air-conditioning, automatic transmission, and a V-8 engine as standard equipment.

Whether four-door sedan, two-door hardtop, or station wagon, the 1971 Ambassador delivered more value per dollar than its full-sized competition. "It might well be called the American Gothic," wrote *Road Test* magazine in August 1971. "Actually, it is the Ambassador SST, American Motors' answer to Chevrolet, Ford, and Plymouth. It is slanted directly toward Middle America—at that vast jury which rejected the Edsel. American Motors still seeks solace in the hope that there are enough citizens who believe in the virtues of a day's work for a day's pay, and an honest product honestly made and sold, to provide a market for their cars." The reviewers weren't alone: 41,674 honest American's though so, too.

The Results

Time magazine's November 29, 1971, issue summed up the year for AMC: "The company reported earnings of $10.2 million on sales of $1.2 billion for the fiscal year ending in September, compared with a loss of $56 million on a volume of $1.1 billion last year. Part of the reason for American's turn-around is the cost-cutting drive of Chairman Roy D. Chapin Jr. Major savings resulted from his decision to forgo styling and engineering changes in 1972 models. As a result, American's operating budget has remained at its 1969 level, while sales have risen 50% since then."

1972

Gremlin

A Gremlin with the heart of a Javelin.

Popular Mechanics wrote, "One of the beefs made by people smitten with the size and shape of AMC's mini has been the lack of a V-8. Well, fault 'em no more on that score."

Since it was based on the Hornet, the Gremlin always had room for a V-8. Now in its third year, the sporty compact finally got optional 304 V-8 power in the Gremlin X. The 304-powered cars also received traction bars on the rear axle to promote better grip on the short-wheelbase vehicle. This wasn't a return of the big-engine/small-car muscle era: emissions equipment was reducing horsepower on all engines, and cars destined for California suffered more dramatically because of tough new laws to reduce the "brown L.A. haze" that Jimmy Buffett sang about.

The automotive industry also changed the way horsepower was measured and reported in 1972. Instead of the traditional SAE gross figures taken on an engine absent all accessories, the new baseline was set with SAE *net* standards taken with basic, power-robbing (but necessary) equipment like alternators and water pumps.

This change had more of a psychological effect than an actual impact on vehicles and their performance. Numbers influence how people perceive something—$0.99 seems much less than $1.00—and 1972 cars seemed less powerful than the previous year, but this was mostly illusory. For AMC's 304 two-barrel V-8, reported output was 210 gross horsepower in 1971; a year later, it was listed as 150 net horsepower. Sure, actual power was a bit less than before, but not nearly as much as the numbers would suggest.

V-8 buyers paid a price in fuel economy, but, oh, what fun the 304 provided! Total Gremlin production was up to 61,717 for the model year as the car continued to grow in popularity.

BELOW AND FOLLOWING PAGES: AMC's popular Gremlin subcompact was reduced to a single model when the slow-selling two-passenger model was dropped for 1972. Electric windshield wipers, for too long an extra-cost option, were now standard equipment. In exciting news, AMC's 304-cu.-in.V-8 was now available as a $154 option. Hooked up to the standard three-speed full-synchromesh transmission, with floor shifter, the V-8 Gremlin was, in the words of one tester, "a poor-man's Corvette." *Tom & Kelly Glatch*

BFGoodrich
Radial T/A

5 Litre
V/8
PLEASANT HILL
AMC

Hornet

The only sporty car you can get with a 360 V-8 without getting in over your head.

The SC/360 was no longer available in 1972, though the 360 V-8 remained an option. All American Motors vehicles in 1972 had a new automatic transmission—the excellent Chrysler TorqueFlite (AMC called it "Torque-Command") three-speed—replacing the durable but aging Borg-Warner unit.

The popular Sportabout was now available in a stylish new edition, thanks to the famous fashion house of Gucci. "Since he comes from Italy, the land of sleek racy automobiles, Dr. Aldo Gucci isn't easily impressed by station wagons," said one ad. "So, naturally, we were pleased when he agreed to add his own special touch to our station wagon."

For $141.75, the Gucci Sportabout option added seats decorated in green and ivory vinyl with green and red stripes, trademark Gucci colors. The doors featured green vinyl with ivory inlays and matching green carpeting. The dramatic headliner was printed in Gucci's well-known double-G logo. Gucci badges were featured inside and out, and exterior paint choices included Snow White, Yuca Tan, Grasshopper Green, or Hunter Green.

Dating back to Helene Rother's designs for Nash in the 1950s, American Motors had pioneered crafting interiors with greater appeal to female buyers. The Gucci Sportabout was yet another expression of that philosophy, also reflecting Roy D. Chapin Jr.'s "philosophy of difference," and 2,584 were ordered out of the 71,055 Hornets produced for 1972.

TOP LEFT: The Hornet SC/360 was dropped at the end of the 1971 model year due to slow sales, but AMC wanted to continue offering performance versions of its popular Hornet line, so the 'X' package was made available on the Hornet two-door sedan. The 'X' included rally stripes, slot-style wheels, bigger tires, and a sports steering wheel. To this could be added a 360-cu.-in. V-8 with two-barrel carburetor and automatic transmission, for breath-taking acceleration, all at a cost of about $2,700.

LEFT: To add some excitement to the Hornet line while increasing sales of its very profitable Sportabout wagon, AMC introduced a new "X" package for Hornet two-door sedans and Sportabout wagons. Although the package itself was mostly cosmetic in nature, additional performance options including the AMC 304-cube and 360-cube V-8 engines, "Twin-Grip" rear axle, and more could be added. The Hornet two-door sedan also could be ordered with a special "Rallye" package that included a handling package, quick-ratio steering, disc brakes, and more.

ABOVE: American Motors had a longtime relationship with the military, having offered its Rambler cars to service members worldwide at very competitive prices. This rarely-seen print advertisement announced the base "military" price for service members interested in buying a Javelin SST was a mere $2,383. It noted that the base engine was a six and that optional engines could be specified to meet any desire. Military members could shop for any new AMC car at their local PX, where an AMC representative could explain standard and optional features and take the order on the spot.

LEFT: In 1971 an American Motors Javelin-AMX won the Trans-Am championship for Roger Penske's team with the legendary Mark Donohue at the wheel. The base Javelin was dropped so the two sporty-car models in the lineup now were the Javelin SST and Javelin-AMX. This move by AMC to discontinue its base models was an effort to simplify production and dealer stocking requirements while greatly improving product quality. Having fewer models meant less chance of mistakes being made during assembly. *Getty Images*

Javelin

If you're going to buy a sporty car, buy one that's been places.

Places like Road America, St. Jovite, and Watkins Glen, all tracks where Javelins won six straight races in the Trans-Am Championship series in 1972. An impressive performance for a production-based racer.

Super Stock and Drag Illustrated magazine was shocked by Javelin/AMX's "running three 14.70's in a row and speeds of 95.5 mph, with the last run

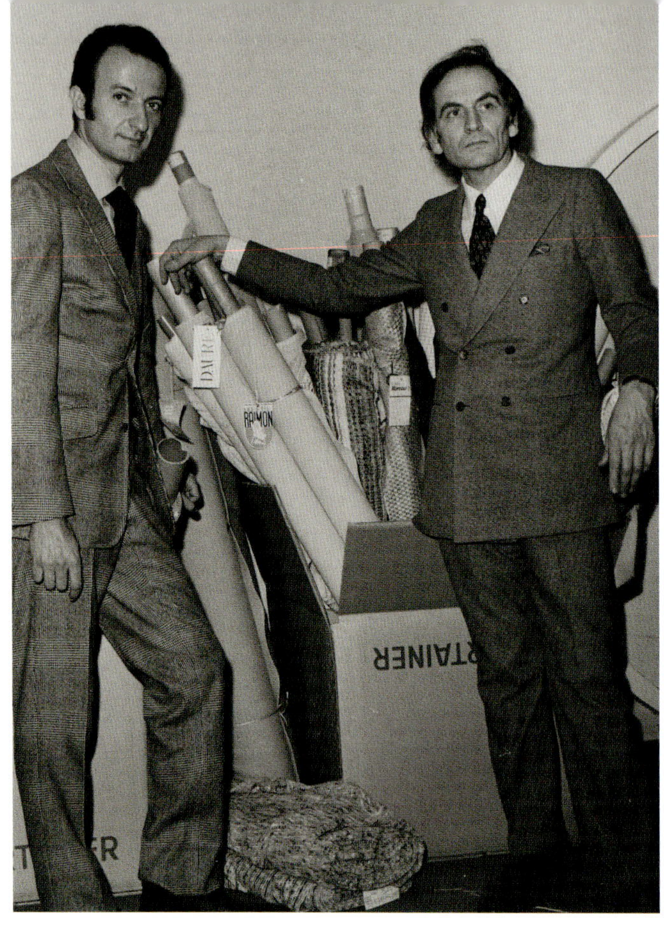

of the day a 14.68 at 95.24. If you have any doubt about the AMX's performance capability stacked up against some other so-called supercars, go back and read the tests in this and other magazines, and you'll be as surprised as we were." Nice.

Prefer style over speed? New for 1972 was the Pierre Cardin Javelin. The French fashion designer believed "People should feel like they're sitting in a living room rather than a machine," and created an interior unlike any other. The basic black interior featured stripes of silver, white, red, and purple that flowed around the seats and door panels before continuing onto the headliner.

"In January 1971 I went to Paris to talk with Pierre Cardin about some ideas for the interior," said Vince Geraci, director of interior design. "We looked over several possibilities, finally settling on one that was bold and quite attractive." At just $85, the option was officially only available with Snow White, Stardust Silver, Trans-Am Red, or Wild Plum paint on Javelin SST models, though a few AMXs also received the treatment. The press release said, "Only Pierre Cardin can make upholstery look so elegant, door panels so classy, and a headliner so chic. And only American Motors can give you a Cardin label at the price of a Javelin." Total Javelin production this year was 26,183, including 2,728 AMXs.

ABOVE: American Motors stylists teamed up with the well-known French fashion designer Pierre Cardin to create a special version of the Javelin. Dubbed the "Cardin Javelin," it included special interior trim that boasted a wild stripe pattern on the seats, door panels, and headliner. Based on Cardin's signature multi-color stripe patterns, the Cardin Javelin was perhaps the most distinctive pony car of all time. Seen here is famed AMC designer Vince Geraci (left) and Pierre Cardin (right) during an extended meeting at Cardin's shop in Paris.

Matador

The best put together cars out of Detroit this year may come out of Wisconsin.

If you watched the popular *Adam-12* TV series in 1972, you'd see officers Reed and Malloy driving a Matador instead of a Plymouth. A year before, the Los Angeles Police Department tested the Matador against its Big Three competition and determined that it "outperformed and exceeded all the other cars." They ended up ordering a fleet of them for patrol duty.

RIGHT: Cardin's designs were modified somewhat by Geraci's American team, chiefly to insure it met U.S. safety and burn standards, along with ensuring it would have accepted wear rates. The design wild interior package, which cost about $85 extra, was popular at the time and has only increased in popularity over the years. Although introductory information says the Cardin trim was not available on Javelin-AMX models, apparently the factory decided to offer them later in the year because we have seen several of them.

LEFT: Can you spot what's wrong with this picture? The new-for-1972 "Cardin Javelin" is shown, but the car is wearing a 1971 grille. This was probably a concept photo to show management what the car would look like, though we can't be certain since the print has no notations or identification explaining the story behind it. The white exterior with black Cardin interior is quite striking.

BELOW: The midsized Matador lineup got a pleasing new grille with fine horizontal bars which updated the look. This Matador station wagon has AMC's uniquely patterned woodgrain applique on the bodysides, which was a popular extra-cost option. Sales of station wagons were very good during the early 1970s, and the Matador wagon, which offered much more interior room than its competitors, was a good seller for the company.

Other agencies ordered Matadors and Ambassadors, too, while the city of Houston bought Gremlins for parking patrols. Then there was the Alabama Highway Patrol, which bought 133 401-powered Javelins in 1971–1972 for high-speed use on the interstate, years before Fox Mustangs and Gen 3 Camaros saw similar deployments in other states. "We like to think of them as our contribution to law enforcement," one fleet flyer said.

Law enforcement was in good company: 54,653 Matador customers felt the same way about their cars.

Ambassador

We back them better because we build them better.

AMC cars were known for high quality, but the past few years had seen that reputation slipping. The company made quality its top priority again, making 216 improvements to its products, then backing those changes up with the best warranty in the business: the AMC Buyer Protection Plan.

"Two things appeal to the consumer," William Luneburg told the *Kenosha News* for the August 26, 1971, edition. "First, that we intend to pay at our expense any costs incurred in fixing what we have

done wrong. . . . And second, if there is any inconvenience to the owner in making these repairs, we are willing to provide a car for him to use during this period. In other words, we have provided a bold new approach that satisfies deep-seated concerns on the part of the consumer." No wonder 44,364 Ambassadors were built for 1972.

The Results

The *Kenosha News*, December 29, 1972, reported: "American Motors came up with the Buyer Protection Plan in 1972 and the plan worked. It sold cars and that made the company money. On Feb. 29 the company announced the highest sales in seven years. . . . By early October American Motors had delivered its 300,000th car, a milestone not reached since 1965."

Over at *Time* magazine, they reported on the results: "Sales of AMC's 1972 autos hit an eight-year high of 303,000 units, up 20% from the previous year; October sales of the '73s were 10% ahead of the same period last year. Next week the company will report a profit of between $25 million and $30 million for the fiscal year that ended in September, also an eight-year high. When the good-news numbers became known this fall, says AMC Marketing Vice President R. William McNealy Jr., 'We poured champagne in the central office for the first time in about 20 years.'"

1973

Hornet

Opens up all kinds of possibilities.

"The styling coup of '73." That's what *Car and Driver* magazine called the new Hornet Hatchback. It was a minor miracle that this new model saw the light of day.

American Motors stylists came up with a very unique "cane-look" side applique for the popular Sportabout station wagon. Introduced as a mid-year option, it's not known how many were made but they are extremely rare today.

A new model in the AMC lineup for 1973 was the attractive Hornet Hatchback. A two-door with a gently sloping fastback, it was originally designed using the 1970–1972 frontal styling, but the sharply creased front fenders of that generation didn't match up well with the smoother, curvier look of the new rear section. The Hatchback was very useful because with its wide opening rear hatch and fold-down rear seat it could carry a lot of cargo when needed, including camping equipment. The tent addition shown here was available for purchase at AMC dealers, turning the little Hornet into a "camper."

According to the *New York Times* of November 5, 1972:

> Richard A. Teague, vice president for styling at the American Motors Corporation, says "we have spent 40 per cent of our time this year" working on bumpers for the new cars. Mr. Teague is proud of the results on the 1973 American Motors models, which have new bumpers designed to meet Federal standards. . . . "It was tough to make them look acceptable," Mr. Teague said. "It was real bag of worms but I think our cars look pretty good. And it's because we spent so much time on it. Of all the safety standard problems we have had, the most severe has been packaging bumpers."

The *Times* also noted, "There was little effort devoted to other areas of the company's cars." This was the new normal in Detroit since the barrage of new regulations consumed so many resources—which is why the Hatchback was such a big deal. It was perfect timing, as General Motors introduced their X-body Chevy Nova and Pontiac Ventura hatchbacks the same year. In fact, there's a good chance GM had caught wind of the coming Hornet Hatchback, hastily adapting a hatch for their existing cars, albeit that their attempt lacked the complete look of the Hornet.

Road & Track magazine, often a critic of American cars, loved the Hatchback. They described it in their March 1973 issue as having "a useful third door and a good big engine. . . . Considering the size of the engine and the restrictive '73 emission controls one would expect fuel economy to take a tumble. Not so. The Hornet averaged 16 mpg over our

ABOVE: AMC executives disliked it when dealers or customers ordered basic Gremlin's because the profit margin was very small. Thankfully, a large percentage of buyers opted for the extra-cost 'X' package, which transformed the little car into something sporty and fun. Retired AMC head of Styling Vince Geraci currently co-owns (with his son) a twin to the Gremlin shown here.

mileage course. Overall, the Hornet represents something of a pleasant surprise. We like the looks and the packaging, and the hatchback body makes it even more attractive."

All Hornets also featured styling changes in the front fenders, hood, and grille treatment, partly to accommodate the new bumpers. The Gucci Sportabout also returned for one last year. Hornet base prices were $2,298 for the two-door sedan, $2,343 for the four-door, $2,449 for the Hatchback, and $2,675 for the Sportabout wagon. Some 102,569 were produced.

Gremlin

Levi's Gremlin with seats of the pants.

Gremlins received a refreshed grille and the required larger bumpers in 1973, but the biggest news was the arrival of the car's own fashion interior package. Unlike the Gucci and Cardin versions of the bigger cars, Gremlin's designer was a bit more blue-collar: Levi Strauss & Company. "My wife went out to a fabric store and bought a bunch of material, and then she washed the hell out of it to get the right look," Vince Geraci recalled. "I took the samples down to the supplier, Milliken, and told them to match that shade, and they produced it with the copper studs and the orange nametag." The material was

LEFT: AMC's popular Gremlin returned for 1973 with a higher price tag and very few appearance changes. The single model continued to be a stark, basic vehicle, with black rubber floor covering and black wall tires with cheap hubcaps. A few dress-up items could greatly change its appearance, such as the whitewall tires and full wheel discs seen here, along with the rally stripe and roof rack. One problem AMC was ignoring was the industry trend towards including more standard equipment in base models.

not the familiar denim used on the jeans, though. "No, it was a spun nylon. Cotton wouldn't have the wear characteristics you need in an automobile interior, or the color fastness. The sun load would cause fading. The material had to look like denim but be tougher." Levi's Edition cars had an orange tag on the front fenders and an extra cost of just $120.45.

The Gremlin now started at $2,059, the inevitable result of added emissions and safety equipment along with the effects of inflation. It didn't matter: the Gremlin's popularity was growing, and 133,146 were built in 1973.

Javelin

The closest you can come to owning the Trans-Am Champion.

Javelin won the SCCA Trans-Am Championship in 1971, and then again in 1972. Since those racers were modified production-based automobiles, the claim used in AMC's subsequent ad campaign was hardly an exaggeration.

New for 1973 was an optional side paint stripe and updated grille treatment. Engine choices remained the same, and the Pierre Cardin edition continued for its second year. Diamond Blue was a new paint color option for the Pierre Cardin package, which was now also officially available on the AMX. Production was up nicely to 30,902 Javelins, including 4,980 AMXs.

The 1973 Javelins were treated to a new grille, one that had hints of AMX to it. If you look closely at the photograph seen here, you'll notice this car has the optional "Cardin" interior trim. The purple exterior paint and black vinyl top combined with the sharp Cardin interior make this Javelin a real head-turner. Although the pony car market was visibly fading, American Motors was in the midst of an outstanding sales year and Javelin sales actually increased.

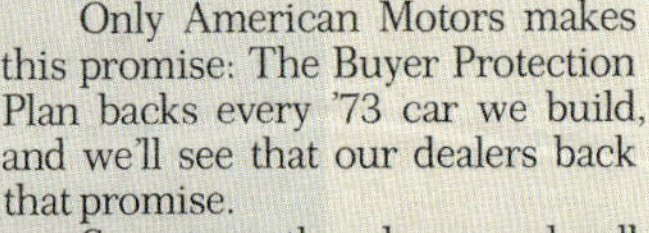

This print advertisement for the handsome 1973 Matador sedan makes a good point: because it shared the same body as the Ambassador, AMC's Matador offered more interior room than other midsize cars. Careful design ensured that the Matador had about the same exterior size as the competition, but much more passenger room. Combined with the famed Buyer Protection Plan, it made Matador a superior value, and one that attracted many buyers that were new to AMC.

Matador

Test drive the Matador with five of your biggest friends.

Writing for *Popular Mechanics*, Michael Lamm compared the 1973 Matador with its predecessor, the 1970 Rebel. He enthused, "American Motors must be doing something right. Or Righter. Its [sic] 1973 Matador is basically the same car as the 1970 Rebel, yet owners rate it higher on many important aspects—quality, ride, and handling. They point out fewer mechanical defects and claim better dealer service." One thing Lamm noticed: nearly half of Matador buyers were over the age of fifty. "When AMC sees Chevelles selling so briskly to young marrieds, it brings tears to their eyes, and that's one reason AMC is putting so much emphasis on Mark Donohue's Matador success in stock-car racing." Also noted was that 54.2 percent of buyers chose the 304 V-8, despite 232-six powered cars averaging 17.9 miles per gallon (7.6 kilometers per liter) highway. Four-door sedans continued to sell best, with 33,822 built, compared with 11,643 station wagons and 7,067 two-door hardtops.

Ambassador

Tailored to family-size comfort with an extra helping of luxury.

Like the other cars in AMC's lineup, there was little change in the Ambassador outside of the mandatory larger bumpers. The familiar SST trim was dropped, so now only the Brougham remained. The emphasis continued to be on improving vehicle quality and backing it up with an even better warranty: the expanded Buyer Protection Plan, available with coverage for twenty-four months or 24,000 miles. For this year, 49,294 were built.

The Results

The *New York Times* declared,

> The smallest of Detroit's Big Four auto makers is counting on its warranty program to increase sales in 1973. The company calls it the Buyer Protection Plan. The American Motors president, William V. Luneburg, says it was "an important catalyst" in 1972 sales, which were at a seven-year high. . . . Under the expanded 1973 plan, additional protection will be available for 24 months, or 24,000 miles. This is double normal 12-month, 12,000-mile protection. It costs the buyer $149. But the optional program includes normal maintenance work, such as lubrication and tune-ups. Furthermore, American Motors says the standard warranty for 1973 cars includes "trip interruption protection." This means that the company will reimburse a car owner up to $150 for food and lodging if his car is kept overnight for repair work and the owner is more than 100 miles from home.

This kind of coverage was unheard-of in the industry, and it greatly boosted the confidence of potential AMC buyers. As Luneburg predicted, "Concentration in small cars and the Buyer Protection Plan were some of the factors that led to recovery for American Motors." In fiscal 1973, AMC's earnings were $44.5 million.

1974

Matador

Newest Midsize for 1974.

You'd swear the new Matador Coupe was designed with the high-speed ovals of NASCAR in mind. It certainly was sleek: the long, sloping hood and sweeping roof looked like it was born in a wind tunnel. Even Bud Lindemann on his *Car and Track* TV show said, "You can't help but wonder how much of this came as a result of Roger Penske and NASCAR racing, the body is far more suitable from an aerodynamic standpoint than last year's flying brick."

In fact, the Matador Coupe was designed in Bob Nixon's studio as a competitor in the popular midsize field against cars like the Pontiac Grand Prix, Chevy Monte Carlo, and Ford Torino. The family-oriented Matador four-door sedans and station wagons were doing well enough, but the boxy, dull Matador hardtop—largely dating back to the 1970 Rebel—just wasn't cutting it.

AMC's big news for 1974 was the completely new Matador Coupe. A two-door pillared hardtop, it replaced the prior Matador hardtop in the midsize lineup. The Coupe was designed by the legendary AMC designer Bob Nixon and received wide acclaim from enthusiast magazines and the public. Product VP Gerry Meyers had approved the program, explaining that, "We get our fair share of the mid-size sedan and station wagon markets, but our share of the two-door segment is very small." The mid-range Matador X was the sportiest version of the new car. *Tom & Kelly Glatch*

"Racing was never a major design issue," said Nixon. "We did talk to Mark Donohue from time to time, but I don't believe it had anything to do with the Matador." *Car and Driver* went so far as to call the new Matador Coupe "1974's Best Styled Car." That was especially welcome praise, since the new Coupe was originally planned to debut at least a full year earlier, with some reports even claiming it was supposed to debut in 1972!

Vince Geraci's interior design team worked their usual magic on the base Matador, sporty Matador X, and luxurious Brougham models. They also worked with fashion designer Oleg Cassini for his take on the Matador. Dick Teague said, "An AMC consumer survey showed that Oleg Cassini would fit the bill. In the area of consumer recognition . . . his name topped the list. So, it was only natural for us to turn to Cassini to carry on our series of fashion-oriented cars."

Based in New York, Cassini was born to Russian nobility, made the news with his engagement to actress Grace Kelly (long before she became Princess Grace of Monaco), and had grown his fashion business to the point that he designed First Lady Jacqueline Kennedy's trademark style. Geraci reported, "For the Matador, Oleg Cassini at first was thinking along the lines of perhaps two automobile interiors—one designed more for daytime use with light colors, and a bright and airy feel: the other more for evening use, something very elegant, with darker, richer colors. Since we were only going to do one interior, it was decided that the more elegant interior theme should be the one. The interior was done in a black and copper motif." The Cassini package was only available on Brougham models painted either black, white, or copper. "My intent," said Cassini, "was to create a look . . . harmonizing every part of the car, outside and inside, with color and texture of fabrics."

Continuing its "Designer" series of models with special interiors, AMC contracted with famed fashion designer Oleg Cassini to create a complete trim package for the new Matador Coupe. Featuring copper accents for the grille, headlamp buckets, and wheel covers on the exterior, the Cassini Matador featured lavish interior fittings including special seat materials with copper accents, special door and instrument panel trim, and plush carpeting. Cassini submitted designs according to the suggestions of AMC's designers, after which Vince Geraci, head of AMC's Interiors Styling Studios, and his team chose the best designs for production, then altered and modified them as needed to fit production and cost realities.

Starting at $3,599 for a basic Matador coupe, *Road & Track* magazine commented, "The Matador's biggest failing is its lack of relevance to the times." There had been no concerns in their minds about relevance, and certainly no apparent obstacles in their path, when Meyers, Teague, and company planned the Coupe. But just weeks after the 1974 models hit the show rooms, the nation was faced with the 1973 oil crisis.

It began on October 6, 1973, when Syria and Egypt launched a surprise attack on Israel in what would become known as the Yom Kippur War. To punish America for its support of Israel during this conflict, the OPEC nations strangled the supply of crude oil, causing the price to jump from $2 per barrel

ROAD TEST: AMERICAN MOTORS MATADOR X

Publication: ***Road & Track*, March 1974**
Author: ***Road & Track* Staff**

AMC has taken another bold step and introduced a dramatically restyled Matador—a car that was until this year so innocuous that the 1973 ad campaign was built around the question "What's a Matador?" The 1974 Matador coupe will not pass unnoticed. It is styled to appeal to the buyer of intermediate-size cars (U.S. carmakers' designation, not ours) such as the commercially successful Chevrolet Monte Carlo and Pontiac Grand Am. As with most cars in this field the styling is all-important: according to AMC the buyer of a domestic "intermediate" is the most style-conscious of all. The Matador coupe—with its long hood and forward-thrusting headlights, sharply raked windshield, concealed wipers, ventless front door glass and fastback roofline blending into the sloping rear deck—hits that market head on.

A Matador driver sits behind a General Motors collapsible steering column, latches up a Chrysler-designed seatbelt interlock system, starts an engine that breathes through a Ford Motorcraft carburetor, puts a Chrysler Torqueflite automatic transmission into gear and steers with GM variable-ratio power steering. This is truly a product of "American motors"! That these components work well together (for the most part) is proof that AMC has chosen wisely.

Judging from the admiring looks it got wherever it went the Matador is a styling success in the context of the traditional domestic market. And though it lacks the refinement of its rivals in several areas it costs considerably less—about $1,000 less than an equivalent Grand Am, Monte Carlo or Olds Cutlass Salon. The Matador's biggest failing is its lack of relevance to the times. A year ago, only people like the editors of *R&T* would have given this a second thought, but in these days of fuel and other resource shortages it is probably hard for anyone to become enthusiastic about any design (not just the Matador's) that places so much emphasis on style and so little on economy of means.

to over $12 in just a few days. Gasoline doubled in price from what had been the average 39¢ per gallon (10¢ per liter), and consumers faced incredibly long lines at gas stations as supplies dried up. The Center for Strategic & International Studies revealed that "The price shock of 1973 is reported to have shrunk the U.S. economy by approximately 2.5 percent, increased unemployment and inflation, and spun the economy into a severe and extended recession (1973–1975)." By March 1974 the oil crisis was over, but the damage to the economy—and to automobiles like the Matador Coupe—was done.

The Gremlin finally got some exterior styling updates for 1974, though they were disappointingly minor. The grille now had thin bright bars for a classier look, and the grille shell was now bodycolor. New safety bumpers featured stylist Bob Nixon's clever "free-standing look," rather than being tied to the body with cheap bodycolor plastic filler panels. The rear quarter panels received pressed "chevrons." Front and rear bumper guards were now standard equipment.

Despite such headwinds, a total of 100,035 Matadors were built, including 62,269 Coupes (with 6,165 receiving the Oleg Cassini touch).

Gremlin

Relieve the fuel shortage.

Advertising for the popular subcompact made a compelling case: "AMC Gremlin is the only US subcompact with a standard six-cylinder engine. Yet for all its engine, the car is very easy on gas. Averages over 18 mpg, depending upon the way you drive. And Gremlin still out-accelerates, weighs more, has a wider track, wider front seat, and wider back seat than any other car in its class. If you want to know what else Gremlin relieves, price one."

The challenges faced by large cars like the Matador and Ambassador were a blessing for the Gremlin. Today, 18 miles per gallon (7.7 kilometers per liter) seems poor, but at the time it was quite respectable. Manufacturers were being challenged by the new regulations to add bumpers that could withstand 10-mile-per-hour (16-kilometer-per-hour) impacts, which increased weight—and weight is the enemy of fuel economy. Stricter emissions regulations added more equipment and a further detuning of engines, thereby reducing the capacity for vehicles to go further with less fuel. The fact that AMC could somehow maintain the Gremlin's traditional efficiency despite this Catch-22 was remarkable.

More than ever, a car like the Gremlin made sense: 131,905 were produced, though a sign of the times was that a mere 12,263 were V-8 powered.

Hornet

Opens up all kinds of possibilities.

Gasoline prices came back down to about 53¢ per gallon (14¢ per liter) by the spring of 1974, though this was still 73 percent higher than it had been before the crisis. In the midst of these changes, the Hornet continued to provide possibilities for AMC.

The models and powertrains were basically the same as the prior year, though the Hatchback received a new Rallye X package that added power steering, manual front disc brakes, a tachometer, and other goodies. Hornet also got its version of the Levi's Edition. *Road Test* said of the Buyer Protection Plan: "This plan has to be the answer to prayers for women and others unsophisticated in things automotive who have been the traditional victims of repair fraud." It's easy to see why the Hornet was more popular than ever: 145,458 were built, including 67,709 of the unique Sportabout wagons.

The 1974 Gremlin X lost a bit of its exclusivity in 1974 since its painted grille shell was shared with ordinary gremlins. But the bold 'X' emblem in the grille and "hockey stick" side stripes added a nice aggressive look, as did the sporty slot-style wheels. The 'X' remained a very popular option package on Gremlins. The car still retained its counter-culture image, as a car you either loved or hated.

Some sales executives within American Motors were dissatisfied with the way the Hornet Hatchback had been marketed within its introductory year, feeling that with such a unique and highly desirable small car the company could have done a better job of selling it. Sales of the Hornet Hatchback had been decent but in truth they failed to meet their volume target. It's difficult to judge, since overall, 1973 sales had been so good for AMC. Here is the mostly unchanged Hatchback for 1974, this one fitted with the optional Levi's interior trim.

Javelin

Control. Head turning styling. Outstanding performance.

Times had changed. Ford replaced the Mustang in 1974 with the Pinto-based Mustang II, which sold like crazy. Chrysler dropped the rival Barracuda and Challenger after the 1974 model year, and there were serious discussions on the fourteenth floor of the General Motors Building about the future of the Camaro and Firebird. Then on January 2, 1974, President Richard Nixon signed the Emergency Highway Energy Conservation Act, mandating a maximum 55 mile-per-hour (88.5 kilometer-per-hour) speed limit on all highways. The law remained in effect until 1995, though how much fuel it actually saved is still debated.

AMC's pony car looked more attractive than ever, and 22,556 Javelin and 4,980 Javelin/AMX models were built for 1974. That was more than the Dodge Challenger (11,354) and Plymouth Barracuda (11,734) from Chrysler, combined. But considering the cost of gasoline and the new national speed limit, the message was clear: pony cars were a dying breed. In addition, as John Conde, former AMC public relations manager, recalled, "We needed [the] manufacturing line to build Pacers on, so we decided to drop the Javelin."

Ambassador

What you don't have to pay extra for that's important.

The Ambassador's strength was its great value. Standard V-8 power, standard air conditioning, and standard upscale interior with Extra Quiet insulation were enough to keep the Ambassador in show rooms. But the oil crisis had wounded large car sales, and though the Ambassador shared at least 90 percent of the components of the Matador, AMC president William Luneburg's relentless pursuit of manufacturing efficiency meant it just didn't make sense anymore in the brave new world of the mid-1970s. That meant the Ambassador was also canceled after 24,971 four-door sedans and wagons were built in 1974, less than half the previous year.

The Results

The *Decatur* (Alabama) *Daily* on January 31, 1974, featured an interview with Chairman Roy Chapin. "The whole question was that the role of the automobile in people's lives, we thought, was changing," Chapin said. "This was the rationale for the direction we decided to take—which was to continue the emphasis on the smaller product. Such decisions helped get the company back on its feet."

AMC manufactured a surprising 431,798 passenger cars in calendar year 1974 versus 392,105 the year before. Combined worldwide sales of AMC cars and Jeeps during the company's fiscal year (October 1–September 30 at that time) totaled an impressive 552,794 units, but after incurring large expenses preparing for the new Matador Coupe and another prospective product, the company recorded a disappointing profit of $27,546.

The biggest culprit was a strike by the United Auto Workers in mid-September, which cost the company $13 million and turned what was expected to be a handsome fourth-quarter profit into a loss. The November 13, 1974, edition of the *New York Times* summarized AMC's position: "The poorer earnings performance came despite a reported 17.6 per cent gain in sales for the year, an increase that set a new company record and raised A.M.C.'s share of the domestic car market from 3.8 to 4.7 per cent. The earnings report was issued at a time when the auto industry, anxiety-ridden over plummeting sales and profits, had laid off more than 68,000 workers, or about 10 per cent of the work force."

The 1974 Javelin-AMX was in many ways the best-looking pony car of 1974. With its beautifully flowing fender bulges front and rear, long hood with a low-set recessed grille and its overall look of power and purpose, there are a lot of reasons why these have become so popular in recent years. The bright orange paint and bold T-stripe on the hood further enhance the appearance of this beautiful machine. Sadly, this would be the final year for both Javelin and Javelin-AMX. The company was introducing a new compact car for 1975 that would require a lot of production space in the plants, with attendant higher profits.

1975-1979
Pacer
MICHIGAN 75
AMC 75
GREAT LAKE STATE

CHAPTER

5

THE DIFFICULT 1970s

Instead of offering a bright, hopeful future, the decade was turning into a continued struggle with extremely high inflation and a resulting decline in the economy. US President Gerald Ford vowed to "Whip Inflation Now." He didn't. His successor, Jimmy Carter, proved helpless against an economy that spawned a new word, "stagflation," meaning a stagnant economy with uncontrolled inflation. Loans for new cars started at 13 percent interest, loans for used cars at 18 percent. This alone made buying an automobile a challenge. At least the flow of oil from the Middle East oil was back . . . until it wasn't.

ABOVE: Sales began to level off and then fall toward the end of the 1974 model year, but American Motors executives remained confident that they could maintain their standing regardless. They knew they had an innovative, all-new car coming out early in the 1975 calendar year, one that they expected would spark sales of all their products. Seen here is American Motors (Canada) President William S. Pickett standing in front of AMC's main plant in Brampton, Ontario, Canada. Newer and much more modern than the Kenosha plant, it supplied cars to Canada, the US, and certain export markets. The car shown is a 1975 Matador coupe.

OPPOSITE TOP AND BOTTOM: In March 1975 American Motors launched its newest small car, the Pacer. A wide, roomy compact, it boasted interior space similar to a midsize American car, but with a trim overall length for easier driving and parking. The Pacer was a bold new product, with styling that was impossible to ignore. Penned by a team led by the brilliant Bob Nixon, the lines were smooth, clean, and near perfect. The public's response to the new Pacer was overwhelming, and the factory was soon put on overtime to fill the flood of orders that came in. In this photo, *top to bottom*, the Pacer D/L, and the base Pacer.

For AMC and the Big Three automakers, lagging sales compounded the huge expenses they were incurring in an attempt to meet the demands of unelected bureaucrats. The NHTSA's Joan Claybrook, for example, knew nothing about the automotive business but demanded, in the name of safety, that speedometers be made to only go up to 85 miles per hour (137 kilometers per hour). In general, the EPA wanted more fuel-efficient cars, and they also wanted cars that polluted less. Laudable goals, but the technology available in the mid-1970s had no chance of meeting such requirements without great sacrifices in power and drivability. Further demands from the NHTSA included developing cars with increased rollover protection, side impact protection, and 5-mile-per-hour (8-kilometer-per-hour) bumpers—all of which increased vehicle weight, which is the enemy of fuel economy.

The burden this governmental Catch-22 placed on the automakers was tremendous. General Motors stated their cost of compliance at that time was over $1.4 *billion*. Chrysler was called on to submit 228,000 pages of compliance documents to the government agencies in 1978 alone; the company, the tenth largest corporation in America at the time, was racing toward bankruptcy.

With a fraction of the resources of the Big Three, what were the odds of American Motors surviving these challenges?

1975

Pacer

The first wide small car.

It's been said that "insanity is doing the same thing, over and over again, but expecting different results." American automotive design has sometimes seemed bent on this form of insanity. Detroit's latest offerings always seem to repeat the errors of the past, oblivious to whatever challenges they may face in the future—and clearly not ready to take them on when they arrive.

AMC had a better idea: face into the wind of technological change with an automobile small on the outside but generous on the inside, with a panoramic, 360-degree view of the road and surroundings, sports car–like steering to avoid hazards, a wide stance for stability, plus a large hatchback and a wider passenger door for easy access. It would be powered by the most advanced internal combustion engine on the planet: a compact, lightweight, two-rotor Wankel rotary-piston engine. This outside-the-box design was the Pacer, possibly the most innovative vehicle ever to come out of AMC.

The fuel-efficient small cars coming over from Japan and Europe were designed for their roads, traffic conditions, even the average size of those countries' citizens, and were less than optimal for most American drivers. Pacer, on the other hand, was designed around the needs and expectations of Americans. "When we started on Pacer in 1971," Product

Manager Gerald Meyers told *Popular Mechanics*, "we took the biggest car we had at the time, the Ambassador. We set a target for ourselves of getting that amount of space in a very small car. Front-seat room, rear-seat room, legroom, hip room, shoulder room. We wanted the roominess of Ambassador in a car smaller than Hornet but no larger than Gremlin. We achieved that objective."

Reaching that goal meant a completely new design. The unibody structure was wider, giving passengers more room than previous compacts, and much more than the imports. The wider stance also contributed to increased stability in emergency maneuvers, and the 100-inch (254-centimeter) wheelbase—in between that of the Gremlin and the Hornet—provided a smooth ride.

The front suspension rode on a separate subframe, which helped isolate occupants from road harshness (a common complaint of unibody vehicles). This was a design used on some small GM cars, but it was a first for an AMC production car. The front suspension was atypical for AMC, with the coil springs riding on the lower control arms. The steering was a superior rack-and-pinion type, just the second American car to feature this highly responsive feature (GM's flagship Corvette would not receive rack-and-pinion steering until 1984). The rear suspension was of conventional leaf spring design, but those springs rode in rubber isolation bushings.

In this rare photo we see the filming of an AMC introductory movie. The new Pacer was especially popular with women, who appreciated its trim dimensions, moderate price, and the range of attractive interior trim and exterior colors offered. Pacers were marketed as small, economical cars and, compared with a big conventional car, they were. However, buyers soon discovered that they weren't getting the sort of fuel economy expected from a compact car. The problem was that Pacer came in way over its weight goal, which hurt fuel economy. *Tom & Kelly Glatch*

These big, individually adjustable seats and the wide space between them illustrate Pacer's great width—it was wider than Ford Granada and offered better interior roominess as well. Pacer's large windows had more glass than nearly every other car on the road and provided unparalleled visibility. Pundits claimed that Pacer looked like a fishbowl on wheels, but the public and road testers of the day loved the car. *Tom & Kelly Glatch*

Meyers described the innovations to *Popular Mechanics*:

> I've been with this company 12 years, and this is the first time we've taken the clean-sheet-of-paper approach on front suspension. We didn't have to. We could have faked it by using an existing system, tacking it under the car and slapping some sheet metal on top. . . . We wanted superior maneuverability. So, we took BMW as the target vehicle. Now there's a car that really whirls around a track. That's what we wanted. We think Pacer is going to live in the future, at least to the end of the decade and possibly into the 1980s. So, we built a car that will handle like a car of the future.

Then there was Pacer's amazing visibility, with drivers treated to an almost unobstructed 360-degree view of what was around them. AMC President Luneburg did his best to quell any rumors about the Pacer, but you know Detroit—a former AMC employee leaked to *Popular Mechanics*: "It's an original. If you go for a lot of visibility, Pacer will have more visibility than any car—except a convertible." The magazine reported that Pacer "will have more glass area than any standard production automobile, past or present; more than 5,500 square inches—almost twice the glass in a Cadillac or Lincoln."

Meyers had his own take on the windows: "We didn't put in a lot of glass for the sake of using a lot of glass. We did some research and found that about 12 percent of the people interviewed have some apprehension about being surrounded by glass. That's psychological. There's no danger. There's no engineering reason to be concerned about the amount of glass." The glass of the side windows was so tall it couldn't roll down all the way into the doors; this called for Vince Geraci's interior team to create door panels that extended above the top of the glass so front-seat occupants could rest their arms on something more comfortable than the window itself.

The short sloping hood of the cab-forward design gave a clear view of the road and greatly reduced aerodynamic drag, which increased fuel economy. Pacer's drag coefficient, the measure of aerodynamic efficiency, was .43 C_d—better than that found in the 1998 Dodge Viper GTS.

Then there was the passenger side door, which was 4 inches (10 centimeters) longer than the driver's, giving easy access to the rear seat. "You don't want a big door on the driver's side," Meyers explained, "because you bang the door getting in and out in parking lots, but you want the extra room on the passenger side, for loading and unloading and getting in the back seat. You'll be able to walk in—not squirm in, actually walk in—on the passenger side of Pacer. Passengers will be able to get in the back seat without the occupant of the of the front seat getting out of the car."

Out back, the large rear hatch provided easy access to the cargo space. When needed, the rear seat folded down for even more room.

What would power this futuristic vehicle? AMC planned to use the revolutionary Wankel rotary-piston engine. Created by German inventor Felix Wankel, the rotary engine has a triangular rotor spinning around a central output shaft within an oval-shaped block, creating three combustion chambers as it spins. NSU Motorenwerke AG, (NSU for short) was the German company that first employed Wankel's engine in the 1960s; by the early 1970s, General Motors was all in on Wankel power, with company president Ed Cole, the engineer behind Chevy's famed Small Block V-8 in 1955, pushing the program. Engineers and accountants loved the Wankel concept because it was half the size and weighed half as much as an equivalent piston engine, and it required half as many components.

AMC briefly considered manufacturing their own Wankel, then placed an order with GM for up to five-hundred-thousand engines. By then, GM's version was almost ready for use in the Chevy Vega and the AMC Pacer. Robert Lund, in his "Detroit Listening Post" column in the January 1974 edition of *Popular Mechanics*, stated that GM was predicting Wankel demand "snowballing to 500,000 units annually by 1977–78." But the Wankel engine soon revealed issues inherent in its design: high fuel consumption, high emissions, and more-than-normal wear on the rotor tip seals. GM believed it had the problem with the tip seals solved, then they made changes to the engine design to reduce emissions and meet 1975 requirements. With that, the engine's reliability went away. The high fuel consumption problem was never solved, and it became an even greater issue with the onset of the 1973 oil crisis.

Apparently, AMC had some sort of Plan B. As far back as February 1973, Lund's column had prognosticated: "If GM can't supply the Wankels by mid-summer of 1975, AMC may go ahead with the car, using an existing engine, and offer the Wankel at a later time, when rotaries become available from GM or elsewhere." Further proof of AMC planning for a possible Wankel-less future came with Gerald Meyers telling *Popular Mechanics*, "We designed the car to accept several different powerplants, current production engines as well as engines we are working on for the future. If our plans develop on the rotary as we anticipate, it could be used in Pacer later on."

The saga continued: Lund's column in May 1974 announced, "AMC was planning to put a Wankel in its new small car the second year after the car was introduced. That would be the '76 model. The car would carry a conventional engine the first year and the customer would be given a choice of a conventional six-cylinder or a rotary the second year."

But it was not to be. On September 24, 1974, Ed Cole postponed GM's Wankel program until solutions could be found to fix the engine's weaknesses. Then Cole retired in the same month, and GM, like the other manufacturers working on Wankel engines (apart from Mazda), soon abandoned the rotary engine program altogether. GM had spent sixty million dollars just on license fees to develop their Wankel, millions more trying to make it production ready.

The Pacer would have to be powered by AMC's much heavier 232 and 258 six-cylinder engines and use existing transmissions and axles. Roy Chapin claimed that, in marketing clinics, potential buyers were ambivalent about the benefits of front-wheel drive. The AMC six-cylinder engine had to be set well back in the chassis, with the rear cylinders actually resting underneath the windshield and cowl, its location dictated by Pacer's low hood and cab-forward design. Serviceability was still generally good, though, aided by the forward-tilting hood.

Then there was the problem of the government's proposed—but not yet settled—side impact rules. As Pacer neared production, AMC's Bob Nixon was ordered to bow the side sheet metal out much further in anticipation of new, probably stronger, side impact regulations, which may (or may not) become the new standard. Pacer wasn't unique in that regard—sit in a mid-1970s GM intermediate and you'll see the doors bow out in a similar

A scene from the AMC final assembly line, circa 1975. Here a worker adds the radiator coolant to a Hornet sedan after which the entire cooling system was pressure-tested to ensure there were no leaks. AMC's assembly lines had been working flat out for a long time, trying to keep up with orders flowing in from US and Canadian buyers, as well as its important export markets, but now the lines were slowing down as the world economy began to shrink.

During the 1960s and 1970s, the best way to boost profits on smaller cars was to entice buyers to load them up with optional equipment. American Motors marketing executives and its Styling staff came up with several desirable packages that grouped many options together at a value price. The combination of appearance enhancements and interior comfort features proved popular. Seen here is the 1975 Hornet Hatchback with the X sport package option.

way—but it exacerbated the Pacer's wide stance (the "ambulatory fishbowl" as *Motor Trend* called it). Nixon later said that, when the final Pacer design was approved, he was shocked at how his "lithe, sleek design" had morphed into something that reminded him of "a fat girl wearing a dress that was too small for her."

Inside, Pacer didn't offer a typical stripped-down "loss-leader" interior. Under Vince Geraci's direction base, models got comfortable Rally Perforated vinyl with full carpeting. The optional Deluxe (D/L) interior trim package added reclining seats and one of the handsomest fabrics ever to grace an automobile, the Basketry Print. The driver-focused, "cockpit-styled" instrument panel was angled toward the driver, much like the 1971–1974 Javelin's.

Starting at $3,299, Meyers predicted, "It's going to be a big-volume car. We're interested in no less than 100,000 cars a year, maybe double that?" Through no fault of the creative minds within American Motors, the Pacer that arrived in show rooms in February 1975 was less athletic than planned yet was wonderfully distinctive just the same. And demand was overwhelming—72,158 were produced during its short 1975 model year, 145,528 for calendar year 1975—making Pacer the most successful new car launch in AMC history.

AMC knew the Pacer would be polarizing. "American Motors has discovered a new word to describe Pacer," *Popular Mechanics* concluded. "The word is controversial. 'It's going to be a controversial car,' says everyone from board chairman Roy Chapin on down. . . . This is the first time in the history of the American auto industry that a car manufacturer has said in advance of bringing out a new product that some people may not like it. That takes guts. That's different. That's Pacer."

Hornet

Style is just one of its strong points.

With all the attention being given to the new Pacer, Hornet received only modest updates. All AMC products were now equipped with standard electronic ignition developed by Prestolite to make its engines more efficient. New catalytic converters required the use

Sales of the AMC Gremlin began to stall during 1975, a result of the poor economy, increasing pressure from US and Japanese small car competitors, and the fact that Gremlin was overdue for restyling. Now in its sixth year, with its increasing weight and large six-cylinder engine, Gremlin couldn't hope to offer the fuel economy of its four-cylinder competition. American Motors management was at fault for not having authorized the development of a four-cylinder engine when it became clear the Gremlin would be an enduring hit. From 1970 to 1974, its six-cylinder engine had been sufficient, but now the market demanded the better fuel economy that only a four-cylinder could provide.

of unleaded, regular-grade fuel. The D/L trim package with imitation wood trim on the Sportabout wagon continued to be a popular option.

Not surprising to anyone, Pacer captured some Hornet sales. Nevertheless, some 87,938 Hornets were produced, mostly on the strength of the unique Sportabout.

Gremlin

The small car that makes it fun to be economical.

Gremlins with six-cylinder engines and manual transmissions got a new option, overdrive from the British firm Laycock de Normanville. Unlike the manual overdrives of the past, this one was controlled by a pushbutton at the end of the turn signal stalk, engaging only above 35 miles per hour (56 kilometers per hour): another effort to eke out more fuel economy. The overdrive option was available with the six-cylinder engines that included a floor-shifted, three-speed manual transmission. A Bravado Grain vinyl top was a new, rather odd-looking option.

Pacer grabbed way too many sales from Gremlin, too, and just 45,848 were built.

Matador

With all this economy you can still have a lot of luxury.

AMC's larger cars received new front sheet metal on sedans and wagons, with single headlights, a protruding Jimmy Durante–style nose, and 10-mile-per-hour (16-kilometer-

LEFT AND BELOW: Two versions of the 1975 four-door Matador: the Matador station wagon, which was still a popular choice for families looking for room and value in a family wagon, and the new Matador Brougham four-door sedan, which was brought out to try to retain some of the people who ordinarily bought the now-discontinued Ambassador. The Matador line received upgrading this year plus an attractive new grille.

ROAD TEST: 1975 AMC PACER

Publication: *Car and Driver*, June 1975
Author: William Jeanes

There is an excitement-generating quality about American Motors' new Pacer that calls to mind the days when we spent most of the fall frothing at Detroit's new cars as they appeared one by one in our hometown show rooms. The Pacer is lovable, and you feel an instinctive urge to take it home—like a rubber ducky, to put in your bathtub to play with. Detroit has finally issued a car to which people are reacting.

For once, an automobile advertising campaign is telling the unvarnished truth: A large man is completely comfortable in the driver's seat or as a front-seat passenger. The same big man can survive in a condition approaching comfort in the rear seat, too. Average-size people will find the rear seat at least as comfortable and roomy as those to be found in the new "precision-size" cars. Compared to the rear compartment of such cars as the Chevy Monza and Ford Mustang II, the Pacer appears to have the proportions of a ballroom.

If ride quality concerns you, you will find the Pacer excellent. While there is admitted insulation from the road, the sensation is not at all like a wallowing full-size car with mushy suspension—it is like a good, well-ordered intermediate car.

Here's what to consider if the Pacer personality appeals to you: You'll get a car made largely from proven components; a car that you can enter or exit without braining yourself; a car that you can sit in and see out of with ease and enjoyment; a car that is pleasing to operate and offers reasonable economy. The small car for the person who doesn't like small cars may at last be in our midst.

per-hour) bumpers. The sleek Matador Coupe returned with the sporty Matador X and the fashionable Oleg Cassini options, and AMC continued offering the Brougham trim with the vinyl top and the opera window that was ubiquitous in cars of this era.

Though Coupe sales faltered, big families and fleets still needed large vehicles, and Matador production remained steady at 59,582 units.

The Results

AMC lost $27.5 million for fiscal-year 1975. Summing up the state of the company in its November 12, 1975, edition, the *New York Times* said, "The 1975 deficit came as no surprise to industry analysts. Company officers had forecast exactly what happened: that profits shown during the last six months of the fiscal year would fail to overcome first-half losses. The losses were caused by a strike during the early fall of 1974 and by recessionary factors thereafter." Once again, the Kenosha union had sabotaged the company that paid them by striking rather than continuing negotiations.

1976

Pacer

Small was never this wide.

In a cover story on the Pacer, *Car and Driver* called it, "The small car for the person who doesn't like small cars." The Pacer's unique concept really took off, so much so that dealers struggled to keep cars in their show rooms. Many customers who wanted to buy the car—or who just wanted to see it—were disappointed. The giant Lakefront Body plant in Kenosha ramped up production, first to 700, then 800 bodies per day. The final assembly line was strained, and more workers were brought in to speed up the process. Component and engine manufacturing also struggled, still more people were recalled from lay-off or newly hired, and overtime became the norm.

Quality inevitably suffers with such rapid expansion, and on the Pacer much of that was visible in its interior equipment and trim installation. In the end, AMC employees stepped up and quality improved once the assembly lines had found their rhythm, but the Pacer's reputation was badly tainted by quality complaints.

For a mere $99, Pacers could now be ordered with a sporty four-speed manual transmission for better acceleration and improved fuel economy. Considering its benefits, and the fact that most other small cars came with a four-speed manual transmission as standard equipment, AMC should have made it standard on all Pacers. The Pacer seemed so modern in appearance but the inclusion of a standard three-speed, along with four-wheel (unassisted) drum brakes and cheap 6.95x14 bias ply tires tarnished its image as an innovator. With many buyers complaining about lackluster fuel economy, AMC should also have made radial tires standard equipment.

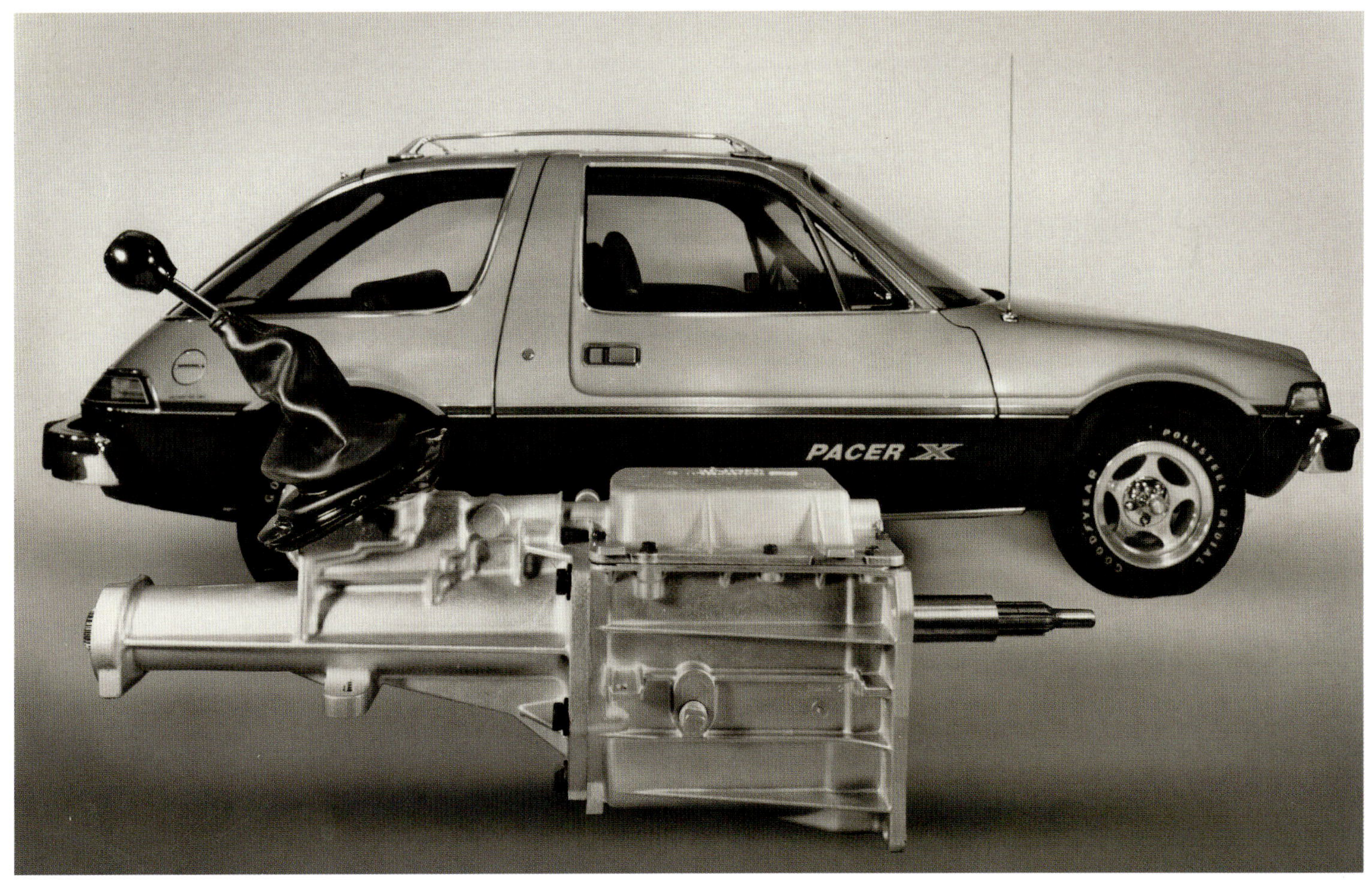

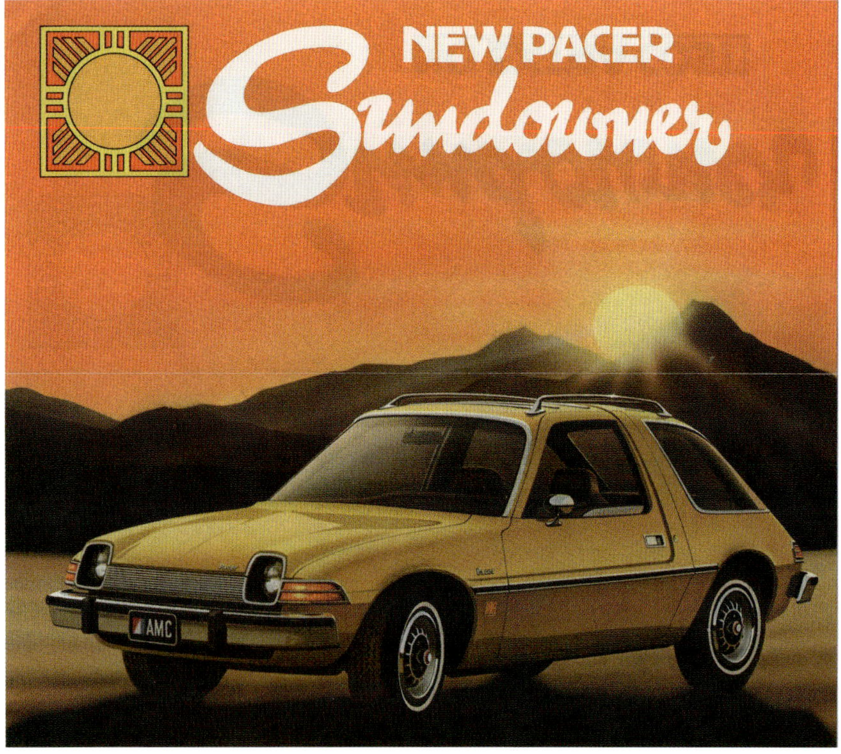

Although production of AMC's Pacer was running strong, retail sales had begun falling off. To counter this trend AMC offered various incentives to customers and dealers. It also introduced this special 'Pacer Sundowner' model towards the end of the 1975 calendar year. A California-Only model, it was intended to lure buyers there, who strongly favored import cars, by offering better value. With a price of $3,599, custom interior, rear window wiper and washer, styled road wheels with whitewall tires, remote control outside mirror and a roof rack—options ordinarily costing $300 extra, were included at no charge. It was an outstanding offer and a very attractive car. Its too bad AMC didn't offer a similar value model to the rest of the country, rather than cheapening its image with rebates.

A larger problem was Pacer's fuel consumption. The published government ratings were hardly realistic for any new car in that era, but inflation was raising the price of gasoline. It hovered around 59¢ per gallon (16¢ per liter), or $3.16 in 2023 dollars, and frugality was everyone's top priority. Pacer offered economy ratings of 18 miles per gallon city/24 miles per gallon highway (7.7 kilometers per liter city/10 kilometers per liter highway) with the 232-six and 17 miles per gallon city/25 miles per gallon highway (7 kilometers per liter city/10.6 kilometers per liter highway) with the 258-six—not good enough for some potential buyers.

To make matters worse, many buyers found that real-world fuel economy seldom, if ever, reached the posted numbers. Many new owners were extremely disappointed in Pacer's thirst for gasoline. In a decade of expensive, often scarce gasoline, a small car was supposed to be an economical car. The fact that Pacer was in effect a midsize car didn't occur to anyone, and they judged it accordingly.

AMC headquarters could see that interest in their crown jewel was dropping rapidly, so they began offering free air conditioning, a savings of $425, making the $3,499 Pacer a fantastic value. An optional four-speed manual transmission also improved efficiency while giving Pacer a sportier appeal. Model year 1976 production was an excellent 117,244 Pacers, but as the calendar year progressed sales declined.

Hornet

Economy cars with a sporty touch you didn't bargain for.

Produced for the US Bicentennial year, a slideshow for AMC salesmen reflected the nation's celebration: "Dimensions of personal liberty and a spirit of independence can also be found in today's '76 Hornet Hatchback. With the utility and cargo capacity of Hornet's hatchback design and its sporty good looks, Hornet Hatchback gives you the liberty to use this car for just about any purpose." The Hatchback offered the best of both worlds, with its striking design, loads of cargo space, and optional Touring interior or X Package for additional style and comfort. Powertrains remained the same, as all manufacturers had to concentrate on just a few select engines due to the time and expense of emissions certification, and both six-cylinder engines lost 5 horsepower in the process.

Production was down more than 19 percent to 71,577, and almost 42 percent of the total was Sportabout wagons.

LEFT: The Gremlin X package was still a popular option, though American Motors probably should have made it a distinct model by this point. The X cross-hatch grille insert with a large red X centered on the grille bar were distinctive styling touches. The X could be ordered with any of Gremlin's fourteen standard color choices for 1976. The V-8 engine was still available. Gremlin six-cylinder models could be ordered with a three-speed plus overdrive manual transmission for maximum fuel economy. For those who wanted improved fuel economy in an automatic-transmission-equipped Gremlin, a special 2.53-1 rear axle ratio was available.

BELOW: The new Touring Interior trim option available on the 1976 AMC Hornet Hatchback and Sportabout included these very comfortable individually adjustable reclining front seats upholstered in tan Sof-Touch vinyl, with matching door panels with carpeted lower panels, plus a matching headliner and sun visors. The Touring Interior option also included tan door pulls, woodgrain overlays for the instrument panel, AMC's Extra Quiet Insulation Package and a sports steering wheel.

Gremlin

Treat yourself to some fun along with big helpings of savings and value.

There were a lot of low-priced econoboxes out there. Then there was Gremlin: roomy, distinctive, and a blast to drive. "Instantly recognizable . . . and now more distinctive than ever with a new grille and squared framed headlamps," said the sales brochure—and it was all that. Despite the success of the Pacer, AMC's fun-size car saw a nice 14 percent jump in production to 52,941.

The AMC Matador sedan and station wagon models returned for 1976 with little exterior change. Extra Quiet insulation and front disc brakes meant Matador was quieter and safer than before, and the very fancy Brougham package could even make it luxurious, but sales of the big AMC cars were going nowhere. Management was no longer interested in its big cars and there were no plans to replace them with all-new designs—a shame.

Matador

Clearly, these are American Motors' finest.

"They look the part and the high level of trim and appointments confirms this impression," said AMC. Outside was a new horizontal motif grille. Inside the new Barcelona package, offered only on the Brougham Coupe, featured "an elegantly tailored interior with individual reclining seats, and unique ornamentation." The Barcelona replaced the Oleg Cassini designer trim, and the black or tan Knap Knit interior was quite attractive. Sadly, the sporty Matador X package was canceled.

Had the Matador Coupe been introduced two or three years earlier, as originally planned, it quite likely would have made a much bigger impact on the market, as the public clearly liked its smooth styling. But budget constraints launched it just days before the oil crisis gripped the nation; now, two years later, only 41,513 Matadors were produced, and only a portion of those were Coupes.

The Results

AMC lost $46.3 million for the year. The *New York Times* reported: "It was the second consecutive 12-month loss for the smallest of the four United States automobile manufacturers. . . . The 12-month loss reported today was the third largest of the nine fiscal year losses the company has had in its 23-year history."

1977

Pacer

The Wide Wagon.

The Pacer Wagon should have been a hot-selling addition to the Pacer lineup for 1977. The Wagon added just 4 inches (10 centimeters) to the Pacer's length and 75 pounds (34 kilograms) in weight, but cargo volume nearly doubled, from 29.5 square feet (2.7 square meters) on the sedan to the wagon's 47.8 square feet (4.4 square meters). Advertising emphasized its wide cargo door. The larger side windows had flip-out quarter windows, while the redesigned rear sheet metal helped make Pacer look more conventional.

The new wagon became the Pacer sales leader, with 37,999 built, but total production was half the previous year's, 58,264 versus 117,244 in 1976.

Over in Germany, another important automobile launched: the Porsche 928. A complete departure from Porsche's traditional air-cooled, flat-six, rear-engine architecture, the water-cooled, V-8-powered, front-engine 928 was the company's response to the possibility of future government regulations outlawing sports cars like the classic 911. It was considered a groundbreaking design, spawning 1980s cars that would include Ford's Sierra (Merkur XR4TI in the US), Tempo, and Taurus, Dodge Charger, and Chrysler Laser.

With sales starting to crash, American Motors was fast running out of product development funds. It managed to introduce one new body style for 1977: the Pacer station wagon. The new wagon was a very clever design using only a new rear section to create what appeared to be a whole-new car. If offered a more conventional appearance and much more cargo space. The company had high hopes that the new wagon would reignite Pacer sales, but that didn't happen. The Pacer wagon sold moderately well, but continuing bad financial news from AMC was causing many potential buyers to stay away from AMC showrooms.

What's this got to do with the AMC Pacer? The Porsche 928 was designed by Anatole "Tony" Lapine, formerly with General Motors Design, where he styled the 1963 Corvette Sting Ray with Larry Shinoda before becoming Porsche's chief designer in 1969. Compare the rear of the Pacer hatchback and that of the 928—the look is quite similar. Lapine later admitted he borrowed the 928's roofline, rear quarters, and hatchback from the Pacer. The stylist of the legendary sports cars saw something in the Pacer that really moved him. It was a revolutionary design.

Hornet

For most people who need wagons Hornet Wagon is really all they need.

As the famous architect Frank Lloyd Wright once said, "Form and function should be one, joined in a spiritual union." Bob Nixon's Sportabout was that rare fusion of form and function, and buyers recognized that: 77,843 Hornets were produced in 1977, with the Wagon again the most popular version.

The storied AMX name returned for the first time since 1974, now on a version of the Hornet Hatchback. AMC's 258 six was standard, the 304 V-8 optional. It wasn't a performance car in the traditional sense, but it looked muscular, handled well, and was much sportier than most of the anemic cars of the day, with *Popular Science* stating: "in looks and performance they remind of, but don't match, yesterday's tire-burning rockets."

The man behind the new Hornet AMX was Jim Wangers, a.k.a. "the godfather of the Pontiac GTO." After leaving Hurst Performance, he'd founded a new company, Motortown, to do the type of post-assembly conversions automakers could not do in-house. His firm

American Motors was trying to respond to the industry trend toward including more standard equipment and luxury features in compact cars by upgrading the Hatchback model with standard bucket seats and sports steering wheel and offering the D/L package on sedans and wagons. The optional X package continued as a popular choice on Hatchback and Sportabout models. With its sharp, sporty lines and low price, it's a wonder the Hornet Hatchback didn't sell more cars than it did.

had already produced the 1976 Mustang Cobra II, Plymouth Volare Road Runner, and Dodge Aspen R/T. "We proposed a package that included a brushed aluminum roof 'Targa Band,' a dramatic front air dam, a rear deck spoiler, and most importantly, a cherished name from AMC's past: AMX," he said. Motortown set up a satellite operation in Kenosha to add the AMX trim items to the Hatchback, and a healthy 5,207 were produced; 3,196 six-cylinder, 2,011 with the V-8.

Ever since the AMX had been dropped from the product lineup customers had been begging AMC to bring it back. The AMX finally returned for 1977 as a trim version of the Hornet. Dubbed the "Hornet AMX" it included a wide range of styling features including body-color plastic fender flares and front air dam, painted bumpers, a black grille, a distinctive bright targa roof band, back window louvers, and dual black side mirrors. On the inside were rally gauges, tachometer, special door panels, floor console, and special instrument panel overlay. For performance folk the larger 258-cu.-in. six-cylinder engine was standard, with the 304 V-8 optional. A four-speed manual transmission was also standard equipment, with automatic optional.

Gremlin

Practicality and value still get top billing.

"For 1977, we've given Gremlin a fresh new look that's bound to make it even more appealing," said AMC. Heaven knows, it was overdue for a makeover.

Up front were restyled, shorter fenders and hood, and a handsome new grille, while out back were large, distinctive taillights, and a much larger hatch window, answering complaints about the lift over height of the original design. The Gremlin also received an advanced single-overhead-cam four-cylinder engine, a 2-liter (121-cubic-inch) once used in Audi 100 and Porsche 924 models. Rated at an impressive 33 miles per gallon (14 kilometers per liter) highway and 21 miles per gallon (8.9 kilometers per liter) city, the four-cylinder engine was available only in a new Gremlin 2.0 Custom model that was priced at $3,248, $253 higher than the base Gremlin tagged at $2,995.

Besides the considerable weight savings of the 2.0 engine, all Gremlins boasted reduced weight for better fuel economy. *Motor Trend* declared, "What AMC is doing, is to lighten Gremlin components wherever possible, including thinner glass and liberal use of 80,000 psi high strength low-alloy steel—especially in the longitudinal framing members from the center door post rearward." That helped efficiency for standard six and optional V-8–powered Gremlins as well as the new four-cylinder.

Of the Porsche/Audi–powered Gremlin, *Motor Trend* concluded, "For the 25-mpg reading, day in and day out, and for the housewife who has orders not to disrupt the second-car gas budget, the Gremlin is expected to succeed in its purpose"—yet Gremlin demand was disappointing this year, with only 46,171 units built, including all powertrains.

For the 1977 model year AMC's neglected little Gremlin finally came in for a significant styling facelift which refreshed the little car's appearance. New front fenders were shorter and smoother, with a new hood to match. A pleasing new argent "eggcrate" grille was used on all models. Out back was a larger rear hatch window and large new taillamps. Gremlin was now 4-inches shorter overall and much more contemporary-looking. It's too bad AMC didn't introduce this redesign for 1975 or 1976, when it might have halted the sales downturn. It's also too bad they didn't make the side quarter windows a little larger, to make Gremlin look more like an all-new design. There were three Gremlin models this year: base Gremlin, Gremlin Custom, and Gremlin Custom 2-liter. Base and Custom Gremlins were fitted with the 232-cube six as standard equipment. Custom 2-Liter models were fitted with AMC's new Audi-designed 2-liter four-cylinder engine. Because the engine was more expensive to build than the longtime 232 six, AMC could offer it only in the higher-priced Custom trim.

Although only in its fourth model year, AMC's Matador coupe was selling very slowly. The product planners had missed the market by specifying a fastback coupe rather than a formal coupe like its competitors were selling. The Oldsmobile Cutlass coupe was one of the hottest-selling cars on the market; buyers loved its elegant half-padded top, opera windows, and hood ornament. Unable to fund a redesign of the Matador coupe, AMC offered the "Barcelona II" option for 1977, which included all of those contemporary styling elements.

Matador

Matador style speaks for itself.

The style leader of the Matador Coupe was the new limited-edition Barcelona II option. This rich-looking package included individual reclining front seats in tan Knap Knit fabric, color-keyed tan custom door trim panels and headlining, tan grille surround and headlight bezels, tan license plate depression and wheel covers, "Barcelona" hood ornament, and more.

But what one segment of the marketplace really wanted was room, and lots of it. The Matador station wagon delivered 95 cubic feet (2.7 cubic meters) of load space with the interior room of a full-sized car, all wrapped in a medium-sized vehicle. It's not surprising that one third of the 30,847 Matadors built in 1977 were wagons.

Overall sales were disappointing. The Coupe never sold as well as in its first year, mainly because the market by then wanted opera-window coupes, not fastback coupes. The Coupe's failure proved the mistake inherent in bringing out a new design two years late.

The Results

On October 21, 1977, Roy Chapin Jr. officially retired, and Gerald Meyers was promoted to chairman and CEO. Forty-nine years old, Meyers was then the youngest CEO in the automotive industry. For fiscal 1977, AMC's profits rose to $8.2 million on sales of $2.2 billion while Big Three sales dropped 21 percent.

1978

Concord

The luxury America wants; the size America needs.

After seven years, the Concord was the major facelift the Hornet desperately needed. Times change, styles change, and the focus on Concord was luxury with economy. The basic Hornet structure and familiar bodies—two- and four-door sedans, two-door hatchback, and four-door hatchback wagon—received the same front sheet metal introduced on the 1977 Gremlin, along with an elegant, bright eggcrate grille and rectangular headlights.

Like other American compact luxury cars, the Concord also had a standup hood ornament, essentially de rigueur back then. On D/L-optioned models, the two-door sedans received a new vinyl roof with opera window treatment that was rectangular in the style of the AMC A-Mark logo. Four-door sedans got a half-vinyl top but no opera windows. Standard Concords used the same roof as the former Hornet. Rear styling featured wide tricolor taillights. The popular D/L package also featured reclining seats, custom door trim and panels, custom headliner, stylish touches of woodgrain highlights plus an impressive digital clock, unique in this price class.

With tooling money almost non-existent, AMC was able to create a competitive new entry in the burgeoning "luxury compact" field with the 1978 AMC Concord D/L. Essentially, the Concord was a Hornet fitted with the shorter front end of the Gremlin, along with a rich new grille and mildly restyled rear. Base Concords were not much different from Hornets, but the reconfigured D/L package turned Concord into a very quiet and luxurious car. The D/L package included a Landau vinyl top with opera-style side windows that replicated the American Motors "A-Mark" logo, plus attractive body-color wheel covers. The D/L was easily the best-selling Concord model for 1978. A Sport package was available on the base Concord Hatchback but few dealers stocked them and few buyers ordered them, despite being well priced and very attractive.

TOP: Inside, Concord D/L was as luxurious as any full-size American luxury car. Features included plush interior trim with well-padded Velveteen Crush fabric individually reclining front seats, walnut burl woodgrain instrument panel trim, a beautiful woodgrain steering wheel, standard Light group, and a quartz digital clock that dazzled people—it was something all-new, and usually reserved for Cadillac-level cars. This particular car is equipped with air conditioning, identified by the air ducts at each end of the lower instrument panel parcel shelf. It also has AM/FM radio and a rear window defogger.

ABOVE: American Motors product planners concluded that the Pacer would sell better if it offered more power and had more conventional styling. Thus, for 1978 all Pacers were given updated frontal styling with a higher hood and "stand-up" eggcrate grille which didn't seem to be an improvement. AMC's 304 V-8 was available as an option, and it provided more power, but at a cost to fuel economy, which was perhaps the largest complaint buyers had about Pacer. The new styling didn't increase sales.

Because of its facelift in 1977, Gremlin had little appearance change for 1978, but still looked fresh and attractive compared with the 1976 versions. This year AMC introduced "2-tier" pricing on all Gremlin models. In seven western states: Arizona, California, Idaho, Nevada, Oregon, Utah, and Washington, Gremlin list prices were $120 lower than in the rest of the country. Thus, this base Gremlin stickered at $3,299 (plus options) in most states, and $3,179 in the seven western states listed. This was an effort to win back customers who ordinarily favored import cars.

For those looking for a sportier appearance, an optional Sport Package included reclining or bucket seats in vinyl or the popular velveteen crush fabric, plus exterior styling touches that included graphics and handsome styled wheels.

Both six-cylinder engines and the 304 V-8 were available with a choice of three- and four-speed manual or three-speed automatic transmissions. The new Concord was a great addition to the AMC lineup and a gratifying 117,513 were built, a nice yet modest 34 percent improvement over the 1977 Hornet.

AMX

If you don't like being the center of attention, drive something a little more tame.

This year AMX became a separate model once more, though some enthusiasts today refer to it as a Concord AMX for clarity. It was similar to the eye-catching 1977 Hornet AMX, available in Firecracker Red, Sunshine Yellow, Quick Silver Metallic, Alpine White, or a special Classic Black with gold accents. Pop culture adopted the car when it was featured on the TV show *Wonder Woman*. But even Lynda Carter driving one couldn't inspire buyers: just 2,540 were built by AMC and Motortown.

Pacer

Now you can get the room and ride of a Pacer with the load space of a wagon.

Pacer received a new raised hood and grille, giving it a more contemporary look. The new hood also provided room for the newly optional 304 V-8 and the breathing space it needed. Even with revised styling and more power, though, production was less than half the previous disappointing year, 21,231, with Pacer Wagon the most popular. Just 11 percent of the 1978 Pacers were V-8 powered.

Gremlin

More fun than a barrel of gas bills.

Other cars could beat the Gremlin's fuel economy now, though in four-cylinder/four-speed form 25 miles per gallon (10.6 kilometers per liter) was possible. But you couldn't get Levi's trim in the others, or an updated instrument panel borrowed from the Concord, new in the Gremlin for 1978.

This was the final year for the Gremlin in America, with production ending after just 22,104 were built. Sales and production of Gremlins would continue in Mexico for that market for several more years.

RIGHT: Introduced as a limited-edition sporty model to lure buyers to AMC showrooms, the 1978 "Gremlin GT" included a bold side strip reminiscent of the original Gremlin "X," large fender flares, spoke-style wheels, DR-70 outline-white-letter tires, body-color bumpers, rally instrumentation, and a whole lot more. Debuting in the 1st quarter of the 1978 calendar year, Gremlin GT was an attractive sporty subcompact, and is highly collectible today.

BELOW: The Gremlin "X" for 1978 got a very attractive new side stripe and featured Levi's interior trim, slot-styled wheels, "Extra-Quiet" insulation, DR-78 steel-belted radial tires, a front sway bar, and more, making it in some ways the nicest Gremlin "X" of them all; a pity since this was to be its last year in the U.S. Gremlin production would continue in Mexico for a while longer. Note this particular Gremlin "X" is on the "Custom 2-Liter" model.

It wasn't long before American Motors realized the new Concord D/L was a smash hit. Its combination of good looks, smooth ride, quiet interior, and lots of value for the money made it an easy car to sell. AMC's launch advertisements were frequent and compelling, bringing many longtime AMC owners as well as many new customers. Here AMC employees celebrate the 100,000th Concord built. The Concord's success allowed AMC another chance to remain in the car business.

Matador

When it's your turn to take the whole team to the game . . .

The luxurious Barcelona II trim was now available on the Matador sedan as well as the Coupe. Only two engines, the standard 258 six and 360 V-8, were available. Matador demand plummeted, with just 10,576 built, and 3,746 of those were the big wagons that were perfect team haulers. Not surprisingly, this would be the last year for the Matador.

The Results

The *Washington Post* gave the final account of AMC's performance in 1978: "Bolstered by the boom in small cars, American Motors Corp. reported record profits from continuing operations of $68.1 million in its latest fiscal year. The company said its sales in both the quarter and year set records, at $831.3 million and $3.17 billion respectively. AMC's new-car sales jumped 14 percent in October while those of General Motors Corp., Ford Motor Co. and Chrysler Corp. fell sharply."

1979

Spirit

Let the Spirit move you today.

"Reincarnation may not exist for humans, but AMC proved once again that it certainly is a fact of life for automobiles," wrote *Motor Trend*. "The awkward little Gremlin has gone the way of the Hornet. . . . It passed away officially at the end of the 1978 model year but has returned for '79 to start a new life as the AMC Spirit."

The Spirit offered a facelifted version of the Gremlin's profile, including a unique new grille and quad rectangular headlights. With greatly enlarged rear side windows for a more contemporary appearance, the Spirit Sedan looked longer and roomier, though it retained the glass hatch and taillights of the 1977–1978 Gremlin.

The big news was the Spirit Liftback, with a sleek new fastback roofline and large hatchback. AMC called the Spirit Liftback "Practicality with a bit of p'zazz." All regular Spirit models were equipped with the four-cylinder as standard, and the 258 six optional. The 304 V-8 was optionally available on Spirit Liftback but not on Spirit Sedan models. Initially, Limited models also included leather interiors, air conditioning, AM/FM radio, and more. Sometime after introduction, the standard A/C was deleted from Spirit Limited in response to complaints about the models' high price tag.

In its February 1979 issue, *Car and Driver* commented, "Something unusual happened while we were testing the AMC Spirit GT. We got looked at. Not just the occasional glance, mind you, but some for-real stares, and even a finger-point or two . . . Though the Gremlin looked truncated, half finished, the Spirit, on the same wheelbase, is proportionally correct. . . . Sitting there, the car looks very right indeed. . . . "

Here's the new Spirit D/L Liftback for 1979. The D/L included bright moldings around the windows and fender lips plus above the rocker panel trim, thicker "B" pillar trim, painted wheel covers, whitewall tires, and a woodgrain dash applique. Spirit D/L also got a custom headliner and sun visors, woodgrain steering wheel, dual horns, courtesy lights, custom door trim panels, and much more. The D/L cost a bit more than the base model but was a better value due to the amount of extra equipment it came with.

ABOVE: Surprisingly, American Motors was able to follow up the success of the Concord D/L by introducing new subcompacts for 1979. The new Gremlin-based cars were the Spirit Liftback and Spirit Sedan. They were offered in three trim series—Base, D/L, and Limited. Even the base models were well equipped, with the 2-liter four-cylinder engine and four-speed transmission, inside hood release, carpeting, bucket seats, full wheel covers, custom steering wheel and much more as standard features. D/L models added a day/night rear view mirror, digital clock, "Extra-Quiet" insulation reclining bucket seats, split folding rear seat, and more. Shown is the Spirit Sedan.

BELOW: The former AMX, a.k.a. the "Concord AMX" was replaced for 1979 by a Spirit-based AMX that was much more performance oriented than the two previous seasons' products. With a unique black grille and headlamp bezels, blackout treatment for the bumpers and exterior moldings, big fender flares, gorgeous Turbocast II alloy wheels fitted with ER60x14 OWL tires, a Rally-Tuned suspension, heavy-duty front disc brakes and heavy-duty rear drums, Performance-tuned exhaust for V-8/four-speed cars, full instrumentation, and so much more, the AMX was a great-handling car and with the standard 258-cu.-in. six or optional 304 V-8, offered better performance than many similar cars.

LEFT: Spirit's top level of trim, the Limited, included power door locks, power liftback release, dual remote-control mirrors, tilt steering wheel, radial ply tires, and leather-covered seats. It was a very comprehensive collection of standard features and was rather expensive when it was first announced. Customer pushback was immediately experienced due to the high price and before long some of the equipment was put back onto the options list and Limited prices reduced. Shown is a Spirit D/L with optional side stripe.

BELOW: The Spirit Liftback model offered a unique GT package that was very attractive and could be ordered on either the D/L or Limited model, though it later was available even on the base Liftback. With spoke wheels, blackwall radial tires, blackout grille and trim, and special instrumentation it offered a sporty car at a value price as low as just $4,037. The GT was a very popular package; it seems a shame it was never offered on the Spirit Sedan, but the factory was not interested in extending the Sedan's range.

This year the AMX was a Spirit model, using the Liftback body. Outside, standard features included front and rear black bumpers with bumper guards and nerfing strips, front air dam and rear deck spoiler with accent stripes, front and rear fender flairs, blackout grille, Turbocast II aluminum wheels, ER60x14 belted radial tires, and much more.

In the smaller, lighter Liftback, there was a higher level of performance from the standard 258 six, and there was still the option of the 125-hp 304 V-8. They were quick for the time, and two specially prepared AMXs took a shocking 1–2 class victory at the 24 Hours of Nürburgring in October 1979. Still, only 3,657 AMXs were produced out of 52,478 Spirits built, which was more than double the number of Gremlins produced the previous year.

Concord

Elegant comfort and exceptional value.

"When we invited AMC owners to list their complaints about the 1978 Concord, a resounding 30 percent put down none. That's an amazingly high percentage and sets the Concord above all 14 cars we surveyed in 1977, including the Honda Accord (18. 9 percent), Thunderbird

(29.1 percent), Grand Prix (21.5 percent) and Diplomat/LeBaron (21.2/18.0 percent)." That's what *Popular Mechanics* had discovered about the new AMC Concord.

Motor Trend added a comment on sales: "In June more Concords were sold than the combined total of all AMC passenger cars in any given month since 1963." Total production was down from the outstanding numbers of 1978, but with the worsening economy and the effects of a new oil crisis, putting out 96,498 Concords was still a satisfying achievement.

All AMC cars featured stronger bumpers front and rear in 1979, meeting the next phase of Federal Motor Vehicle Safety Standards and Regulations safety criteria while reducing weight. Instead of saving money, *Road & Track* estimated the 1973 regulations cost owners $1 billion *more* per year in increased new car prices and higher repair costs. How they arrived at that figure is unknown.

Like the new Spirit, the Concord series now included three trim levels: Base, D/L, and Limited. As before, the D/L was the volume-seller, though fleet sales of the base cars, along with some retail sales, helped overall volume. The Concord Limited was as plush as a Lincoln or Cadillac and as quiet as the tomb, so people who could afford them ordered them. But prices overall had been climbing for years due to the incessant inflation affecting the country and, coupled with extremely high interest rates on car loans, made sales more and more difficult to get.

Pacer

An exceptional blend of big car room, ride, and comfort.

When the Pacer was launched in 1975, it was hoped the little car would lead AMC into the 1980s. As predicted, by 1979 they were still being built, though only 10,215 saw the light of day, and the message was clear.

The Results

On January 16, 1979, the Shah Mohammad Reza Pahlavi fled Iran at the beginning of the Iranian Revolution. This was the start of a series of events that, over the next eighteen months, initiated the decade's second oil crisis. The effects were long term: oil prices did not return to previous levels until the mid-1980s, and the panic produced by gasoline shortages may have negatively affected the way teenagers viewed automobile transportation as they reached driving age.

In its November 19, 1979, issue, *Time* reflected on AMC's current position:

> President W. Paul Tippett Jr. of American Motors Corp. used to joke that his company actually had a three-word name: "Ailing American Motors." Now Tippett and his colleagues are laughing for a different reason. AMC has pulled back from the brink yet again, chiefly by cutting its work force, consolidating plants and concentrating on a few small cars and specialized vehicles. Last week, like proud parents of a sickly

ROAD TEST: 1979 AMC SPIRIT GT

Publication: *Car and Driver*, February 1979
Author: Mike Knepper

The Spirit is proof there's been a dramatic change in thinking at AMC. For years it tried to out-VW VW, out-Datsun Datsun, and out-Toyota Toyota, only to be met with less and less success. . . . So what to do? Abandon the economarket and start giving 'em luxury in small packages. The Pacer was the first step in that direction, the Concord the next, and now, enter the Spirit.

After several attempts at almost getting it right, Teague and Company have come up with quite a handsome automobile. Though the Gremlin looked truncated, half finished, the Spirit, on the same wheelbase, is proportionally correct. The new front end boasts rectangular headlights, framing a tastefully aggressive, matte-black grille. The slope of the fastback is just "fast" enough. Sitting there, the car looks very right indeed.

So the car gets a mixed review. We give it high marks for styling, its long list of standard equipment, its interior appointments, and for the general level of improvement over the Gremlin. But the handling and the anemic V-8 take the luster off what could otherwise have been one of the real highlights of the 1979 season.

> child who suddenly won the bantam championship, AMC announced that profits more than doubled, to a record $83.9 million on sales of $3.1 billion for the fiscal year ended in September. AMC has rested its survival strategy on what Chairman Gerald Meyers calls a "three-legged stool" of small cars, Jeeps and steady Government contracts for postal vehicles and military tactical trucks.

American Motors also signed an agreement with French automaker Renault, who would use AMC's dealer network to expand their US sales.

The production upswing that had begun in 1978 with the introduction of the Concord extended into 1979. At one point the company was running low on four-cylinder engines and four-speed transmissions. Rather than lose orders or have to delay them, a quick fix was instituted. Some Spirit models ordered for stock were fitted with the 232-cu.-in. six and three-speed manual transmission in place of the standard four-cylinder/four-speed. This picture is from a marshalling yard at the Kenosha, Wisconsin plant.

1980-1983

CHAPTER

6

THE CARS OF THE EARLY 1980s

As the 1980s began, the "malaise" (as President Jimmy Carter described it) that had affected the United States for much of the 1970s had reached a tipping point. Inflation and economic stagnation continued, and the second oil crisis was pushing the nation to the brink. The entire auto industry was reeling: Chrysler was on the verge of bankruptcy, thanks to poor sales, poorer management, and the excessive cost of complying with government mandates. The automaker was deemed too big to fail, since it was the tenth largest company in the US at the time, and the Chrysler Loan Guarantee Act, signed into law on December 21, 1979, gave them $1.2 billion in government loans that were eventually paid back in full, with interest.

ABOVE: The 1982 AMC Spirit Liftback with optional GT package was as sharp as ever, even more so when equipped with the optional Turbo II alloy wheels seen here. However, high inflation had made cars much more expensive than just three years earlier, while high interest rates continued to pummel consumers. The poor economy had many potential buyers worried about their job security, all of which soured retail demand. There was nothing dealers could do but work harder to find customers and wait for better times. Sales of the Spirit Sedan model were never very high, and by midyear a decision was made to end production prior to the end of the model year.

OPPOSITE TOP: American Motors had an established reputation as a company that could develop new cars on a shoestring budget—it proved this yet again in 1980 with the new Eagle series of four-wheel-drive automobiles. Consumers had shown a growing interest in four-wheel-drive sport utility vehicles (SUVs) since the beginning of the 1970s, but now they wanted better fuel economy than what the big American SUVs could offer. The Eagle fit into a niche all by itself, one that handily served these buyers. Sales exceeded projections right from the start.

OPPOSITE BOTTOM: There wasn't much new in terms of appearance for the 1980 Spirit Sedan, but it continued to be built solidly and priced competitively in the subcompact market. More of the Spirit's competitors were turning to a front-wheel-drive chassis layout, however, making their products lighter and roomier, as well as more fuel efficient. Even if most consumers didn't understand what front-wheel drive was, they wanted it because it was seen as the next big thing.

Researchers Stephen Cooney and Brent D. Yacobucci of the Library of Congress' Congressional Research Service wrote about the American auto industry at that time: "While the drama over Chrysler was being played out, the Big Three automotive industry more broadly was affected by the impacts of the Iran crisis of 1979, the so-called "second oil price shock" that also hit in that year, and the onset of a recession in 1980. Car production fell from 14.7 million units in 1978 to 9 million in 1980. A total of 800,000 workers in the automotive and related industries were laid off, because of reduced demand, and the unemployment rate within the industry stood at 30%."

Chrysler may have been too big to allow it to fail, but what about American Motors? With a fraction of the resources of the Big Three, the independent company's burdens were even more challenging. Banks stopped lending to them, but the company at least had a lifeline with increasing investments by Renault. Over its history, AMC had had a remarkable ability to introduce the right vehicles at the right time. Would American Motors' uncanny luck continue into the 1980s?

1980

Eagle

The Eagle has landed . . . on all fours.

AMC announced: "Introducing the American Eagle. Totally new, totally exciting and totally right for the 1980s!"

A four-wheel-drive automobile for daily use had never been successfully launched—until now. Four-wheel drive was nothing new, but it had only been available on off-road vehicles.

Otto Zachow and William Besserdich created the first four-wheel-drive vehicle in 1908, after Zachow declared, "Who ever heard of a mule walkin' on only two legs?" In 1915 they developed a 1 ½-ton (1,360-kilogram) truck for the US Army. The Thomas B. Jeffery company, then Nash after its purchase of Jeffery, had built thousands of similar Nash Quad trucks during World War I. But those pioneering 4×4s, along with later Willys Jeeps and Dodge Power Wagons, used solid axles front and rear, and a permanent transfer case to send power to both axles. Later systems allowed disengaging the front axle, but that involved stopping the vehicle, shifting the transfer case, stepping outside, then manually disengaging each front hub in whatever weather conditions were calling for the four-wheel-drive in the first place.

That was acceptable for commercial and off-road vehicles, perhaps, but Roy Lunn had a better idea.

Royston C. "Roy" Lunn was no ordinary engineer. Born in England in 1925, he began working for Ford of England after World War II. Moving to the US in 1958, he took over as manager of the Ford Advanced Vehicle Center, where his immense talents were critical in fulfilling Henry Ford II's mission to win the 24 Hours of Le Mans. Lunn led the development of the Ford GT Mark II and Mark IV that defeated Ferrari in 1966 and 1967.

There were two things that helped American Motors rush the new Eagle to market quickly. Chief Engineer Roy Lunn had been tasked with developing an all-new line of light, fuel-efficient senior Jeep models to replace Cherokee and Wagoneer. As part of his investigation into lighter drivetrain components, he had studied a new full-time 4WD transfer case that was lighter, quicker, and much more full efficient. Lunn realized that a version of the new transfer case could be fitted to the AMC Concord to create America's first 4WD automobile. Lunn developed the new car in secret, not even telling CEO Gerry Meyers until he reached a point where he needed more money to complete development. The new Eagle drivetrain is seen here.

Raj Nair, Ford's president of Ford North America in the late 2010s, recalled Lunn's central contributions to Ford's successes. "His legacy as the godfather of the original Ford GT40 was well known throughout the company, and he helped bring Ford a performance car that is just as legendary today as it was in the 1960s."

In 1971, after Ford's racing ambitions had ended, Lunn was hired by AMC's Jeep division. Within a few years, he'd adapted Jeep running gear for a Hornet, but found the result too trucklike. "I wanted it to be a full-time four-wheel-drive vehicle that was as smooth to drive as a normal production car. I had done some earlier work on four-wheel-drive automobiles at Toledo, but they were terrible. I read in an English engineering magazine that someone developed a transfer case that used something called 'silly putty' that was very smooth. I incorporated that idea on the XJ Cherokee, and realized I could use it on a car."

Lunn made the simple yet ingenious system the centerpiece of his "8001 Plus Four" project. His paper for the Society of Automotive Engineers stated, "A key factor was a full-time transfer case with a viscous biasing differential. The viscous unit had been invented and developed by FF Developments Ltd. of Coventry, England. They had sold the manufacturing rights to GKN Ltd., which arranged a prototype development with the FF Company."

FF Developments had been born when Major A.P.R. "Tony" Rolt and Freddie Dixon began developing 4WD systems for road cars in the 1930s, with industrialist Harry Ferguson financing the venture in the 1950s. Rolt was a driver for Team Jaguar Racing and was co-driver of the Le Mans-winning Jaguar C-Type in 1953. Rolt and Ferguson created a viscous coupling using a thick silicone product (the "silly putty" mentioned by Lunn), which transferred power to any of the four wheels that still had traction without the weight and complexity of a central differential. The Ferguson P99 Formula 1 racer (the only 4WD F1 racer to win in competition) and Andy Granatelli's Novi and turbine Indy 500 cars used the system, as did the expensive Jensen FF sports car.

ROAD TEST: 1980 AMC EAGLE WAGON

Publication: *Car and Driver*, February 1980

Author: Don Sherman

Here we have a rare phenomenon: The whole is way more than the sum of its parts. Little AMC, which you'll agree is anything but America's prince of technology, took one obsolete car line, jacked the body three inches skyward, stuck in enough gears and fluid couplings to make all the wheels drive, and called it Eagle. And the thing flies! It's got to be the most impressive piece of automobile engineering in America today. What's more, it drives well. There's actual road feel in the steering wheel. The brakes work great. It goes straight down the highway. And it produces only a little more wind whistle and road noise than your average conventional car. The wagon version even looks right perched up on its tippy-toes. The only things I don't like about the Eagle are its lack of a manual transmission, and the Modern American Funky interior it comes with. The seats in particular look like furniture you'd expect to find in a really wacko shrink's office. All of which fades into insignificance the instant you're confronted with bad roads or rotten weather. If you've got ten grand to spend on mobility insurance, this Eagle will do you a whole lot more good than State Farm.

Lunn adapted his transfer case to the upcoming Concord, adding a Dana 30 front differential and Spicer half shafts to modified Concord components. He also specified 15-inch (38-centimeter) wheels and raised the new car three inches to increase ground clearance. Tough Krayton plastics were used for the fender flairs and body cladding to reduce off-road damage.

Lunn created a revolutionary automobile, the first mass-produced four-wheel-drive passenger car, which added only $600 to the manufacturing cost of the Concord yet could be sold at a profitable premium. One more benefit: the EPA classified the Eagle as a "truck," which exempted it from the Corporate Average Fuel Economy (CAFE) mandates that AMC and the Big Three were struggling to meet.

David E. Davis Jr., publisher of *Car and Driver*, stated, "To say that I loved the Eagle would be the understatement of the year. When I got home, I bought 200 shares of American Motors stock. The Eagle had convinced me that AMC was a hot property. . . . The Eagle has landed and is about to scream." The public agreed: 46,381 were built the first year despite the oil crisis and economic woes of 1980.

Concord

Very tempting to consider; very gratifying to own.

Concord continued with its blend of luxury and value. All Concords were updated with a horizontal bar grille and full-width taillights. Four-door sedans got their own opera windows, still considered chic, added to the C-pillar. The ever-popular wagon remained, but the sleek Hatchback was discontinued.

In 1980, all American Motors cars received a new rust-proofing process called Ziebart Factory Rust Protection. Much more than the sprayed-on undercoating available at the Ziebart dealers, this comprehensive rust prevention treatment was built into the automobile, included aluminized trim screws, plastic inner fender liners, galvanized steel in every exterior body panel, and a deep-dip bath in a special primer. AMC backed it up with a five-year No Rust Thru warranty added to its now-famous Buyer Protection Plan. Buyers responded favorably, and 80,456 Concords were built for 1980.

ABOVE: The 1981 Concord D/L two-door saw a rapid decline in sales this year as customers began to prefer the ease of having four doors over the luxury coupe appearance of the Concord two-door. AMC stylists experimented with different roof types for the two-door sedans, hoping to find one that would attract more buyers. To this end, they arrived at a squared-off, formal appearance that was attractive, though nothing was ever put into production. A shame.

BELOW: The 1980 Concord D/L four-door sedan was as handsome as ever, and a decent seller for dealers. But the body design was becoming a bit stale—not surprising since it had been introduced in the fall of 1969 and had only minor facelifts since. As it happened, American Motors Styling staff was even then working on a reskinning of the basic body in the hope of extending Concord's market relevance. The redesign would use the same basic body but square off and extend the rear fenders for a longer look; it would square off the roofline as well for a more formal appearance while also giving the feeling of greatly increased interior room.

The Spirit Liftback didn't experience many observable changes for 1980, but its sporty styling and obvious solid construction made it a strong competitor. Shown in this car, the GT package was an attractive option that was ordered on a good percentage of Spirit Liftbacks. This particular car has been upgraded with the optional Turbo II alloy wheels and fatter tires. The color-keyed body scuff molding was a good idea to order, as the car's width and curved door sides were an open invitation to nicks and scratches.

Spirit

There's more to Spirit than meets the eye.

Both Spirit and Concord received a new standard engine, the 2.5-liter (151-cu.-in.) Iron Duke from General Motors. This engine was created by taking one bank of the famous Pontiac V-8, one of the finest engines Detroit had produced in the 1960s. *Popular Mechanics* wrote of the switch, "It's much better suited to those cars' size and weight specs than the previous smaller, shakier and noisier VW-based Four. . . . Four-speed (instead of three speed) manual transmission is now standard on all AMC passenger cars (except Eagle). One unfortunate effect of the ever-toughening CAFE standards, however, is that the zippy 304 V-8 is on longer available in AMC cars." Thanks to the second oil crisis, the Spirit was the right car for the times: 71,032 were manufactured that year, but only 865 saw light as the sporty AMX models.

Pacer

Big car room and riding comfort.

Pacer rolled into the 1980s with one minor change: a blacked-out grille. Then, in December 1979, the last Pacer rolled out of the Lakefront Body Plant in Kenosha with no fanfare, after only 1,746 were built for the year. There were still brand-new Pacers on dealer lots in 1981.

Former CEO Roy Chapin Jr. opined, "I don't think we marketed it as well as we should have. . . . I think we should have positioned it more as an alternate to the intermediate cars than as a small car because in terms of interior space, and ride, and handling it really (was) much more of an automobile than it appeared to be just by looking at the dimensions." Still, Pacer had all the components needed to be successful: an innovative concept, a superb though polarizing design, and advanced engineering. Just one piece was missing . . . luck.

ROAD TEST: 1980 SPIRIT LIFTBACK

Publication: *The Boston Globe*, August 10, 1980
Author: John R. White

It's nice to hear somebody ooh and aaah over an American-built car—even if the somebody is a sixth-grader. (One does get tired of the wallowers in guilt who proclaim Americans can't do anything right anymore.)

We had the kids in this shiny American automobile delivering them to the fun and games of soccer camp. The car is American Motors' Spirit Liftback, a two-door with conventional rear-wheel drive, a six-cylinder engine that's been around a while, good styling, few flaws, no detectable bad habits, fine performance and decent economy—and, in this case, loaded with options.

The Spirit is rated 22 miles per gallon city, 35 highway with the manual four-cylinder; 22 city, 31 highway with the automatic four; 18 city, 26 highway with the six automatic or manual. We almost never hit the EPA ratings in a test run and with this six with its juice drive, the A/C going full blast, and weighing in around 2600 pounds, we certainly expected to come in well under the EPA. Surprise! In spite of lead foot, jackrabbit starts and all the other mischief, we posted 18.1 miles-per-gallon.

Nobody pretends that Spirit is a sports car—and it doesn't deliver sports car performance—but it comes a lot closer to that standard than one foreign pretender to the title of sports car that we've tested and it delivers better than a number of the sporty set in general.

The more we drove this car, the better we liked it. With the six economy is fair; with the four and stick, this shapes up as American economy alternative to the imports. And, it is bigger than those little econoboxes; at 2500 to 2600 pounds, if you hit something, there is more car to absorb the blow.

The Results

The *Washington Post* broke the dismal news that closed out 1980 for AMC: "American Motors Corp. reported today that it lost a record $197.52 million last year as revenues declined 16.6 percent from their 1979 level. The full-year loss, which amounted to $6 a share, compared with a profit of $70.6 million ($2.24 a share) in 1979. Worldwide sales of cars and Jeeps were 327,808, down 22 percent from 418,204 in 1979. Car sales rose one per cent to 228,937 for the year. This included 37,792 cars imported by Renault."

With AMC on the brink of failure, Renault purchased a 22.5 percent share of the company. The French company was expanding in other areas, too, purchasing 10 percent of Mack Trucks.

1981

Eagle

Experience driving in the 4th dimension.

Popular Science extolled the virtues of the Eagle: "It rides easily, stops quickly on icy roads, and is designed for doctors, firemen, people who drive snowplows and others in rough climes." And in 1981, AMC proclaimed: "Experience what lies beyond the sports car." Adding Roy Lunn's four-wheel-drive system to the Spirit created something new and exciting: the Eagle SX/4 and Kammback.

Fitting the Eagle's four-wheel-drive system to the "Series 50" Spirit was easy: it bolted right up, and only new body-side cladding needed to be tooled. The Spirit Liftback was transformed into the Eagle SX/4, while the Spirit Sedan became the Kammback, named after the German aerodynamicist Wunibald Kamm, who discovered the drag-reducing effect caused by slicing off a car's trunk. Priced from just $5,995, the Kammback was $725 less than the SX/4 and geared toward first-time buyers and fleets. The SX/4 also added a new dimension to the already sporty Liftback.

Jean Lindamood in the *Car and Driver* of May 1981 wrote: "Dateline: Snow Belt, U.S.A. Undoubtedly, American Motors' 1981 Eagle SX/4 Sport is great for winter driving in a city like Ann Arbor, which is notorious for its abominable road upkeep. The four-wheel-drive SX/4's sure-footed grip is comforting when surrounding cars get stuck in their driveways and slide sideways through the slush. But to satisfy the Stump Jumpers and Brush Busters of

AMC marketing executives made a mistake in not pushing Eagle Kammback sales harder than the weak effort made. The Gremlin/Spirit basic body styling was greatly improved by the addition of fender extensions and the Kammback's new grille. In addition, the Kammback's price was lower than the SX/4's, and it offered much more rear seat headroom and better visibility. The base price of all 1981 Eagles included impressive standard features such as power steering and power front disc brakes, four-speed manual transmission, automatic four-wheel drive with transfer case skid plate, 15-inch (38-centimeter) radial ply tires, front stabilizer bar, dual horns, quad rectangular head lamps, dent-resistant Krayton fender flares and lower body treatment, inside hood release, and more. Dealers who stocked them had no problem selling them.

ABOVE: The 1981 Eagle SX/4. When equipped with the optional Sport package, the baby Eagle transformed into a tough, aggressive-looking, sporty car. It was capable, as AMC bragged, of out-cornering a Porsche on less-than-ideal surfaces such as snow, ice, or dirt. With black bumpers, grille, and window moldings, the car changed from a sporty hatchback with luxury touches into a true GT. The 15-inch (38-centimeter), five-spoke alloy wheels seen here, fitted with Goodyear OWL tires, look particularly sharp on the Eagle.

ABOVE: Right from its very first model year, the Eagle station wagon was the most popular variation in the Eagle lineup. Its combination of roominess, ease of entry and exit, good cargo space, and attractive styling appealed to a many buyers. Because the standard drivetrain on senior Eagles (that is, the 30 series) for 1981 included the 2.5-liter four-cylinder engine and four-speed manual transmission, the advertised fuel economy rating was as high as 22 miles per gallon (9.4 kilometers per liter) city and 29 miles per gallon (12.3 kilometers per liter) on the highway. Of course, most of the senior Eagles were ordered with the six-cylinder engine, because the four banger was noisier and a trifle underpowered. The six only came with an automatic transmission, with the rating for that combo being 16 miles per gallon (6.8 kilometers per liter) city and 22 miles per gallon (9.4 kilometers per liter) highway.

ABOVE: All American Motors automobiles received Ziebart Factory Rust Protection, which came with a five-year, no-rust-through warranty, along with the American Motors Buyer Protection Plan. The Ziebart Factory Rust Protection was not the same as aftermarket Ziebart protection, which was sold at many dealerships, of all brands, strictly as an after-sale purchase. Because AMC's rust protection was applied as the car was being built, the company didn't need to drill holes in the body to spray in the sealant. And the Rust Protection meant buyers didn't need to spend the extra $300–$400 that competitive dealers charged for the aftermarket treatment.

America, the SX/4 needs to be put through more strenuous paces." She tried her best to bury an SX/4 on her family farm in midwinter, but failed, stating, "With its ground clearance and selectable four-wheel drive, AMC's new Eagle SX/4 doesn't require pavement to be fun."

As Lindamood mentioned, an important new option was Select-Drive, which allowed Eagles to be switched from 4WD to 2WD when stopped. *Popular Mechanics* said, "This should give AMC salespeople a 20-miles-per-gallon (EPA city) Eagle to brag about and will do much to enhance Eagle's reputation as a relatively fuel-thrifty 4wd." Demand was good: 17,340 SX/4 and 5,602 Kammback Series 50 Eagles were manufactured, but the economy reduced sales of the larger, more expensive Series 30 Eagle sedans and wagons to about one quarter of 1980's production, 14,485 units.

BELOW: With the new roof treatment, which included opera or quarter windows, a revised grille, and elegant new wheel covers, the Concord D/L sedan looked a bit more luxurious than it had before, and it was still a strong seller, though noticeably less so in this difficult year for the auto industry. As always, Concord offered excellent value for the money, in a car that was comfortable and strongly reliable. And like all American Motors automobiles, Concord was protected by its singular Buyer Protection Plan, a comprehensive twelve-month, 12,000-mile (19,312-kilometer) warranty with unique benefits.

Concord

One Tough American Economy Car.

Concord remained much the same, but all AMC cars benefitted from an updated 4.2-liter (258-cu.-in.) six-cylinder engine. It was 90 pounds (40.8 kilograms) lighter, smoother, quieter, and more fuel efficient. Removing unneeded iron from the engine block provided a 30-pound (13.6-kilogram) reduction, with another 12 pounds (5.4 kilograms) removed from the cylinder head. Finally, the stamped valve cover was replaced by a new glass-filled nylon piece, saving 19 pounds (8.6 kilograms). In all, 55,097 examples of the lighter, more efficient Concords were built.

Spirit

These cars are built to last.

AMC announced that "Spirit is offered in 2 body styles: sedan and liftback. The liftback's efficient design allows for exceptionally easy cargo storage. And room enough to hold what many larger cars just can't handle. The Spirit sedan offers traditionally appealing design and comfort. Inside, the fold down rear seat provides extra cargo space." With prices starting at $5,090 for the base sedan, $5,589 for the upscale D/L

There was little that could be done to update or refresh the Spirit line for 1981, and the company was short of development funds due to its heavy investment in the upcoming new Renault R-9 sedans to be produced in Kenosha, along with the all-new Jeep XJ wagons that were to replace the J-Series Jeep wagons. As before, the D/L had an excellent value story to tell, and it had a reputation as a strong, well-built subcompact. In a better market it probably would have sold much better than it did.

ABOVE: All American Motors automobiles received Ziebart Factory Rust Protection, which came with a five-year, no-rust-through warranty, along with the American Motors Buyer Protection Plan, Because AMC's rust protection was applied as the car was being built, the company didn't need to drill holes in the body to spray in the sealant as was the case with aftermarket application. World War II veteran Buell Martin of Connecticut, bought this Concord D/L new and drove it for years.

BELOW: Here's a 1981 AMC Spirit Sedan dressed up with a neat rally side stripe and wire wheel covers, plus a handy—and handsome—roof rack. This car may actually be a Styling Department mockup, as the rocker panel molding doesn't appear to be the same as that used on production models. All Spirits this year were given a new grille treatment with a bright cross centered in it, giving them a slight appearance change. AMC stylists experimented with luxury and sporty appearance option packages on several Spirit mockups; all were attractive, but they couldn't convince management to authorize production.

Liftback, these durable compacts made a good case for buyers. But with the economy slowly starting to improve and gas prices becoming manageable again, Spirit's appeal was fading: 44,619 were produced, 26,413 less than the previous year.

Although most enthusiasts don't know it, American Motors offered several fleet versions of its four-wheel-drive Eagle models. The so-called Fleet Eagle could be ordered in Base Concord interior and exterior trim to effect a lower price. These were useful for companies that needed a light 4WD vehicle but wanted to save on the expense of buying a full-size truck or SUV. The Fleet Eagle also provided them with much better fuel economy. Some police departments also ordered Fleet Eagles with base interior trim but heavy-duty suspension and brakes suitable for police work. Seen here is one the many Eagles operated by the California Highway Patrol.

The Results

On December 18, 1981, the *New York Times* announced: "The company has reported losses totaling $88 million this year, in addition to a loss of $156 million in 1980." Renault increased its share of AMC to 46.4 percent by the end of 1980. Since Renault had been nationalized in 1946, the French government now essentially owned the fiercely independent, proudly American AMC.

1982

Eagle

It's a switch from every other car in the world.

That switch was the unique Select-Drive transmission, standard on all Eagles beginning in 1982. The only downside to full-time four-wheel drive was reduced fuel economy, but with Select-Drive, the Eagle could change over from 4WD to 2WD at

RIGHT: The Eagle Kammback for 1982 continued to offer excellent value for money in a small 4WD automobile. However, both the factory and its dealers mostly ignored the Kammback's potential, and sales were accordingly dismal. In a short message to dealers sent midyear, the factory announced it was ending production of the Kammback prior to the end of the model year. This meant that the Spirit Sedan would also be dropped from the line, since the two models shared the same body.

BELOW: Although sales of the attractive Eagle SX/4 never reached their expected heights, due to the poor economy experienced nationally from 1980 to 1983, it was a fun car to drive and extremely capable in light off-road driving. The five-spoke alloy wheels seen on the car were an expensive option and thus rarely seen today.

the flip of a switch. That sounds more convenient than it was in practice, because the vehicle would first have to be stopped before engaging or disengaging the four-wheel drive. A small inconvenience, though, since the savings was 1 mile per gallon (.43 kilometer per liter) or more in 2WD mode.

Eagles were now available with a five-speed Aisin Seiki manual transmission, a first for AMC. While Series 50 production was down (10,445 SX/4, 520 Kammback), the bigger Series 30 Eagles almost doubled to 26,958, mostly wagons.

Concord

Born tough.

The entire auto industry had moved away from making major changes to models every year to the incremental approach George Romney had promoted in the 1950s. Again, Concord's updates were minor trim changes, but 43,810 were assembled, with almost half of those four-door sedans.

Spirit

The high mileage Spirit.

The slow-selling Spirit Sedan was due to be canceled, but 820 were built early in the model year, possibly to use remaining components in inventory. Spirit (and Concord) were just marking time until the new AMC/Renault compact car arrived. Still, 20,182 Spirit Liftbacks were built that year.

ABOVE: An attractive optional paint treatment was offered for 1982 on Concord D/L and Limited models, although it may have been a bit too bold for many customers, even if it brightened up dealer showrooms. This Concord Limited two-door, with wire wheel covers, is a handsome and obviously luxurious car for folks looking to downsize from the typical big American cars while retaining all the luxury and quiet smoothness that big cars offered.

BELOW: The Concord D/L station wagon for 1982. The woodgrain side treatment was standard on the D/L wagons, but occasionally a dealer would order a car for stock without it, just to be able to offer something with a different look. Woodgrain panels on station wagons, long in vogue, were beginning to go out of favor with the buying public. The optional spoke wheels seen on this wagon are a nice touch and make the car look younger and sportier. But 1982 was one of the worst years ever for the auto industry, as a poor economy caused sales to dry up even more.

The Results

On January 6, 1982, the *New York Times* offered a grim assessment: "The automobile industry closed the books today on its worst sales year in almost two decades, recording total car sales of 7,978,487, a 6.3 percent decline from 1981 and the weakest performance since 7.55 million were sold in 1963." AMC posted a loss of $153.5 million.

Then the *Washington Post* announced on January 16, 1982,

> Gerald C. Meyers resigned as chairman and chief executive officer of the struggling American Motors Corp. yesterday in a shakeup of top management that appears to have been engineered by AMC's French partner, Régie Nationale Des Usines Renault. Meyers' departure after four years as chairman surprised auto industry analysts on Wall Street. . . . AMC announced after a meeting of its directors that Meyers, 53, will be succeeded as chairman and chief executive officer by W. Paul Tippett Jr., 49, who had been president for the past three years. The new president, viewed by industry analysts as the key figure, is Jose J. Dedeurwaerder, a former Renault executive who joined AMC in October. "This looks like another step in the Renault takeover of AMC," said David Healy, auto industry analyst at Drexel Burnham Lambert.

1983

Eagle

Intelligent Choices for Family Travel.

The 1983 dealer brochure asked, "Just how reliable is the remarkable Eagle? Ask the National Ski Patrol. They've named the American Eagle their official vehicle. And remember, they're the people who have to get to the slopes, often when roads are impassable to ordinary cars." The California Highway Patrol also purchased Eagle wagons for their mountain regions. Rural letter carriers, who purchase their own vehicles, loved Eagle wagons. That was a significant measure of the Eagle's capabilities.

This is the Eagle SX/4 for 1983. Not much was new, which is understandable because this was scheduled to be the final year for the smaller Eagle automobiles. The Kammback had been dropped months earlier (along with the Spirit Sedan), and the company was also dropping its conventional two-wheel-drive models, Spirit and Concord. One can't help but wish the company had tried to rebuild sales volume with simple additions like a Concord GT, a Spirit Sedan GT, or variations of Eagle models, but the effort wasn't made.

ABOVE LEFT: The final year for the AMC Spirit was 1983, and for that year the company dropped the base model, although it may have produced some at the beginning of the model run or perhaps for a fleet order. This year, AMC added the Spirit GT as a model rather than an option package. This was a good move, since customer interest was trending toward better-equipped, better-trimmed cars. With a base price of $6,495, the six-cylinder GT was a value-oriented, sporty car that was great fun to drive.

ABOVE RIGHT: The Concord base models were likewise gone for 1983, though whether any may have been produced for fleet sales is unknown. Detailed production records for the last years of AMC were not available at the time of writing. The Concord line was now being pitched as The Tough Americans, as AMC car styling had become stale after so many years with little change. It's a shame the company didn't authorize the new sheet-metal changes created by the styling staff: they could have increased sales dramatically. But Renault, now effectively owners of AMC, did not want to spend any money to keep the AMC brand alive. Their only interest was in Renault-branded products.

The poor-selling Series 30 two-door sedan was dropped from the lineup in 1983. The Iron Duke four-cylinder remained the standard engine initially, only to be replaced later in the year by AMC's own four-cylinder, the 150-cu.-in. Hurricane, adapted from its famous 258 six.

Roy Lunn explained, "Unlike most engines available today (it) was not designed for passenger cars and then adapted for trucks. We specifically developed it with our Jeep vehicles and Eagle in mind. That's the reason that performance and durability were of such prime consideration from the very beginning."

Now AMC no longer paid a markup to GM for the Iron Duke, and the more powerful Hurricane would be the standard powerplant on the all-new 1984 Jeep Cherokee. Just 2,259 of the Series 50 SX/4 Eagles were produced, while 3,093 four-door sedans and 12,378 four-door wagons of the larger Series 30 Eagles were built.

Concord

Known by the standards we keep.

The Concord carried on with just the four-door sedan and wagon. Starting at $6,995, Concords were fully equipped with full vinyl top, 258-cu.-in. six, reclining front seats, and

RIGHT: This photograph, dated November 1979, shows the styling direction that American Motors designers were planning for the next facelift of the Concord sedan. The reskinned Concord, which might have been introduced for 1983 or 1984, had a much more contemporary look, much like the popular Chrysler LeBaron, yet would have required only minor retooling. The rear fenders have been extended to provide a more substantial look while improving trunk space. The sail panel is squared off and the rear window more vertical, to improve rear seat headroom while also imparting a lighter, airier feel to the cabin. The opera windows are now a part of the door assembly. Thick wheel opening moldings lend a feeling of elegance and taste.

BELOW: AMC stylists and modelers also created an elegant new look for the Concord two-door sedan. In this view, the sail-panel opera window has been eliminated, replaced by a half-vinyl top with a bright band that creates the opera-window look instead. Most of the four-door sedan versions of the restyled Concord sedan didn't use a vinyl top at all, which would have created a noticeable savings in production costs.

much more, including Ziebart factory rust protection and the five-year no rust-through warranty. But the future was clear: only 4,433 sedans and 867 wagons were built.

Spirit

Does a Number on the Competition.

That number was $6,495, fully equipped. The only engine offered now was the 258 six, and the only model available was the sporty Spirit GT liftback. With a legacy dating back to the 1970 Gremlin, it was clear the Spirit's days were short, especially since AMC was preparing a thoroughly modern compact for introduction. Just 3,491 Spirits were assembled in its final year.

ABOVE: From the 1983 sales brochure: a Spirit GT with a burning foundry fire in the background, which was meant to impress possible buyers with the great strength and durability of AMC cars. The 1983 Spirit GT goes into the history books as the last new model introduced by American Motors. It's too bad not many were sold, as they were fine cars to drive, with the feel of a true grand touring automobile. But after this year the only AMC-branded cars sold in America would be Eagles.

The Results

The Renault Alliance was launched in June 1982 as a 1983 model. The new model, available in two- and four-door sedan versions, won major industry awards like "Motor Trend Car of the Year" and ranked first on *Car and Driver*'s "Ten Best" list. *MotorWeek* described it as "a fine, thrifty, good-handling, roomy, highly-domesticated European sedan that's made in the U.S." Renault spent $150 million updating the Kenosha Lakefront plant for Alliance production, shifting the remaining AMC automobiles to the Brampton, Ontario, plant outside Toronto.

United Press International brought more troubling news of AMC's fortunes: "American Motors Corp. Tuesday reported its fourth straight annual deficit—a 1983 loss of $146.7 million—but broke a string of 14 quarterly losses by reporting a $7.4 million fourth quarter profit. The No. 4 automaker's 1983 loss means AMC has lost $637.5 million in the last four years."

On a positive note, the AM General division of AMC won its initial Army contract to produce 55,000 High Mobility Multipurpose Wheeled Vehicles (better known as Humvees) over a five-year period. That's right, the iconic military Hummer was originally an AMC product!

RIGHT: This painting of the proposed reskinning of the Concord—which would have been shared with the Eagle models—shows how rich and elegant it might have looked. The rear view shows how wrapping the taillamps around the bodysides would have added visual width to the body, as would the longer bright trim molding between the taillamps. Thicker, heavier-looking bumpers would lend a feeling of strength and solidity to exterior. The wire wheel covers here are an extra-nice touch.

MOTOR TREND
CAR OF THE
Kenosha
CLEARANCE
14 FT. – 0 IN.

Foreshadowing the end of AMC-branded car production, the walkway over 52nd street in Kenosha announced the company's new Renault Alliance, which had been named *Motor Trend* Car of the Year. It was a great honor, one that hadn't been bestowed on an AMC car since 1964, but by this time it was a sad one. Notice that the Renault name is bigger and stands over American Motors. Also, even though this photo was taken in the heart of Kenosha, most of the cars on the road are not AMCs.

1984–1988

CHAPTER

7

THE EAGLE YEARS

It was an exciting time at American Motors. In 1983 the Kenosha Plant began producing the Renault Alliance, an Americanized version of the Renault 9, a family sedan that sold well in Europe. It was the familiar AMC storyline: the right automobile at the right time. America was still mired in the economic malaise that permeated the country in the late 1970s, and with high inflation, continuing unemployment, and intractable gas prices, AMC and Renault had found the perfect time to stage a comeback.

ABOVE: The Eagle sedan for 1984. The four-cylinder engine and four-speed transmission were still standard equipment, even though almost no one ever ordered them that way. Eagle was a high-end product that attracted high-end buyers used to the best. One wonders why AMC didn't at least make the five-speed transmission standard equipment, since it offered a better fuel economy rating while also making the four-cylinder engine a viable choice. Another question remains: why didn't AMC offer the optional Sport Package on the Eagle sedan this year? It would have been easy to do and certainly would have boosted sales.

OPPOSITE TOP: Under orders from their Renault masters, AMC's marketing people dropped the two-wheel-drive models from the AMC line, leaving the Eagle 4WD models as the only AMC-branded cars remaining. The Eagle line had been progressively trimmed as well: the SX/4 was dropped, and the Kammback and Eagle two-door sedan had been discontinued earlier. AMC dealers were left with just the senior Eagle four-door sedan in a single trim level, roughly equivalent to the old D/L designation used on Concord/Spirit, with four-door station wagon in that trim and also as a Limited model.

OPPOSITE BOTTOM: A January 1980 mockup of a restyled Eagle sedan. This is probably the restyled Concord mockup seen earlier, but it now wears Eagle wheel covers and has been jacked up to imitate a four-wheel-drive setup. Note that this car lacks the Eagle fender flares and, as observed under high magnification, wears a Concord Limited badge on the front fender. Other mockups have been found sporting wheel flares. It's a shame the company couldn't convince Renault to let them perform the minor restyling that could have allowed AMC cars to remain in production a little longer.

This print advertisement for the 1984 Eagle Limited station wagon is eye catching, but we wonder how many prospects felt its claim was exaggerated. Rest assured, the Eagle could go through just about any sort of terrain, even high banks of snow. When equipped with a powerful six-cylinder engine and automatic transmission, Eagle's full-time four-wheel-drive would constantly adjust power and torque to each axle to make its way through any conditions, even ice or snowy hills. The full-time system was especially helpful when driving on highways that were a mix of dry and wet, as the driver didn't need to shift in and out of 4WD to meet conditions. Select Drive could handle any road.

As part of this effort, the Jeep division announced its most important product ever, the 1984 Jeep XJ Cherokee. This was the first truly modern sport-utility vehicle (SUV), with AMC's famed unibody construction in two- and four-door versions. Cherokee offered as an option the innovative new Selec-Trac four-wheel-drive system, similar to the one fitted to the Eagle, and the standard engine was AMC's new 2.5-liter (150-cu.-in.) "Hurricane" four-cylinder, an engine developed from the famed 4.2-liter six.

As always, AMC was a pioneer in other areas. Both the Alliance and the Cherokee were created using cutting-edge 3D computer-aided design, thanks to Renault's partnership with French aerospace company Dassault Systèmes. The rest of the 1980s would be interesting indeed.

1984

Eagle

We just bought our four-year-old an American Eagle.

With all the new products flowing out of the AMC/Renault partnership, little attention was given to the existing AMC automobiles. For 1984 the Spirit was dropped. So were the sporty Eagle S/4, Kammback, and two-door sedan models. That left the Eagle four-door sedan, and the Eagle and luxury Eagle Limited station wagon as the sole survivors.

Advertising for the Eagle changed. The car's off-road capabilities were no longer emphasized, and this would be the last year the Eagle was the official vehicle of the National Ski Patrol. Now Eagle's on-road assets were promoted: safety and security in bad weather. Marketing studies showed Eagle owners rarely went off-road, just like few SUVs and Crossovers today ever leave the pavement.

The GM-sourced Iron Duke four was replaced by the new AMC Hurricane I-4 engine as the standard engine. The company stated, "All major engine functions are microprocessor controlled including spark, fuel, air injection (pulse air) and carburetion." This was high tech

This photo, taken in 1984, shows an AMC employee working at his machine in the AMC Stamping Plant where the bodies and structural panels were stamped out on huge, expensive stamping machines. During 1984, AMC operations were working regular shifts plus some overtime, as the new Renault Alliance and Encore models were selling at a very good pace. The market for subcompact cars was going strong at this point, but it soon faded as consumers once more became interested in big cars and, especially, SUVs.

for the time, but the Hurricane was too underpowered for the Eagle, and just 184 were built. The trusty AMC 4.2-liter six was again a popular option, delivering a fine 20 miles per gallon (8.5 kilometers per liter) city, 28 miles per gallon (12 kilometers per liter) highway.

The Results

AMC's Kenosha plant ramped up to 900 cars per day to keep up with the demand for the compact Alliance sedan and the new Encore hatchback. Jeep's XJ Cherokee and Wagoneer were also major successes, keeping the Toledo operations humming. The Brampton plant, however, produced just 25,535 secure, stylish Eagles, 4,241 sedans, and 21,294 wagons.

MAKE	AMC	
Model	Eagle Sedan	Eagle Station Wagon
Passengers	5	5
Doors	4	4
Wheelbase (inches/centimeters)	109.3/278	109.3/278
Engine (Standard)	151 cu. in., OHV I-4, 82 hp	151 cu. in., OHV I-4, 82 hp
Engine (Optional)	258 cu. in., OHV I-6, 110 hp	258 cu. in., OHV I-6, 110 hp
Production	4,241	21,294

Total American Motors Production: 25,535

Taken inside the American Motors Styling Studios, this photo shows how nice the Eagle Kammback (and Spirit Sedan, for that matter) could have looked if only someone in management had authorized production. Fitted with a flatter Concord hood and senior Eagle grille, plus blacked-out B-pillars and fat tires mounted on wire wheels, this vehicle still looks fresh and attractive today. It wears a Spirit badge, so it could be viewed as either a Spirit GT sedan or an Eagle Kammback. To enhance the Eagle viewing, taller jacks would have been placed underneath it. The car wears 1979 Michigan license plates, so apparently it was registered and probably driven on the road. We wonder if it survives somewhere, an unknown treasure waiting to be discovered.

1985

Eagle

Get the best of weather. Fight back.

Make it Eagle.

Marketing analysis also discovered another interesting fact: most Eagle buyers were affluent. A TV ad for the Eagle showed a wagon pulling out of a garage with a Mercedes-Benz parked next to it. The scene then moved inside the Eagle, with a confident mother reassuring a worried child that bad weather would not be an issue. This was the Eagle difference, something no other automobile at the time could provide.

The 1985 Eagle received a minor styling update—the domed hood and grille from the defunct Eagle S/4—while the only engine now available was the excellent 110-horsepower, 4.2-liter inline six.

The Results

AMC's Kenosha plant was no longer struggling to keep up with the demand for compact Renaults. The economy was rapidly improving, and auto buyers' interest was moving on to bigger vehicles. Jeep's Toledo plants were still busy building their traditional Wrangler, J-10 pickup, and full-sized Grand Wagoneer along with the very successful smaller XJ Cherokee and Wagoneer.

The Brampton plant assembled 16,190 Eagles, 2,655 sedans, and 13,535 wagons.

MAKE	AMC	
Model	Eagle Sedan	Eagle Station Wagon
Passengers	5	5
Doors	4	4
Wheelbase (inches/centimeters)	109.3/278	109.3/278
Engine (Standard)	258 cu. in., OHV I-6, 110 hp	258 cu. in., OHV I-6, 110 hp
Production	2,655	13,535

Total American Motors Production: 16,190

American Motors finally was able to make a very minor styling update to the Eagle cars in 1985, when it began installing the old Gremlin/Kammback/SX/4 hood and grille on the senior Eagles. The change was minor, but at least it made the cars look a little different than previous models. To add to its basic value, while also reducing complexity on the assembly line, the 4.2-liter AMC six-cylinder engine and five-speed transmission were made standard equipment. This combination was actually ordered by a fair number of buyers, though the six/automatic drivetrain was by far the most popular.

1986

Eagle

The beauty of four-wheel drive.

If you've ever been caught in an unexpected thunderstorm or snow squall, you know the beauty of four-wheel drive. And the finest in the flock of 4WD options was the Eagle Limited: "The security and practicality of 4WD plus 'first class' accommodations . . . that's Eagle Wagon Limited. This most elegant Eagle includes all of the thoughtful standards on the base wagon plus supple leather upholstered seats, plush 18 oz. carpeting (12 oz. in the cargo area), a smart woodgrain steering wheel, a convenient parcel shelf, dual chrome, remote-control rearview mirrors, and wire wheel covers."

The 1986 Eagle Limited station wagon. American Motors offered the same three models this year as it had in 1985, with little change other than some minor improvements. Fuel economy ratings for the Eagle this year were 16 miles per gallon (6.8 kilometers per liter) city and 19 miles per gallon (8 kilometers per liter) highway with the automatic transmission, and 17 miles per gallon (7.2 kilometers per liter) city, 22 miles per gallon (8.9 kilometers per liter) highway with the standard five-speed manual transmission. As more efficient new cars and SUVs were coming to market, these fuel economy numbers were not as attractive as they had been in previous years.

There was also an optional Eagle Wagon Sport package with special black accenting and 4×4 graphics, steel-belted radials, halogen headlamps and fog lamps, black remote-control rearview sport mirror, and a leather-wrapped steering wheel. There were still plenty of reasons for an affluent suburbanite to buy one for their family, but with Renault calling the shots, few knew the Eagle still existed. The success of the modern XJ Cherokee and Wagoneer also greatly eroded sales.

The Results

Like their namesake, the great American bald eagle, 1986 Eagles are rare: 8,217 were built, 1,274 sedans, and 6,943 wagons.

MAKE	AMC	
Model	Eagle Sedan	Eagle Station Wagon
Passengers	5	5
Doors	4	4
Wheelbase (inches/centimeters)	109.3/278	109.3/278
Engine (Standard)	258 cu. in., OHV I-6, 110 hp	258 cu. in., OHV I-6, 110 hp
Production	1,274	6,943

Total American Motors Production: 8,217

1987

Eagle

Hustlin'

And relaxin' and loadin' and haulin' and pickin'. What little marketing effort the company put into promoting the Eagle emphasized its versatility and safety. AMC had carved a comfortably profitable niche for its product, something the company had always been best at—just look at the success of the 1956 Rambler, 1958–1963 American, 1968 Javelin and AMX, 1970 Hornet and Gremlin, and so many other landmark automobiles.

The Results

Just 5,203 Eagles were built at the Brampton plant, 751 sedans, and 4,452 wagons.

On March 10, 1987, the headline in the *Washington Post* read: "Chrysler to Buy American Motors." The story continued.

> Chrysler Corp. yesterday announced plans to buy American Motors Corp. for a total of more than $1.5 billion in a deal that would reduce to three the number of home-grown U.S. car manufacturers. The buyout proposal is contained in a letter of intent signed by Chrysler and French auto maker Regie Nationale des Usines Renault, which owns 46.1 percent of AMC. . . . AMC, which has lost a total of $858.6 million since 1980, was

ROAD TEST: 1988 EAGLE WAGON

Owner: Alan Strang, Texas

On December 7, 1987, I went to my local AMC dealer to see a 1988 Eagle sales brochure. I was told by the sales manager that none were available, and that the AMC line was going to end on December 15 since Chrysler had decided to stop production. I was upset! What could we do? The end of AMC was just a week away, but perhaps I could save the last AMC built.

Alan Strang

The next day, I called the AMC Brampton plant and talked to the production manager. Sure enough, the Eagle line was shutting down on Friday, December 11—just four days away. I told him I wanted to buy the last AMC. On December 10, Alan McPhee, AMC Public Relations Manager called me. He told me that the car was not presold, and it was going to a dealership in Oklahoma City. As soon as I had the information on the car, I called the dealer. I told them that they would be getting the last Eagle built and I wanted to buy it. I made arrangements to drive to Oklahoma City and dolly the car back to California. I arrived on January 19, 1988, completed the necessary paperwork, and left as the owner of the last AMC!

The 1986 Eagle Limited station wagon was an attractive car, especially with the alloy wheels seen here. The entire Eagle lineup, from beginning to end, was really America's first example of crossover SUVs: they combined a passenger-car chassis and body with four-wheel drive. In Eagle's case they were perhaps the best crossover vehicles of all time because the driveline was essentially the same as that used on the Jeep XJs and senior Jeeps. Although the Eagle's transfer case lacked the low range offered on Jeep vehicles, the combination of AMC's tenacious Select-Drive 4WD system and a chassis that sat much higher than a conventional car made the Eagles far superior in snowy, icy, or off-road driving, compared with a Subaru or similar 4WD automobile. *Tom & Kelly Glatch*

> too short of cash and product lines to survive much longer, according to auto industry analysts and officials. And with Renault experiencing severe financial and labor problems at home, it was only a matter of time before AMC's French benefactor took decisive steps to end its hemorrhaging in the United States, analysts and officials said.
>
> AMC's strength has been in its Jeep products—four-wheel-drive sports-utility vehicles such as the Jeep Wrangler and Wagoneer, and pickups like the Comanche. But the Japanese are zeroing in on those models also, leaving AMC desperate for new ammunition and the kind of undisputed marketing savvy exhibited by Lee Iacocca's Chrysler.
>
> "This merger can't do anything but good for us," said Peter Zourdos, director of the National Automobile Dealer Association's AMC dealers' group. "Chrysler has the wherewithal to do something for us. I'm very happy about this," said Zourdos, who was also president of Courtesy AMC-Jeep in Rockville.
>
> In addition to its Jeep lines—all technically classified as trucks—AMC will continue to manufacture, at least for the time being, its four-wheel-drive passenger car, the Eagle, according to company officials.

After the sale, Bob Lutz, Chrysler's then-president and chief operating officer—and one of the finest automotive minds in the industry—stood in awe of what AMC had accomplished, writing, "With almost no resources, and fighting a vastly superior enemy, they were able to roll out an impressive succession of new products."

MAKE	AMC	
Model	Eagle Sedan	Eagle Station Wagon
Passengers	5	5
Doors	4	4
Wheelbase (inches/centimeters)	109.3/278	109.3/278
Engine (Standard)	258 cu. in., OHV I-6, 110 hp	258 cu. in., OHV I-6, 110 hp
Production	751	4,452

Total American Motors Production: 5,203

1988

Eagle Wagon

With no fanfare and no advertising, Chrysler's new Jeep-Eagle Division fulfilled the existing orders and consumed the remaining component inventory of what they now called the Eagle Wagon. The window stickers, owner's manuals, and vehicle labels all still showed AMC's name and logo. The Eagle with the highest serial number was 2CCCK3866JB702306, but since AMC assigned the car's vehicle identification number at the acceptance of the order, not by assembly sequence, it was not the last Eagle assembled. A total of 2,305 1988 Eagle Wagons were produced, all of them before the end of the 1987 calendar year.

The Results

On December 11, 1987, Eagle 2CCCK3866JB701986 rolled off the Brampton line, the last Eagle—and the last AMC product—ever.

MAKE	EAGLE
Model	Eagle Wagon
Passengers	5
Doors	4
Wheelbase (inches/centimeters)	109.3/278
Engine (Standard)	258 cu. in., OHV I-6, 110 hp
Production	2,305

Total American Motors Production: 2,305

The final model year for Eagle was 1988, though all of the Eagles for this year had been produced toward the end of 1987. By this time, the line had shrunk to just a single station wagon model. Standard equipment included air conditioning, rear defroster, Extra Quiet insulation, halogen head lamps, AM/FM E.T. stereo, tilt steering wheel, and much more. There was no Limited model; instead, leather upholstery was an optional extra. A leather-wrapped steering wheel was standard. The initial AMC Data Book for the 1988 models says the styled wheel covers were standard, but at some point AMC made wire wheel covers standard instead.

1968–1975

Mech John Evans
Charlie Adams
CRANE Cams
Grant
REBEL ★ SST
DONOVAN
CHAMPION
SCHIEFER
JARDINE
GOODYEAR
VALVOLINE
RICHMOND
RAMBLER
SPARK O MATIC
MILFORD PA

CHAPTER

8

ON TRACK, AMC IN COMPETITION

"Because the only race Rambler cares about is the human race!" That ad from 1963, approved by AMC's then-President Roy Abernethy, summed up American Motors' philosophy on auto racing.

Under George Romney, American Motors had been against racing and joined the 1957 Automobile Manufacturers Association ban on the Detroit automakers from supporting competition. While the Big Three began ignoring the prohibition by the early 1960s, Romney and Abernethy were adamant in refusing to race. But when Roy Chapin Jr. was promoted to chairman in 1967, he knew the company had a huge image problem with the expanding youth market.

OPPOSITE TOP: Another well-known AMC racer, Grant Rambler, shown here with driver Charlie Adams's name emblazoned on the door.

OPPOSITE BOTTOM: The young but already well-known racer Jesse Snyder (in T-shirt), posing in front of the 1967 Rambler Rogue hardtop that he built for racing. In time Snyder's car became known as "the Fastest Rambler in the World." One of Snyder's enthusiastic sponsors was Richmond Rambler, a Rambler dealership in Staten Island, New York. Note the Rambler's redline tires, a high-performance car must for the "right" look.

LEFT: The big show for American Motors' early racing efforts was the popular Trans-American Championship series, which saw many of the era's pony cars competing with each other for glory—and the usual resulting uptick in dealer sales. Shown here is the new team at a pitstop during its initial race at Sebring in Florida. AMC's red-white-and-blue racing colors dazzled the crowd, who hadn't been expecting to see such a bold a car from the company.

AMC's sudden involvement in motorsports competition was out of character for the company. This ad shows the multipronged assault AMC was making in the field, and the surprising success they were having in all forms of racing. *Tom Glatch Collection*

On September 26, 1967, AMC's manager of product information, Carl Chakmakian, was promoted to manager of the newly formed Performance Activities Department. "Basically, the program is intended to assist our dealers and customers by developing the 'hardware' required for competition on the drag strips and in sedan racing," said AMC's vice president of marketing, William McNealy.

Chakmakian began contacting the major performance parts manufacturers, first to discover what they currently made for AMC engines, and then to encourage them to develop new products. Those performance components were added to the dealers' Parts Catalog F-14072. In the catalog, regular parts were arranged by vehicle location: Group 1–Engine, Group 9–Rear Axle-Propeller Shaft, Group 17–Standard Parts. Chakmakian used an available slot for what became the famous "Group 19–High Performance Equipment."

In the January 1969 issue of *Car Life*, Allan Gridler wrote, "Few Javelin or AMX owners will run at Bonneville, or in professional road races, but they are showing up at dragstrips and slaloms in rapidly increasing numbers. What the professional does serves as a good example for the amateur racer, or the driver who simply wants a more satisfying car."

American Motors would never be the same.

Land Speed Records

The all-new AMX was going to launch at the 1968 Chicago Auto Show. How to make the event unforgettable? Why not hire the fastest man and woman on earth, Craig Breedlove and his wife Lee, to set multiple land speed records with the new AMX? In 1965 Craig drove his jet-powered "Spirit of America – Sonic I" to 600.601 miles per hour (966.57 kilometers per hour) on the Bonneville Salt Flats, while Lee drove the same car 308.506 miles per hour (496.49 kilometers per hour), both world records.

Craig Breedlove had pitched a similar record-setting concept to Ford and Chevrolet to no avail, but, as he told author Richard Truesdale,

> December 1, 1967, I got a phone call from AMC's Performance Activities Manager Carl Chakmakian to discuss putting the AMX through its paces. He asked if I would be interested. The problem was the time constraints, the AMX was to be introduced at the Chicago Auto Show on February 23, 1968, and AMC wanted to make a big splash. Carl said that he could get me two cars before Christmas. They actually arrived at my shop in Torrance (California) on December 17, 1967. This meant that we would have less

than six weeks, rather than the six months we really needed, to get the cars properly prepared. Right off I knew we would have a big problem in that the 10-mile course at Bonneville wouldn't be available in February due to the seasonal flooding. Since I owned a Goodyear tire store at the time, I was able to secure the use of their five-mile circular track in San Angelo, Texas, for the run.

The plan was to run two cars, one powered by the AMC 290-cu.-in. engine for Class C records, and the other with a 390-cu.-in. engine for Class B. Both engines were built by Traco Engineering, the Culver City, California, shop that had backed Billy Vukovich's 1953–1954 Indy 500 victories. Founders Jim Travers and Frank Coon turned their expertise into one of the most successful engine builders then in motorsports.

For the Breedloves' run, the United States Auto Club (USAC) was on hand to sanction any national and international closed course records, as well as American and national unlimited records.

"We ran the Class C car first. The plan was to go as hard as possible for twenty-four hours." That record run was not without pitfalls, as Lee had a flat tire while running 156 miles per hour (251 kilometers per hour), and Craig had the headlights go out in the dark desert night, but they completed the twenty-four hours. A few days later they made the same attempt with the Class B AMX, but the transmission failed after eight hours. They couldn't make repairs for another attempt as "we were out of time since the cars had to be shipped to the Chicago Auto Show the following week."

Yet the 290 AMX covered 3,378 miles (5,436 kilometers) in twenty-four hours at an average speed of over 140 miles per hour (225 kilometers per hour), 38 miles per hour (61 kilometers per hour) over the old record, breaking every Class C record from

This press photo, taken in February 1968 at the Chicago Auto Show, shows some of the main spark plugs behind AMC's new performance image. *Left to right:* AMC Performance Activities Manager Carl Chakmakian, who joined Nash-Kelvinator before AMC was formed; AMC President William Luneburg; race car drivers Lee Breedlove and her husband, Craig Breedlove; and AMC CEO Roy D. Chapin Jr. Behind them is Lee Breedlove's record-setting AMX coupe.

15.5 miles (25 kilometers) to twenty-four hours, for a total of ninety new records. And the 390 AMX set sixteen new Class B records in its shortened run; one of those, for 621.371 miles (1,000 kilometers) standing start, the AMX averaged 156.548 miles per hour (251.939 kilometers per hour)—the old record had been 148.702 miles per hour (239.312 kilometers per hour).

"In looking back on the effort it's really remarkable all that we accomplished," said Craig Breedlove. "After all, American Motors was a small company in comparison to GM and Ford, but the AMX was a remarkable car."

Later in 1968, Craig took three specially prepared production Javelins to the Bonneville Salt Flats. Record runs that year were thwarted by flooded salt, but Breedlove's 304-powered Bonneville Speed Spectacular Javelin, equipped with the special "Breedlove" roof-mounted spoiler, still set a flying mile mark of 161.733 miles per hour (260.284 kilometers per hour) in the C/Production class, the rear tires spinning on the wet salt. The record stood for several years.

Trans-Am

Even before AMXs were heading toward Craig Breedlove's shop, two Javelins were on a truck to Ronnie Kaplan Engineering in Elk Grove Village, Illinois. Veteran racers Ronnie Kaplan and Jim Jeffords were hired by Carl Chakmakian to prepare the newly launched Javelins for the SCCA Trans-Am Championship series for 1968.

Like Breedlove's record-breaking AMXs, Trans-Am racers were production based, driving under strict rules that allowed only minor modifications and safety equipment. Any new developments would need factory part numbers and be added to Group 19. With minimal performance parts to work with, Kaplan's task would be difficult. At least he had the services of two of the finest drivers of the era, George Follmer and Peter Revson. They turned to Traco Engineering for the team's first engines, AMC 290 V-8s bored to the 305-cu.-in. maximum allowed, before building their own.

The team missed the series opener at the 24 Hours of Daytona in January but tested in February at Riverside Raceway for the next event, the Sebring 12 Hours in March. Both cars were surprisingly fast at Sebring, but Follmer dropped out while Revson finished 12th. In May, the red-white-and-blue Javelins were 2nd and 4th at New Mannford, Oklahoma, and at Mid-Ohio the pair qualified 1–2.

By the end of the season, AMC was the only factory-sponsored team to complete all twelve races, finishing second six times and placing third and fourth twice each behind champion Mark Donohue and his Roger Penske Camaro. AMC placed third in the manufacturers' points, with 51 to the factory Ford Mustang team's 59 in second. "We are making progress all the time, but the Javelins are making more progress faster," Donohue told *Autotopics* magazine. "They could catch up."

NASCAR also created a new Grand Touring Division with Trans-Am–like cars racing on ovals and road courses. Paul Connors of West Palm Beach, Florida, ran a few races in 1968 in his

Javelin. The following year, veteran driver Jim Paschal in Goodyear distributor Ross Huggins's well-funded Javelin earned five victories and placed third in the manufacturer standings.

The Trans-Am team should have done better in 1969, too, but internal feuding between Kaplan and Jeffords and the loss of drivers Follmer and Revson to other teams made the year a complete disaster. Donohue and Penske's Camaro won for the second straight year, and the best the Javelins could muster was two 4th place and one 5th place finish, resulting in just fourteen points.

AMC wasn't happy with Kaplan's results, and Penske was himself unhappy with Chevrolet's lack of support despite delivering two championships. Penske reached out to AMC, and a three-year contract rumored to be worth $2 million or more made the Roger Penske/Mark Donohue dream team AMC's. The two-page ad in *Car Life* for June 1970 said it all: "From Zero to Donohue in 3.1 Years!"

Donohue called out the foundation of Penske Racing for an "unfair advantage" of engineering, preparation, and a focus on doing things different from the competition. The team built two 1970 Javelins to their immaculate standards, with Penske's longtime partner, Traco Engineering, supplying the 305-cu.-in. engines. Penske bragged they would win seven races in 1970, but this was the only year all pony car manufacturers had factory-supported teams in Trans-Am: Ford, Chevrolet, Pontiac, Dodge, Plymouth, and AMC. Parnelli Jones and his Bud Moore Boss 302 Mustang won the championship on the strength of six victories out of eleven races.

Penske's boast of winning seven races might have been realized, but engine reliability issues early in the season handed three of those races to Jones. Still, Donohue and the Javelin

The number 25 Javelin is quickly back in the race and is seen here blowing through a corner at high speed. This photograph was taken by someone hired by AMC's Carl Chakmakian to record the new team's first year in Trans-Am racing.

The legend and his works. Performance Manager Carl Chakmakian poses here with many of the projects he conceived and sponsored on behalf of American Motors. Included are a pair of Javelin Trans-Am cars, the Grant Rebel Funny Car (showing off its chassis and engine), plus the three Javelin Speed Spectaculars used as prizes in a countrywide AMC contest. The race cars brought glory and recognition to American Motors and its dealers, while the Speed Spectaculars also brought in many prospective customers.

finished the year in second with three wins. It was "basically a who's who of American racing," factory Dodge driver Sam Posey told author Gary Witzenburg. "The fact that Donohue and Jones dueled with each other for the championship was so significant, because Parnelli was the apotheosis of the Indy driver of the time, the best there was, and Mark was competitive with him. Those two guys defined the competitiveness and excellence of that series."

NASCAR changed the race's name to the Grand American Division, and Jim Paschal was a victor in ten races out of thirty-five, finishing second in the championship. It was Paschal's last season in the series, which only continued for one more year.

For 1971, Penske and Donohue based their new cars on the updated Javelin body, building to even higher standards. Penske sold the old cars to privateer Roy Woods Racing, who updated them to the 1971 body. AMC would be the only manufacturer backing a Trans-Am team this year, with the Big Three canceling their support of most forms of motorsport. Donohue now claimed seven victories out of ten races (including six straight), plus George Follmer took the last race of the season with Roy Woods's Javelin. The championship was AMC's, scoring 82 points to Ford's 61 and Chevrolet's 17.

Penske's Javelins were sold to Roy Woods Racing for 1972, since Penske and Donohue wanted to focus now on NASCAR. With George Follmer again at the wheel, the Woods Javelins claimed four wins out of six events, and Follmer was crowned champion. This would be the last year of the pony car–based Trans-Am series—and AMC went out a winner!

NASCAR

And for Donohue and Penske's next act—NASCAR. The series was expanding out of its Deep South roots, which would give Penske's sponsors greater visibility. They commissioned the famed duo of Dick Hutcherson and Eddie Pagan to build their 1972 Matador Coupe, hired former Holman-Moody crew chief Ray Elder, and tapped Traco Engineering to provide the 355-cu.-in. AMC engines. As usual, the best of everything, yet they knew they were in unfamiliar territory. "We are coming down here very humbly," said Donohue.

Running a limited schedule of twelve out of thirty-one races in 1972, Mark Donohue competed in four events, Dave Marcis in seven, and Donnie Allison in one. Their best finish was 3rd on June 18 at Riverside with Allison driving.

Penske again ran ten out of thirty-one races in 1973 with the "flying brick" Matador. Donohue started the year off right with the team's first NASCAR victory, at Riverside in the January 21 Winston Western 500. One of Donohue's unfair advantages was using four-wheel disc brakes, common in most forms of racing then but not in NASCAR, which was slow to adapt. Mark led 138 of the race's 191 laps on the California road course, telling *National Speed Sport News*, "My brakes were better . . . I could go deeper into the turns." Donohue ran one more race, then commitments in other series had NASCAR's Dave Marcis and Penske's Indy car driver Gary Bettenhausen take over. Marcis finished 8th at the Mason-Dixon 500 at Dover in June.

ABOVE: Ike Knupp in the very fast T.E.A.M.-created Number 60 AMX race car. The appearance of the red-white-and-blue competition cars from American Motors created mixed reactions, some folks welcoming AMC to the racing community, others loudly making fun of the company. Most of the critics soon found they had to shut up, as the Javelins and AMXs proved surprisingly competitive even in their debut years.

LEFT: Once American Motors became committed to racing, many of its employees wanted to join the effort. In this photo, taken in front of American Motors headquarters on Plymouth Road in Detroit, we see Product VP Gerry Meyers (*in suit*) with the racing team known as T.E.A.M (Technical Employees of American Motors), which put forth a racing effort with talented driver Ike Knupp (*standing in front of the car*). The tall man standing next to Knupp and Meyers is T.E.A.M manager Jim Alexander, from the Styling Department. *Left to right:* Byron Gaugh, George Cude, Phil Toney, two unidentified men, Ron Erwin, Eric Kugler (also from Styling), and Dennis Scheuleter

Rambler 6 at Indy?

If you think you're surprised, you should have been at the brickyard!

A lot of eyebrows went up when the Navarro Engineering Special was rolled out for test runs. The mere idea of a Rambler-powered Indy "500" car trying to clock in at better than 160 mph left the wags limp with laughter. But when they learned that the engine was producing 550 bhp at an easy 6000 rpm, they began to wonder. Les Scott passed his rookie driver's test with ease, and then clocked lap speeds of better than 150 mph...the fastest Six ever at Indy.

People started talking. And asking questions.

"We didn't choose a Rambler engine for sentimental reasons," says Barney Navarro. "We chose it because we knew it was a rugged engine that would run hard for a long time."

The Rambler Six he chose was the basic 199 cu.-in. engine that comes in the car you can buy for $1839.* Navarro used a stock head, rockers, block, and a seven-main-bearing crankshaft; plus a stock cam that was reground. Further modification from there, plus turbosupercharging, brought the horsepower up to competitive level.

So how come you didn't see it in the starting lineup? With time running out, the turbosupercharger and carburetor combination never did get ironed out to cover the range of rpm's needed. And Rome wasn't built in a day.

American Motors builds your kind of car.

Ambassador · Rebel · Rambler American

*Based on manufacturer's suggested retail price for Rambler American 220 2-dr. sedan, federal taxes included. State or local taxes if any, destination charges, optional equipment extra.

MOTOR TREND / SEPTEMBER 1967 7

In 1974 the team finally had a car that could compete on the superspeedways: the sleek new Matador Coupe. Bettenhausen could only finish 7th at the Riverside road course, and 12th in the Daytona 500. Donohue had retired from driving, totally burned out from the dual burdens of driving and engineering the team's various race cars, and NASCAR veteran Bobby Allison was hired to pilot the Matador for the final seven races of the season. Allison was the perfect choice: an elite driver, he was also a team owner known for his ability to set up a stock car.

"A lot of times with other team owners my input on car set up and so on wasn't always appreciated," Allison said. "When I started working with Roger, Mark Donohue walked in and told me, 'We'll put whatever you want on the car, set it up however you tell us you need it.' I'll always admire the way Roger Penske approaches racing; he builds his race teams with quality people and makes sure that you have everything you need to compete at the highest level."

The final race of the season was the Los Angeles Times 500 on November 24. Run at the Ontario Motor Speedway oval in Southern California, it was all Allison's, where he led thirty-four laps to victory.

The ad in the September 1967 issue of *Motor Trend* told the implausible story of Barney Navarro's Indianapolis 500 entry powered by a turbocharged AMC 199-cu.-in. six-cylinder engine. Navarro was a noted California engine builder and performance parts manufacturer who determined that the AMC six had the free-breathing cylinder head, bulletproof seven-bearing bottom end, and displacement near the 209-cu.-in. maximum that made it perfect for Indy. *Tom Glatch Collection*

Allison was again cruising to victory in 1975, first in the Winston Western 500 at Riverside, then running second in the Daytona 500. He won both races at Darlington, the Rebel 500 on April 13, and the grandaddy of stock car races, the Southern 500 on September 1. "The AMC Matador was a great little car," said Allison. "Aerodynamically, I felt like it was one of the best cars in the field. The grille on the car wasn't the greatest, but the rest of the body lines and shape were really favorable. Every race we ran that year that we finished, we finished in the top-five a total of 10 times to be exact, including the three wins."

"There had been some changes at American Motors at the time and the focus was really shifting away from motorsports," Roger Penske recalled. "After the 1975 season, there was an opportunity for our team to move in another direction." Allison drove Penske's Mercury in 1976, then in 1977 he took over Penske's Matador equipment, running it out of his Hueytown, Alabama, shop. Without factory backing, his "Bull Fighter" could only record five top-five finishes during the season, and the Matador era in NASCAR was over.

Indianapolis 500

"Rambler 6 at Indy? If you think you're surprised, you should have been at the brickyard!" The full-page ad in the September 1967 issue of *Motor Trend* sure grabbed everyone's attention.

The car was a three-year-old A. J. Watson creation and the engine a turbocharged

Rambler 199 six-cylinder. "We didn't choose a Rambler engine for sentimental reasons. We chose it because we knew it was a rugged engine that would run hard for a long time," said the project's mastermind, Barney Navarro.

Bernard Julian Navarro was one of those rare people with an innate understanding of the internal combustion engine. An East Coast transplant to California, he was a highly successful Ford flathead builder, as well as manufacturing speed parts for Bonneville and the SoCal drag and dry lakes scene. He also developed a heart-lung machine that was used for years in a Los Angeles hospital, and he created a line of concrete saws whose design is still used in construction projects today.

Quiet yet friendly, with a powerful intellect, Navarro was not your average hot rodder. He told author Paul D. Smith, "You don't violate the laws of nature. You can't; they're inviolate. If you understand the basic physics, you have the problem beat. Now it's a matter of ingenuity and figuring out the limitations of what the rulebooks allow you, working within those parameters."

The Indianapolis 500 is the greatest prize in American racing, and with USAC allowing production-based engines of up to 209 cu.-in. to compete against the exotic powerplants dominating Indy, Navarro determined the free-breathing head and seven-bearing crankshaft of the new AMC 199 six fit those parameters perfectly.

With a proven track record of success, Roger Penske could attract million-dollar budgets, top sponsorship money, and the best drivers. Outside that hot rod circle, Barney Navarro was unknown and could only muster $12,000 and a station wagon from AMC.

Norm Hall attempted to qualify the Navarro Injection Special in the 1967 Indianapolis 500. While the turbocharged engine produced competitive horsepower (550 horsepower at 6,000 rpm), the whole package was not fully developed in time for the event. Despite high levels of boost (105 pounds; .5 kilonewtons), Navarro used stock AMC crankshafts with no issues. *IMS Photo*

AMC test driver Les Scott drove Barney Navarro's more powerful Indy racer in 1969. That's Navarro filling the fuel tank on his creation. The addition of a second Garrett AiResearch TE06 turbo and Navarro's boost management system had the Rambler Six producing 640 to 700 horsepower by 1970. His A. J. Watson chassis finished second in the 1964 Indianapolis 500, with Rodger Ward driving, but it was woefully antiquated by 1969 and not up to a repeat performance. Navarro was later granted two US patents for his turbocharging system. Barney's favorite quote was "there's nothing more fun than learning." *IMS Photo*

Navarro developed mechanical fuel injection and a single turbocharger system for the six, and the 550-horsepower the engine generated was encouraging. But all he could afford was the ancient Watson chassis, one that was hardly state-of-the-art even when new, and the only drivers he could get to pilot it were unknowns, including AMC test driver Les Scott.

As his car was variously called, the "Navarro Injection Special" or "Navarro Engineering Special" either crashed during practice or didn't qualify for the 500 from 1967 through 1969. More determined to succeed, Navarro returned in 1970 with the same car, now with the Rambler Six boosted by an ingenious twin-turbo system producing almost 200 horsepower over the Offenhauser and Ford engines. The second turbocharger was activated only on straightaways, turning the Rambler into a straight-line rocket; but the obsolete chassis was hopelessly outclassed, and with a lack of proven driving talent they didn't qualify again for the next three years.

Outside of Indianapolis, Navarro was mildly successful. In 1969 at the two races on the 1-mile (1.6-kilometer) Trenton oval, they started 12th and finished 11th in the first, qualified 25th and finished 20th in the second. At the two 1971 Rafaela Indy 300 races at Autodromo de Rafaela, Mexico, Dave Strickland started 20th and finished 19th in the first race, qualified 19th and finished 15th in the second. Out of money, 1972 would be his last appearance at Indy, yet for his efforts Barney Navarro was granted two US patents for his unique dual-turbocharger system.

Another California hot rodder turned performance parts entrepreneur, Fred Carrillo, brought AMC back to the Speedway in 1976–1977, this time with a turbocharged V-8. Installed in a more competitive AAR Eagle chassis, it was the only stock-block to qualify either year. Jerry Grant started 20th and finished 27th in the 1976 500, Jim McElreath started 20th and placed 23rd after turbo failure on lap 71 in 1977. "Basically, these were 209-cu.-in. engines, and I worked with Champion [spark plugs] on them," Carrillo told *Hemmings*.

The *Indianapolis Star* in February 1976 published an interview with Dick Jones, Champion's West Coast racing manager: "The company felt that even though it had almost 100 per cent of the field," Jones said, "it would be shirking its responsibility if it didn't look into means of reducing cost to car owners. So they let me do this." Jones reported the stock-block AMC was about half the cost of the Offy or Foyt engines used then. "This possibility was one of the determining factors for why Champion opened its Long Beach shop for the development work." Jones also noted, "the project was entirely funded by Fred Carrillo and Champion authorized me to do the design and development."

Carrillo said he "built the crank, rods, pistons and pretty much everything else, and they [Champion] put it together. It was a destroked 343 block, the Trans-Am block. . . . Originally, we were supposed to get an aluminum block and heads from AMC, but I guess AMC was running out of money, so we had to go with the iron block. . . ." The AMC weighed about 138 pounds (62.6 kilograms) more than the venerable Offenhauser, and "for that reason, it would use up the tires real quick and fuel economy was always a problem," said Carrillo. The AMC generated an incredible 1,050-horsepower, and McElreath was winning the Texas race when they consumed their allotted fuel and had to drop out.

Wealthy California businessman Warner Hodgdon bought the AMC/Eagle and headed for the Speedway, this time with an aluminum block and heads created by his well-funded team. At Indy in 1978, Roger McCluskey qualified a stunning 11th, but clutch failure placed him 25th in the race. Crew chief Dennis McCormack said, "With the headers and turbo, the aluminum AMC was 20 pounds lighter than the Cosworth DFX. We put tons of test miles

Fred Carrillo, a manufacturer of racing connecting rods, came to the Speedway in 1976–1977 with a 1973 AAR Eagle chassis fitted with a turbocharged AMC V-8. The 209-cu.-in. engine was based on AMC's Trans-Am block, creating an incredible 1,050 horsepower. AMC had promised Carrillo aluminum block and heads but could not deliver, so the iron V-8 was too heavy, upsetting cornering and increasing tire wear and fuel consumption. Jerry Grant started 20th and finished 27th in the 1976 500. *IMS Photo*

on it at Ontario with [Jim] McElreath, McCluskey, and Neil Bonnett, and at times, we could run right with them." At Phoenix that year, the McCluskey team again showed its potential, starting 14th but finishing 19th with a fuel leak. Finally, Jerry Sneva qualified 21st for the 1979 Indianapolis 500, but turbocharger failure placed him 31st. After that, Hodgdon concentrated solely on his growing involvement in NASCAR, and AMC became a footnote to Indianapolis 500 history.

Drag Racing

Funny Cars are a shock to the senses, and the sight of a flamethrowing AMC Rebel Funny Car in 1967 was simply outrageous! Shortly after his promotion, Carl Chakmakian offered a contract to Grant McCoon, owner of Los Angeles-based piston ring manufacturer Grant Industries, to construct and race the Grant Rambler Rebel Funny Car.

"Famous Amos" Saterlee built the 438-cu.-in. AMC engine fitted with a GMC 6-71 blower and fuel injection, which was installed in a Logghe tube chassis with a one-piece fiberglass Rebel body. "Banzai Bill" Hayes first drove the beast, painted red with a blue racing stripe and white stars. Then, with Hayes recovering from an injury, famous Chevrolet racer Hayden Proffitt began driving duties, travelling the quarter mile (.4 kilometer) in 7.5 seconds at 170 miles per hour (274 kilometers per hour). A new car was built in 1968 and renamed the Grant Rebel SST. Now sporting the vertically striped, red-white-and-blue paint scheme that most AMC pro racers were adopting, Hayden Proffitt and the flamethrowing Rebel was an image changer, one quarter mile at a time.

Jim McElreath started 20th and placed 23rd in the 1977 Indianapolis 500. Fred Carrillo admitted the iron AMC was "some 138 pounds over an Offenhauser engine" and would have benefited from aluminum block and heads. Still, Carrillo's AAR Eagle was very fast, with McElreath leading the American Parts 200 at Texas World Speedway that year before running out of fuel and finishing sixth. *IMS Photo*

Legendary driver Wally Booth became known for campaigning a Gremlin X drag car in Pro Stock. Booth's car was equipped with the American Motors 360-cu.-in. V-8 destroked to 340-cu.-in., hooked up to a Borg-Warner transmission. Fitted with two Holley four-barrel carburetors sitting on an Edelbrock Tunnel Ram manifold and boasting 13.2:1 compression, the 2,300-pound (1,043-kilogram) Gremlin could fly! By the time this photo was taken, Booth was already a five-time national NHRA meet runner-up and had been voted "One of the Top 10 Pro-Stock Drivers" by *Hot Rod* magazine.

By March 1969, it was reported 160 AMC dealers had a drag racing program of some kind. With strips outside large cities and near small towns, drag racing was truly grassroots motorsports. Nearly a decade earlier, Rhode Island Ford dealer Bob Tasca discovered that when the racers he sponsored at the local dragstrip won, his sales spiked the next day. He coined the term "win on Sunday, sell on Monday" and all of Detroit's racing activities—from Le Mans, Indianapolis, and Daytona to the smallest dragstrips and parking lot slalom courses—followed that formula throughout the 1960s.

Hurst Performance, which was already building the Hurst SC/Ramblers, was tasked with creating a series of special AMX racers for Super Stock drag racing. Kenosha assembled the fifty-two white 390-powered cars in one batch, VINs A9M397X213560 to A9M397X213611, before sending them to Hurst's facility in Ferndale, Michigan, for final preparation.

For AMC, placing those AMX SS racers in the hands of performance-oriented dealers throughout the nation was essential to spreading the word about their performance capabilities. One of those Hurst racers was shipped to the nation's largest automobile market: Southern California. The driver would be Shirley Shahan, the first woman to win a national drag race.

"Late in 1968, we were approached by American Motors to run a '69 AMX," she told *National Dragster* magazine in 2008. "As they were offering a salary and wanted us to campaign in the Los Angeles area for the Southern California AMC Dealers Association, we decided to make the switch. We felt we needed to be closer to home for our kids." Shirley and her engine-builder husband H. L. Shahan had been traveling the country racing Super Stock Plymouths far from their home in Visalia, California. It was on the road that she notched her first professional event victory at the 1966 National Hot Rod Association (NHRA) Winternationals in Pomona. Eventually, after having three children, she gave up the gypsy life of a traveling racer and settled back in Visalia.

Throughout the 1974 season, Ed Howe and his green Brand X Javelin surprised the Chevy and Ford racers with its performance, including Michigan legend Bob Senneker in the blue number 84 Camaro. *Howe Racing Enterprises Archives*

Shirley and H. L. received AMX SS number 35, the thirty-fifth built in Kenosha but the first completed by Hurst Performance, as a token of the impact she'd had on the field of drag racing as the "Drag-on Lady." "What a neat car and so fun to drive! I was back to a stick shift, yeah! In 1970, we won our class at the Winternationals, setting both E.T. and mph records during the season. We did do some match racing with the AMX but stayed pretty close to the Los Angeles area. The AMX was such a kick to drive. I think everyone was a little amazed when I stood it on the bumper at Lions Drag Strip." Racing in the SS/D class, her fastest time was 10.97 seconds at 125.69 miles per hour (202.28 kilometers per hour).

Other successful AMX SS racers included the "Gold Digger" (number 12) from Manhattan Rambler in New York City; Pete Peterson's "Pete's Patriot" out of Kearney, Nebraska (number 39); and the last AMX SS built (number 52), Ivan Fletcher Jr.'s "American Dream" from Sunset Motors in Anchorage, Alaska. That defines grassroots motorsports!

In 1971 AMC had Shirley and H. L. racing a Hornet two-door sedan in the second year of the new Pro Stock category, but that class had quickly evolved to be completely dominated by Hemi 'Cudas, Challengers, and Demons. With the Hornet uncompetitive and the contract with AMC ending, Shirley retired from racing.

Late that year, AMC offered the Berkley, Michigan, team of driver Wally Booth and engine master Dick Arons the opportunity to race in Pro Stock. Booth-Arons had worked their way up to the elite of the Super Stock ranks in Chevys and Mopars, but Pro Stock was now attracting more attention. The dominance of the Hemi Mopars forced the NHRA to revise the class rules, allowing smaller engines with lighter-weight racers. The time was right for another Pro Stock attempt.

AMC gave Booth $75,000 to develop a Pro Stock Gremlin. The team built engines of 342-, 354-, 362-, 368-, 376-, and 385-cubic-inches in an attempt to find the ideal displacement/weight combination. Booth told *Elapsed Times* magazine, "I started with 376 cubic inches and kept dropping the displacement down in order to be able to carry less weight in the car," finding the sweet spot at 362 cu. in. Designed by Bob Riley and built by Ron Fournier, their Gremlin X was one of the first high-tech tube-frame Pro Stock racers, but it never quite reached the performance needed to win.

For the 1973 season, Dick Maskin and Dave Kanners had built a Pro Stock based on the new Hornet Hatchback body. Thinking the Gremlin's aerodynamics might be an issue, Booth tested both cars side by side with identical power. He discovered the Hornet was 0.15 seconds quicker and 3.5 miles per hour (5.6 kilometers per hour) faster. "It was like we were racing a car with a parachute attached to it," he said. Tom Smith's Wolverine Chassis in Romulus, Michigan, created a new tube-frame Hornet Hatchback for Booth. Then, on March 17, 1974, the Booth-Arons Hornet stung Jack Roush's Mustang II at the NHRA Gatornationals, 8.97 to 9.01 seconds. Booth and Arons would go on to win five NHRA national events, including the biggest prize in drag racing—the U.S. Nationals in Indianapolis in 1976. They also won the NHRA World Finals by defeating Dave Kanners in the Maskin & Kanners Hornet Hatchback while going on to earn the Pro Stock National Championship that year. Booth and Arons also won two IHRA events in 1975, and the 1976 AHRA Dragnationals in Kansas City. Booth retired from driving in 1979, still racing the amazing Hornet.

Short Track

The upper Midwest in the 1970s was the scene of the most competitive short track stock car racing in the nation. A driver could race four or five times a week on these asphalt ovals of one-half mile or less; if successful, they could earn a nice living doing so. From this area future NASCAR stars and champions would hone their talents: names like Dave Marcis, Dick Trickle, Arkansas transplant Mark Martin, Alan Kulwicki, and Matt Kenseth,.

Tom Reffner, "The Blue Knight" from Wisconsin Rapids, won a stunning sixty-seven stock car races across the Midwest in 1975 in his Howe Javelin. He tied the number of victories in one season set by his childhood friend, Dick Trickle ("The White Knight") in 1972. No driver since has approached this performance. Reffner also earned pole position in 81 of the 116 events he ran in 1975. That's dominance! *Stan Kalwasinski Photo*

Dick Trickle ("the White Knight") was the winningest short track stock car driver in history by 1972, having earned sixty-seven victories in this red-hot racing environment. Many thought the feat could never be duplicated. Three years later, Trickle's childhood friend, Tom Reffner ("the Blue Knight"), also won sixty-seven events! The cover story in *Stock Car Racing* said it all: "The Blue Knight Rides a Rambler."

Trickle and Reffner had both raced 351-powered Mustangs against the more popular small-block Camaros. They grew up as schoolmates in Wisconsin Rapids, Wisconsin, and, though fierce competitors on the track, shared a shop together for their race cars. But it was over the winter of 1974 that Reffner took a different path to success: he commissioned famed chassis builder Ed Howe to create a 1974 Javelin stock car. Howe ("the Green Hornet") had raced a similar Javelin with surprising success in his native Michigan area earlier that year, having painted his "unlucky" bright green with the name Brand X on the door.

Why did Howe switch from his already successful Chevy? His son Chas recalled, "I know that he went to AMC because of Bobby Allison. Bobby hooked him up with the factory, who sent him to Traco for engines. The first two engines, a 355 and a 390, blew up in short order, and he shipped them back. They rebuilt them, and they blew up again, so instead of sending them back again, he decided to build his own using parts from both engines. The block, crank, and heads were from the 390; the rods, pistons, valves, and valve springs were from a 350 Chevy and then he couldn't kill it. He tried to re-up the deal with AMC for '75 for a full program with Tom Maier driving, but the factory didn't have the budget." Howe converted the "Brand X" into a Camaro, and Tom Reffner purchased Howe's AMC engine along with a new Howe-built Javelin.

At the first race of the season, at Capitol Speedway in April 1975, Reffner's Javelin turned a wheel for the first time. "Yea, I came in from hot laps with a big smile on my face," he told Stock Car Racing. "I knew it would be a good season when I first stepped on the gas after

Warner Hodgdon's well-funded National Engineering team purchased Carrillo's equipment for 1978, then created the aluminum engine components needed to make the AMC V-8 successful. For the 1979 Indianapolis 500, Jerry Sneva qualified 21st, but turbocharger failure placed him 31st. Warner Hodgdon then left Indy to concentrate on his growing involvement in NASCAR, and American Motors was no longer a challenger in "the Greatest Spectacle in Racing." *IMS Photo*

Many racing enthusiasts consider Mark Donohue to have been America's greatest racer. A happy, friendly man, he was known as "Captain Nice." Sadly, Donohue died at age thirty-eight in 1975 in Graz, Austria, during a race practice.

warming up the engine." He could not have anticipated just how well the season would go. "I couldn't believe what we had done. We'd go the 100 miles to Madison [Wisconsin], then over to Michigan, up into Canada, back to Michigan, over to Ohio, and back to Michigan—all in one week." The result was one for the record books. "Just as Dick had won 67 features in 1972, I did in '75. Dick never tried to hold me back. I also had fast time in 81 of the 116 events."

Reffner continued with the Howe Javelin in 1976, then had Bill Bembinster's Bemco Engineering build a Hornet Hatchback for 1977, relegating the Javelin to backup duties. Though never approaching the record-tying victories of 1975, Tom Reffner and his Hornet were competitive until 1981, when new rules required him to switch to a smaller third-generation Camaro. His last racing victory was in 1999 at age 58, and he passed away at 82 in October 2023, still sharing the record of sixty-seven wins with his childhood friend, Dick Trickle.

Off-Road and Rally

The headline shouted: SC/RAMBLER WINS AT BAJA. In just a few years the off-road Baja 500 had become the ultimate endurance race, competed over the rugged desert of Mexico's Baja California peninsula. Dune buggies, dirt bikes, and specially prepared 4×4 trucks ruled this event. Yet here was the press release: "Ensenada, Baja California, Mexico: An American Motors SC/Rambler from James Garner's American International Racing team won the PASSENGER CAR category June 11th–12th (1969) in the Baja 500 Off Road racing event, an automotive enduro race that stands as a challenge to both vehicle and driver."

Motor Trend reported, "The object was to field a series of ten (10!) off-road racing sedans to carry the red, white and blue colors of American Motors into the desert wilds of

Mexico's finger-like peninsular projection called Baja, California. James Garner's American International Racing organization, not content with their triple entries in Formula A racing, thought that off-roading could produce fun as well as profit, thus did the Rohrbacher shops in Hemet, California, move heaven and earth to fit the SC/Ramblers with the accouterments peculiar to this zany new sport in time to make the recent Baja 500 race."

Veteran Grand Prix racer Bob Bondurant with co-driver Tony Murphy crossed the finish line after nineteen hours and five minutes of racing. "The performance of our SC/ Rambler was truly remarkable," said Bondurant. "We experienced no mechanical trouble despite the tremendous pounding our car took on the course." Three more of actor James Garner's SC/Ramblers finished in 3rd, 5th, and 13th place in Class I before the event was halted at the end of thirty hours.

Two of the SC/Ramblers raced by Garner's team were converted to four-wheel drive using Jeep front axles and transfer cases. Carl Jackson and Jim Fricker finished fourth in the Category IV Class in seventeen hours and thirty minutes. "This four-wheel-drive vehicle was a real 60-day wonder," said Elmer Waring, chief Inspector for the Baja 500 technical crew, "for it was created in two months and placed into competition against units with years of development and dozens of open competitive events."

Four-wheel drive passenger cars? A decade later that idea became reality when the revolutionary AMC Eagle was introduced. Talk about an unfair advantage: the small Eagle SX/4's four-wheel drive and sports car–like handling were perfect for SCCA ProRally, an American racing series from 1973 through 2004 that was like a domestic version the World Rally Championship today.

In 1981 Guy Light and Jim Brandt's Eagle SX/4 finished 2nd place in total points for both driver and co-driver and gave AMC 3rd in the Production Manufacturer standings for the season. They finished the year winning their class at the Reno, Nevada, event with a dominating eight-minute victory in the Production Class, as well as placing 10th overall.

The "Big Bend Bash" rally in Alpine, Texas, started the 1982 ProRally season, with Gene Henderson and Jim Kloosterman taking the Production Class in their Eagle SX/4. That would be the team's only victory that year, but consistent finishes throughout the season earned American Motors another 3rd place in the Production Manufacturer standings.

Then, at the third rally of the season, the 1983 Nor'wester rally held in Tumwater, Washington, conditions could not have been better for the Henderson/Kloosterman SX/4—rain, cold, and stages covered with more than 6 inches (15 centimeters) of snow. They won the Production class, finishing an amazing fourth overall. "It was perfect conditions for our 4wd (AMC) Eagle. We love that slop," Henderson told *Rally Racing News*. At season's end, Henderson and Kloosterman ranked second in the drivers' championship, while AMC was again third among the Production Manufacturers.

After 1983, a few Eagle SX/4s competed in the series until 1988, but without factory support the victories were now a memory. And sadly, so too was American Motors.

EPILOGUE:

American Motors Today

Most of American Motors' physical assets are gone today. The big factories in Kenosha and Milwaukee were knocked down years ago to make room for apartments and condominiums. AMC's beautiful old headquarters building in Detroit, so full of memories of a great American company during America's greatest century, was demolished more recently. The men and women who worked there continue to take pride in the legacy of a distinctive company that struggled mightily against enormous odds and succeeded for more decades than anyone thought possible.

But in many ways, American Motors is still with us.

Jeep is the most prominent survivor of AMC's operations. During the 1970s, the employees of American Motors managed to turn around Jeep Corporation, which was rapidly fading away under Kaiser's management. AMC grew Jeep sales by some six-hundred percent, and today America's favorite four-wheel-drive vehicle is a leader in its field, built and sold around the world.

The men and women entrusted with designing new Jeep vehicles have a heavy responsibility for ensuring that Jeep will always meet buyers' expectations. Because AMC understood that, and most of AMC's design team was hired by Chrysler, that sense of heritage has been instilled in the staff who remained and their successors. Even today, when a new Jeep is being readied for the market, certain retired AMC/Jeep designers are asked to review the product and, hopefully, bestow their approval.

Another overlooked American Motors success story is AM General Corporation, the company that builds the military Humvee. That vehicle became part of American culture during Operation Desert Storm, when it gained a status similar to the Jeeps driven in World War II. AM General was founded by American Motors, and the Humvee was designed by AMC engineers.

The former AMC assembly plant in Brampton, which had produced a wide range of vehicles over the years, is currently scheduled to receive a major overhaul in preparation for manufacturing the next-generation Jeep Compass.

So perhaps the best way to summarize the ongoing influence of AMC is to note that, of all the major independent car companies that once existed, portions of only one—American Motors—continue manufacturing products in the automotive industry today.

And Americans Motors enthusiasts share the heritage of a gutsy little David that battled the Goliaths for more years than anyone expected. As legendary AMC designer Vince Geraci has said on many occasions, "it's up to you, the enthusiasts who collect and preserve AMC cars, to make certain that the great story of American Motors is never forgotten."

About the Authors

One of America's best-known automotive writers, **Patrick R. Foster** has spent over 30 years studying the automotive industry. The leading authority on AMC and its predecessors, Pat has written several books on that subject along with many others, including *Jeep*, *Studebaker*, *Hudson*, *Kaiser-Frazer*, and *Metropolitan*. His popular columns appear in *Hemmings Classic Car* and *Old Cars Weekly*, and he has won awards for his books and articles from the AACA (Antique Automobile Club of America) and SAH (Society of Automotive Historians). In 2011, he was honored with the Lee Iacocca Award—one of the most coveted awards in automotive writing. His website is The Olde Milford Press (oldemilfordpress.com).

Since 1983, **Tom Glatch** has contributed hundreds of stories and photographs to major collector, Corvette, Mustang, muscle car, and Mopar magazines. Tom grew up during the muscle car era, and his first car was a very quick 1970 Plymouth Duster 340. Tom and his wife, Kelly, have contributed photographs to books by other Motorbooks authors, as well as Motorbooks' Corvette calendars. When not pursuing old muscle cars, Tom works for a Fortune 500 corporation as a data and systems analyst and developer. He lives in southeastern Wisconsin.

Index

A

Abernethy, Roy, 62, 69, 72, 75–79, 81, 84, 86, 89, 91–92, 215
Adams, Charlie, 214–215
Advanced Styling Studio, 125
air conditioning, 19
Airflyte styling, 8, 25, 43
Aisin Seiki transmission, 196
Alexander, Jim, 100, 221
Allison, Bobby, 230
Allison, Donnie, 221–222
All-Season Air Conditioning system, 19, 21, 30, 33
AM General, 116, 119, 233
Ambassador, 86–87, 90–93, 101–103, 106–107, 122–123, 132, 139–140, 144, 150, 155
See also under Nash; Rambler
Ambassador by Rambler, 42–43, 46, 49, 52, 57
AMX, 99–101, 105–106, 120–121, 123–125, 128, 168, 174, 178–179, 216–218, 221
SS, 227–228
Anderson, Edmund "Ed," 16, 21, 25, 31, 43–44, 51, 58, 62
Arbib, Richard, 26–27, 33
Arons, Dick, 228
Audi 100, 169
Austin Motor Company Ltd., 25, 44

B

Barit, Abraham E., 11
Bembinster, Bill, 231
Bemco Engineering, 231
Bendix Eletrojector, 34–35
Besserdich, William, 184
Bettenhausen, Gary, 221–222
Bogart, Humphrey, 14
Bondurant, Bob, 232
Bonnett, Neil, 226
Booth, Wally, 227–229
Borg-Warner, 41, 112, 136, 227
Bosch, 35
Brandt, Jim, 232
Breedlove, Craig and Lee, 100, 216–218
Bresnahan, Timothy F., 10
Buick, 11, 13
Buyer Protection Plan, 140, 144–145, 149, 187, 192, 194

C

Cadillac, 11, 13, 166
Eldorado Brougham, 33
Cardin, Pierre, 138, 143
Carrillo, Fred, 224–226, 230
Carrousel, 78
Carrozzeria Touring, 14
Carter, Jimmy, 153, 183
Cassini, Oleg, 146, 162
Cavalier concept, 117
Chakmakian, Carl, 100, 216, 218–220, 226
Chapin, Roy D., Jr., 14, 40, 43–44, 52, 68, 92, 96–97, 101, 113, 116, 119, 132, 136, 151, 158–159, 171, 188, 215, 217
Chapin, Roy D., Sr., 92
Chapman, B. A., 81
Chevrolet, 9–11, 13, 33, 40, 216, 219
Bel Air, 60
Camaro, 97, 218–219, 230
Chevelle, 64, 78–79
Chevy II, 71
Corvair, 51
Corvair Spyder, 85
Corvette, 34–36, 99, 105, 155
Corvette Sting Ray, 168
LeBaron, 180, 200
Malibu, 79
Monte Carlo, 145
Nova, 97, 129, 141
Vega, 115, 157
Chicago Auto Show, 84, 88, 100, 131, 216–217
Chrysler, 15, 45, 59, 150, 154, 176, 183–184, 211–213, 233
300C, 34, 36
300D, 35
Laser, 167
Turbine, 71–72
Valiant, 51
Chrysler Loan Guarantee Act, 183
Classic series, 74
Claybrook, Joan, 154
Clean Air Act (1963), 116
Cole, Ed, 157–158
Concord, 172–174, 176, 178–181, 185–187, 192–193, 197–201
Conde, John, 150

Connors, Paul, 218–219
Coon, Frank, 217
Cooney, Stephen, 184
Corporate Average Fuel Economy (CAFE) mandates, 186, 188
Cude, George, 221
Custom Flying Scot OHV engine, 61

D

Dassault Systèmes, 206
Davis, David E., Jr., 186
Dedeurwaerder, Jose J., 198
DeLorean, John Z., 42, 122
DeSoto, 11, 15, 51, 59
  Adventurer, 35–36
Dixon, Freddie, 185
D-Jetronic system, 35
Dodge, 11, 15, 51, 219
  Aspen R/T, 169
  Challenger, 150
  Charger, 84, 167
  Coronet, 94
  D-500, 35
  Diplomat, 180
  Monaco, 106
  Power Wagons, 184
  Viper GTS, 157
Doehler-Jarvis, 56, 66
Donohue, Mark, 123–124, 137, 144, 146, 218–222, 231
Donovan, Leo, 27
Doss, H. C., 12–13
Double Safe unibody construction, 30
drag racing, 226–229

E

Eagle, 182–186, 190–192, 195–196, 198–199, 201, 204–206, 208–212
  Kammback, 190, 192, 196, 198, 206, 208
  SX/4, 190–192, 196, 198, 232
  Wagon, 186, 211, 213
  Wagon Limited, 210
Edelbrock Tunnel Ram manifold, 227
Edelman, Herb, 99
Elder, Ray, 221
Emergency Highway Energy Conservation Act, 150
Environmental Protection Agency (EPA), 116
Erwin, Ron, 221
Evans, Robert Beverley, 91–92, 97, 113
Extra Quiet Insulation, 165–166, 213

F

Fashion Safety Arch, 31
Federal Motor Vehicle Safety Standards and Regulations, 180
Ferguson, Harry, 185
Ferrari, 184
FF Developments Ltd., 185
Fisher & Ludlow Ltd., 25
Flajole, William J., 25
Flashaway Hydra-Matic, 34
Flash-O-Matic transmission, 41
Fleet Eagle, 195
Fletcher, Ivan, Jr., 228
Follmer, George, 218–220
Ford, 9, 11, 15, 40, 45, 176, 216
  Anglia, 44
  Edsel, 55, 115
  Explorer, 57
  Fairlane, 64, 79, 94
  Falcon, 51, 71, 97
  Galaxie, 60
  Granada, 156
  GT Mark II, 184
  GT Mark IV, 184
  GT40, 185
  LTD, 106
  Maverick, 116, 119, 129–130
  Mustang, 76, 84, 87, 97, 115, 218–219, 230
  Mustang Cobra II, 169
  Mustang II, 150, 229
  Sierra, 167
  Taurus, 167
  Tempo, 167
  Thunderbird, 180
  Torino, 84, 145
Ford, Gerald, 153
Ford, Henry, II, 10, 184
Fournier, Ron, 229
Fricker, Jim, 232
Funny Cars, 226

G

Gabriel Air Shocks, 112
Garner, James, 232
Gaugh, Byron, 221
General Motors, 10, 154, 157–158, 168, 176
Geraci, Vince, 81, 94, 120, 138, 142, 146, 156, 159, 233
GKN Ltd., 185
Goodyear tires, 129, 191
Granatelli, Andy, 185
Grant, Jerry, 224–225
Grant Industries, 226
Grant Rambler, 214–215
Gremlin, 115–117, 119–121, 130–131, 133–135, 139, 142–143, 148, 155, 160, 165, 169–170, 175, 177, 200
  GTO, 175
  Pro Stock, 228
  X, 130, 133, 165, 175, 227, 229
Gridler, Allan, 216
Gucci, Aldo, 136

H

Hadsall, Guy, Jr., 97, 99
Hall, Norm, 223
Hayes, "Banzai Bill," 226
Healy, David, 198
Hemi Mopars, 228
Henderson, Gene, 232
Hepburn, Audrey, 14
High Mobility Multipurpose Wheeled Vehicles (Humvees), 201, 233
Hillman Minx, 44
Hodgdon, Warner, 225–226, 230
Holden, William, 14
Honda, Accord, 179
Hornet, 114–115, 117–119, 128–130, 136, 140–142, 149, 155, 159–160, 164, 168–169, 228
  AMX, 168–169
  Hatchback, 140–143, 150, 159, 164–165, 168–169, 229, 231
  SC/360, 129–130
  Sportabout, 129, 136, 142, 168
  X, 136
  See also under Hudson
Howe, Ed, 228, 230–231
Hudson, 8, 22, 40
Hornet, 9, 12–13, 16, 20, 26, 33. *see also* Hornet *entry*
  Hornet Club Sedan, 12–13
  Hornet Hollywood Hardtop, 17

Hornet Six, 27
Hornet Special, 29
Italia, 8, 14, 20
Jet, 8, 15, 20
Step-Down series, 8
Super Wasp Hollywood, 16
Wasp, 9, 19–20, 26–27, 29, 33
Wasp Custom, 20
Huggins, Ross, 219
Hurricane engine, 199, 206, 208
Hurst Performance, Inc., 109, 112–113, 121–122, 227–228
Scrambler, 109–111
SC/Rambler Hurst, 109–113, 121, 231–232
Hutcherson, Dick, 221
Hydra-Matic transmission, 36

I

Iacocca, Lee, 212
Imperial, 11
Indianapolis 500, 222–226, 230
Isbrandt, Ralph, 28, 56, 59–60, 64

J

Jackson, Carl, 232
Jaguar, C-Type, 185
Javelin, 97–100, 103–105, 120–121, 123–129, 137–139, 143, 150–151, 216, 218–221, 229–231
AMX, 125–129, 137, 143, 150–151
Mark Donohue Edition, 123–124
Trans-Am Edition, 124
X, 228
Jeep, 116, 123, 151, 181, 185, 199, 206, 233
Cherokee, 199
Comanche, 212
Grand Wagoneer, 209
Wagoneer, 185, 208–210, 212
Wrangler, 209, 212
XJ Cherokee, 185, 206, 208–210
XJ wagons, 193
Jeffery company, Thomas B., 184
Jeffords, Jim, 218–219
Jensen FF, 185
Jet Stream Styling, 41
Johnson, Miller, 94
Jones, Dick, 120, 225
Jones, Parnelli, 219–220

K

Kaiser, 28
Kaiser Jeep Corporation, 116, 124
Kaiser-Willys, 9
Kamm, Wunibald, 190
Kanners, Dave, 229
Kaplan, Ronnie, 124, 218–219
Kelly, Grace, 146
Kelsey-Hayes wheels, 121
Kennedy, Jacqueline, 146
Kenosha Auto Transport Corporation (KAT), 71
Kenseth, Matt, 229
Kloosterman, Jim, 232
Knupp, Ike, 221
Kohler, Walter J., 22–23
Korean War, 9
Kornmiller, Allan, 16
Kugler, Eric, 125, 221
Kulwicki, Alan, 229

L

Lamm, Michael, 119, 144
land speed records, 216–218
Lapine, Anatole "Tony," 168
Lawson, Charles T., 12–13
Laycock de Normanville, 160
Levi Strauss & Company, 142–143
Lewis, Shari, 117
Light, Guy, 232
Lincoln, 11
Aviator, 57
Lindamood, Jean, 190, 192
Lindberg, Paulette, 131
Lindemann, Bud, 130, 145
Lowey, Raymond, 86
Lund, Robert, 157–158
Luneberg, William V., 92, 128, 139–140, 144–145, 150, 156, 217
Lunn, Royston C. "Roy," 184–186, 190, 199
Lutz, Bob, 212

M

Machine Go package, 131
Mack Trucks, 189
Maddox, George, 119
Maier, Tom, 230
Marcis, Dave, 221, 229
Margulies, Walter P., 113
Marlin, 91, 95
Martin, Buell, 194
Martin, Mark, 229
Mashigan, Chuck, 125
Maskin, Dick, 229
Mason, George W., 10–13, 16, 21–22, 25, 39
Matador, 121, 130–131, 138–139, 144–148, 160–162, 166, 171, 176
Coupe, 145–148, 151, 162, 171, 176, 221–222
McCahill, Tom, 22, 25, 95
McCluskey, Roger, 225–226
McCoon, Grant, 226
McCormack, Dennis, 225–226
McElreath, Jim, 224–226
McNealy, R. William, Jr., 124, 129–130, 140, 216
Mercury, 11, 15, 47, 222
Comet, 94
Cougar, 97
Metropolitan, 18–19, 25, 32, 37, 40, 42, 44, 49, 54–55, 59, 62
See also under Nash; Rambler
Meyers, Gerald, 116, 119, 129, 145–146, 155–157, 159, 171, 181, 185, 198, 221
Mobilgas Economy Run, 32, 34
Motorotown, 168
Murphy, Tony, 232

N

Nance, James J., 11, 28
NASCAR, 145, 218–222
Nash, 8, 10, 40
600 series, 8
Ambassador, 8, 16, 19, 21, 29, 33–34. *see also* Ambassador *entry*; Rambler
Ambassador Country Club, 16, 28
Ambassador Custom, 22–23, 28
Ambassador Eight, 21, 30
Ambassador Six, 21
Ambassador Special, 29–30

Metropolitan, 8, 15. *see also* Metropolitan *entry*; Rambler
Nash-Healey, 8
Rambler, 8, 11, 58
Rambler Cross Country, 13
Rambler Custom, 16
Rambler Deluxe, 16
Statesman, 19, 21–22, 25, 29–30
Nash, Charles W., 10
National Automobile Dealers Association (NADA), 21
National Highway Traffic Safety Administration (NHTSA), 116, 154
National Hot Rod Association (NHRA), 227, 229
National Traffic and Motor Vehicle Safety Act (1966), 116
Navarro, Barney, 222–224
Nixon, Bob, 71–72, 76, 84, 119–120, 145–146, 148, 153, 158–159, 168
NSU Motorenwerke AG, 157

O

O'Connell, Wade, 120
off-road racing, 231–232
Oldsmobile, 11, 13, 47, 55
Cutlass, 171

P

Pacer, 153–159, 162–164, 173–174, 180, 188
Wagon, 167–168, 174
Packard, 9, 11, 16, 21, 45
Pagan, Eddie, 221
Page, Bettie, 27
Pahlavi, Shah Mohammad Reza, 180
Paschal, Jim, 219–220
Penske, Roger, 123, 137, 145, 218–223
Perkins, H. G., 11
Peterson, Pete, 228
Pickett, William S., 153
Pininfarina, Nash-Healey, 21
Plymouth, 11, 15, 51, 59, 219
Barracuda, 97, 150
Fury, 35–36
GTX, 94
Valiant, 97
Volare Road Runner, 169
Pontiac, 13, 55, 62, 188, 219
Firebird, 97
Grand Prix, 42, 145, 180
GTO, 122
Tempest, 78
Ventura, 141
Poole, Chris, 80
Porsche, 191
924, 169
928, 167–168
Posey, Sam, 220
Potter, David, 28
Prestolite, 159
Proffitt, Hayden, 226
Pure Oil Economy Trials, 54

R

Rambler, 20, 22, 24–25, 27, 30–32, 34, 38–41, 43, 45–46, 56, 59–60, 109, 112, 222–223
Ambassador, 40, 60, 65–67, 73–74, 78–81. *see also* Ambassador by Rambler; Ambassador *entry*
American, 43–46, 49, 52–54, 58–63, 66–73, 77, 85–86, 88–91, 95–96, 98, 103–104
American Custom, 54–55
American Rogue, 88, 90
American Rogue Typhoon, 88–90
Classic, 43, 48, 56–57, 61, 64–66, 69, 73, 75–76, 78–80, 91
Classic Custom, 60
Coast-to-Coast Economy Run, 46
Cross Country, 13
Custom, 36
Custom Cross Country, 32
Deluxe, 32
Marlin, 76, 81–84, 86, 91
Metropolitan, 44, 50. *see also* Metropolitan *entry*
Rebel, 34–37, 40–41, 51
Rebel V-8 Custom Cross Country, 51
Rogue, 87, 103, 214–215
Six, 36, 46, 51, 224
Typhoon, 75, 78, 88
See also under Nash
Rebel, 46, 94–95, 102–103, 107–108, 120–122
Funny Car, 226
Machine, 121–122
Reddig, Bill, 31, 58
Reffner, Tom, 229–231
Renault, 181, 184, 189, 195, 198, 205, 210–212
9, 205
Alliance, 201–203, 205–208
Dauphine, 44
Encore, 207–208
R-9, 193
Revson, Peter, 218–219
Riley, Bob, 229
Rolls-Royce, 101
Rolt, A.P.R. "Tony," 185
Romney, George W., 12–13, 16, 25, 28, 30–31, 37, 39–40, 45–46, 49–50, 52, 60, 62, 65, 68, 72, 78, 197, 215
Rother, Helene, 24–25, 136
Roush, Jack, 229
Roy Woods Racing, 220

S

Sabrina, 14
Safety View headlights, 21
Saterlee, "Famous Amos," 226
Scena-Ramic windshield, 21, 33, 51
Scheuleter, Dennis, 221
Scott, Les, 224
SC/Rambler Hurst, 109–113, 121, 231–232
Sebring 12 Hours, 218
Select-Drive, 192, 195–196, 212
Selec-Trac four-wheel-drive, 206
Senneker, Bob, 228
Shahan, H. L., 227–228
Shahan, Shirley, 227–228
Shift-Command transmission, 99
short track racing, 229–231
Sinoda, Larry, 168
Smith, Paul D., 223
Smith, Tom, 229
Sneva, Jerry, 226, 230
Snyder, Jesse, 214–215
Society of Automotive Engineers, 24, 185
Spirit, 177–179, 188, 193–195, 197, 200, 206
GT, 181, 200–201
Liftback, 177–179, 183, 188–189, 195, 197

Sedan, 178–179, 182–183, 190, 194, 196–198
Sports Car Club of America (SCCA), 123, 143, 218–220
Strickland, Dave, 224
Studebaker, 9, 11, 91–92, 116
Avanti, 86
Lark, 51
Starliner, 86
sunroofs, 131
Super Flying Scot L-head six, 49
Super Stock drag racing, 227

T

Tarpon concept car, 76, 81, 84
Tasca, Bob, 227
Teague, Richard Arthur "Dick," 62, 72, 78, 80–81, 84, 86, 95, 117, 119, 124–125, 128, 141, 146
T.E.A.M (Technical Employees of American Motors), 221
Telovac Shifting controls, 41
Tippett, W. Paul, Jr., 180, 198
Toney, Phil, 221
Torque-Command, 75, 80, 88, 136
Torque-Flo V-8, 29, 33
Traco Engineering, 218–219, 221
Trans-Am series/Championship, 123, 137, 143, 215, 218–220
Travers, Jim, 217
Trickle, Dick, 229–231
Truesdale, Richard, 216
Turbo II alloy wheels, 183
Turbocast II wheels, 178–179
24 Hours of Daytona, 218
24 Hours of Le Mans, 184
24 Hours of Nürburgring, 179
Twin Grip, 49
Twin Travel Bed seating, 21, 30, 33, 68
Twin-Stick transmission, 66–67, 88
Twin-Ultramatics, 21
Typhoon engines, 94–95

U

Uni-Side Construction, 64
United Auto Workers strikes, 123, 151
United States Auto Club (USAC), 217

V

VanDerzee, N. K., 12–13
Venturi, 97
Vixen concept, 117
Volkswagen, 103, 115, 119–120
Beetle, 44, 96, 120
Vukovich, Billy, 217

W

Wahlberg, Nils Erik, 19
Wangers, Jim, 122, 168–169
Wankel, Felix, 157
Wankel rotary-piston engine, 157–158
Ward, Rodger, 224
Waring, Elmer, 232
Watson, A. J., 222–224
Weather Eye climate control system, 19, 33
Wells, Rich, and Greene, Inc., 94–95, 99, 103
Wherry, Joseph H., 34
Willys Motors, 72, 184
Witzenberg, Gary, 220
World War II, 8
Wright, Frank Lloyd, 168

Y

Yacobucci, Brent D., 184
Yom Kippur War, 146–147

Z

Zachow, Otto, 184
Zern, Ed, 30
Ziebart Factory Rust Protection, 187, 192, 194, 200
Zourdos, Peter, 212